Berlitz® Audio Aids   Only $7.95 / £4.95

Just listen and repeat!

60 minute cassettes teach you basic expressions with the right accent before you depart. 32 page script included, with pronunciation and complete text.

	Cassettes Quantity	LP Records Quantity	8-Track Quantity
Arabic	218		
Danish	200	225	
Dutch	212	237	
Finnish	201	226	
French	202	227	802
German	203	228	803
Greek	204	229	
Hebrew	205	230	805
Italian	206	231	806
Japanese	207	232	
Norwegian	208	233	
Portuguese	214	239	
Russian	209	234	809
Serbo-Croatian	215		
Spanish (Castil)	210	235	810
Spanish (Lat Am)	213	238	813
Swedish	211		

English for Visitors

			LP USA
For French			246
For German			247
For Italian			248
For Spanish*			249
For Danish			
For Dutch			
For Finnish		860	
For Norwegian	320	870	
For Swedish	330		Total Units
For Japanese	Cas. BRIT 340	Cas. USA 345	
* also available as 8-Track	890		

Please count the total number of units requested and complete the reverse side of this order form.

11403

$	£
From New Jersey	**From London**
Total units _____	Total units _____
at $7.95 each	at £4.95
Total amount enclosed	Total amount enclosed
$ _____	£ _____
(N. J. residents add sales tax)	(VAT is included)

Name _____

Address _____

_____

_____

Please complete and return this order form to:

Traveller's
Shopping Service   or
600 Grand Avenue
Ridgefield, NJ 07657
USA

Traveller's
Shopping Service
8, Trident Way
Brent Road
Southall
Middlesex UB2 5LS
England

Please order Berlitz books through your bookseller. Should you encounter any difficulties, write directly to any of the distributors listed on the back cover.

11403

BERLITZ®

EUROPEAN
PHRASE BOOK

By the staff of Editions Berlitz

Library of Congress Catalog Card Number: 73-20997

7th printing 1981

Printed in Switzerland

Editions Berlitz
1, avenue des Jordils
1000 Lausanne 6, Switzerland

Contents

Preface

You're about to visit several countries in Europe and we've attempted to provide you with a useful phrase book featuring key phrases in 14 different European languages.

Our book is simple to use, since the language sections are divided into topics, from arrival to eating out, from shopping to emergencies. Each expression appears with a code to pronunciation next to it. Simply read this imitated pronunciation as if it were English, stressing the syllables that are printed in bold type.

This European Phrase Book is made up of key extracts from 14 complete phrase books published by Berlitz. If you plan to spend a longer period of time in one country or language area, you'd be well advised to obtain a complete 192-page single language phrase book. It contains detailed travel information and tips, as well as useful phrases.

The phrases featured in each language of this book are also available in cassette form to help you prepare for your trip. The cassette is also available with a full-length phrase book at booksellers and record shops as a "Cassettepak" or "8-track Cartridgepak".

Bon Voyage!

DANISH

Guide to Pronunciation

Letter	Approximate pronunciation	Symbol	Example	

Consonants

b, c, f, h, l, m, n, v	as in English			
d	1) when at the end of the word, or between two vowels, like **th** in **this**	dh	**med**	mehdh
	2) otherwise, as in English	d	**dale**	da**r**ler
g	1) at the beginning of a word or syllable, as in **go**	g	**glas**	glahss
	2) when at the end of a word after a long vowel or before unstressed **e**, like **chs** in Scottish lo**ch**, but weaker and voiced	ǧ	**kage**	kar**ǧ**er
	3) usually mute after **i**, **y**, and sometimes mute after **a**, **e**, **o**		**sige**	seeer
j, hj	like **y** in **yet**	y	**ja**	yah

DANISH

k, p, t	1) when at the beginning of a word, as in **k**ite, **p**ill and to	k	**k**affe	**k**ahfer
		p	**p**ude	**p**oodher
		t	**t**ale	**t**arler
	2) otherwise like **g**, **b**, **d** in **g**o, **b**it and **d**o	g	læ**kk**e	leh**g**er
		b	sto**pp**e	s**d**ober
		d	sæ**tt**e	seh**d**er
l	always as in **l**eaf, never as in be**ll**	l	ve**l**	veh**l**
r	pronounced in the back of the throat, as in French	r	**r**ose	**r**oaser
s	always as in **s**ee	s/ss	**sk**ål	**sg**awl
			ha**s**ter	hah**ss**derr
sj	like **sh** in **sh**eet	sh	**sj**ælden	**sh**ehlern
w	for Danes this is the same as **v**			
z	like **s** in **s**o	s	**z**one	**s**oaner

Vowels

Vowels are generally long in stressed syllables when followed by *at most* one consonant. If followed by two consonants (or more), or in unstressed syllables, they are generally short.

a	1) when long, like **a** in c**ar**; it can also be pronounced like **a** in bad, but longer	ar	b**a**de	b**ar**dher
	2) when short, like long **a**, or more like **a** in c**ar**t	ah	h**a**t	h**ah**d
	3) you will also hear, as alternatives to the above, a more or less "flat" pronunciation of **a**, which can be like **a** in h**a**t, or tend towards **e** in l**e**t; it can be long or short	ai	t**a**le	t**ai**ler
		æ	t**a**k	t**æ**g
e	1) when long, the same quality as **a** in pl**a**te, but longer, and a pure vowel, not a diphthong	ay	m**e**re	m**ay**rer
	2) when short, somewhere between the **a** in pl**a**te and the **i** in h**i**t	ay	f**e**dt	f**ay**d
	3) when short, also like **e** in m**e**t	eh	l**e**t	l**eh**d
	4) when unstressed, like **a** in **a**bout	er	gamm**e**l	gahm**er**l
i	1) when long, like **ee** in b**ee**	ee	b**i**de	b**ee**dher
	2) when short, like **ee** in m**ee**t	ee	l**i**ter	l**ee**derr

o	1) when long, like **aw** in s**aw**, but with the tongue higher in the mouth; quite like **u** in p**u**t	oa	**skole**	sg**oa**ler
	2) when short, more or less the same quality of sound	oa	**bonde**	b**oa**ner
	3) when short, also like **o** in l**o**t	o	**godt**	g**o**d
u	1) when long, like **oo** in p**oo**l	oo	**pude**	p**oo**dher
	2) when short, like **oo** in l**oo**t	oo	**nu**	n**oo**
y	put your tongue in the position for the **ee** of b**ee**, but round your lips as for the **oo** of p**oo**l; the vowel you pronounce like this should be more or less correct	ew	**byde** **lytte**	b**ew**dher l**ew**der
æ	1) when long, like the first part of the word **air**	ai	**bære**	b**ai**rer
	2) when short, like **e** in g**e**t, but next to **r** it sounds more like the **a** of h**a**t	eh æ	**ægte** **værre**	**ehg**der v**æ**rer
å	1) when long, like **aw** in s**aw**	aw	**åben**	**aw**bern
	2) when short, like **o** in **o**n	o	**ånd**	**o**n
ø	like **ur** in f**ur**, but with the lips rounded; can be long or short	ur	**frøken** **øl**	fr**ur**gern **ur**l

Diphthongs

av	like **ow** in n**ow**	ow	**hav**	h**ow**
ej	like **igh** in s**igh**	igh	**nej**	n**igh**
ev	like **e** in g**e**t followed by a short **u** as in p**u**t	ehoo	**evne**	**ehoo**ner
ou	like **o** in g**o**t followed by a short **u** as in p**u**t	ooo	**lov**	l**ooo**
øi	like **oi** in **oi**l	oi	**øje**	**oi**er
øv	like **ur** in h**ur**t followed by a short **u** as in p**u**t	uroo	**søvnig**	s**uroo**nee

N.B. 1) Many Danish speakers put a glottal stop in or after long vowels (like the Cockney pronunciation of **t** in wa'**er**). Although it has a certain distinctive role, you will be understood perfectly well if you do not use it, so we have not shown it in our transcriptions;

2) **dd** and **gg** between vowels are pronounced like **d** in **d**o and **g** in **g**o;

3) the letter **d** is not pronounced in **nd** and **ld** at the end of a word or syllable (*mand* = **mahn**, *guld* = **gool**) or before unstressed **e** or before **t** or **s** in the same syllable (*plads* = **plahs**).

DANISH

Some basic expressions

Yes.	Ja.	yar
No.	Nej.	nay
Please.	Vær så venlig.	vair saw **vehn**lee
Thank you.	Tak.	tahk
Thank you very much.	Mange tak.	**mahng**er tahk
That's all right.	Å, jeg be'r.	aw yay bayr

Greetings

Good morning.	Godmorgen.	goadh**mo**rern
Good afternoon.	Goddag.	goadh**dai**
Good evening.	Godaften.	goadh**ahf**dern
Good night.	Godnat.	goadh**nahd**
Good-bye.	Farvel.	fahr**vehl**
See you later.	På gensyn.	paw **gehn**sewn
This is Mr. . . .	Det er hr . . .	day air hehr
This is Mrs. . . .	Det er fru . . .	day air froo
This is Miss . . .	Det er frøken . . .	day air **frur**gern
I'm very pleased to meet you.	Det glæder mig at træffe Dem.	day **glai**dherr migh aht **treh**fer dehm
How are you?	Hvordan har De det?	**vor**dahn harr dee day
Very well, thank you. And you?	Fint, tak. Og De?	fint tahk. o dee
Fine.	Fint.	fint
Excuse me.	Undskyld.	**oon**sgewl

Questions

Where?	Hvor?	vor
Where is . . . ?	Hvor er . . . ?	vor air
Where are . . . ?	Hvor er . . . ?	vor air
When?	Hvornår?	vor**nawr**
What?	Hvad?	vah(dh)
How?	Hvordan?	vor**dahn**
How much?	Hvor meget?	vor **migh**erd

How many?	**Hvor mange?**	vor **mahng**er
Who?	**Hvem?**	vehm
Why?	**Hvorfor?**	vor**for**
Which?	**Hvilken/Hvilket?**	**vil**gern/**vil**gerd
What do you call this?	**Hvad hedder dette?**	vahdh **heh**derr **deh**der
What do you call that?	**Hvad hedder det?**	vahdh **heh**derr day
What does this mean?	**Hvad betyder dette?**	vahdh ber**tew**derr **deh**der
What does that mean?	**Hvad betyder det?**	vahdh ber**tew**derr day

Do you speak ... ?

Do you speak English?	**Taler De engelsk?**	**tai**lerr dee **ehng**erlsg
Do you speak German?	**Taler De tysk?**	**tai**lerr dee tewsg
Do you speak French?	**Taler De fransk?**	**tai**lerr dee frahnsg
Do you speak Spanish?	**Taler De spansk?**	**tai**lerr dee spahnsg
Do you speak Italian?	**Taler De italiensk?**	**tai**lerr dee eetahlee**aynsg**
Could you speak more slowly, please?	**Vil De tale langsommere?**	vil dee **tai**ler **lahng**somerrer
Please point to the phrase in the book.	**Vær så venlig at pege på sætningen i bogen.**	vair saw **vehn**lee ahd **pigh**er paw **sehd**ningern ee **baw**(g)ern
Just a minute. I'll see if I can find it in this book.	**Et øjeblik. Jeg vil se, om jeg kan finde det i denne bog.**	ehd **oier**blig. yay vil say om yay kahn **finn**er day ee **deh**ner baw(g)
I understand.	**Jeg forstår.**	yay for**sdawr**
I don't understand.	**Jeg forstår ikke.**	yay for**sdawr igger**

Can ... ?

| Can I have ... ? | **Kan jeg få ... ?** | kahn yay faw |
| Can we have ... ? | **Kan vi få ... ?** | kahn vee faw |

Can you show me ... ?	Kan De vise mig ... ?	kahn dee **vee**sser migh
Can you tell me ... ?	Kan De sige mig ... ?	kahn dee **see**yer migh
Can you help me, please?	Vil De være så venlig at hjælpe mig?	vil dee **vai**rer saw **vehn**lee ahd **yehl**per migh

Wanting

I'd like ...	Jeg vil gerne have ...	yay vil **gehr**ner **hai**(wer)
We'd like ...	Vi vil gerne have ...	vee vil **gehr**ner **hai**(wer)
Please give me ...	Vær så venlig at give mig ...	vair saw **vehn**lee ahd **gee** migh
Give it to me please.	Vær så venlig at give mig det.	vair saw **vehn**lee ahd **gee** migh day
Please bring me ...	Vær så venlig at hente ... til mig.	vair saw **vehn**lee ahd **hehn**der ... til migh
Bring it to me, please.	Vær så venlig at hente det til mig.	vair saw **vehn**lee ahd **hehn**der day til migh
I'm hungry.	Jeg er sulten.	yay air **sool**tern
I'm thirsty.	Jeg er tørstig.	yay air **turrss**tee
I'm tired.	Jeg er træt.	yay air trehd
I'm lost.	Jeg er faret vild.	yay air **farr**erd veel
It's important.	Det er vigtigt.	day air **vig**dee(t)
It's urgent.	Det haster.	day **hahss**derr
Hurry up!	Skynd Dem!	sgurn dehm

It is/There is ...

It is/It's ...	Det er ...	day air
Is it ... ?	Er det ... ?	air day
It isn't ...	Det er ikke ...	day air **ig**ger
There is/There are ...	Der er ...	dair air
Is there/Are there ... ?	Er der ... ?	air dair
There isn't/There aren't ...	Der er ikke ...	dair air **ig**ger
There isn't any/ There aren't any.	Der er ingen.	dair air **ing**ern

A few common words

big/small	**stor/lille**	sdoar/**lil**ler
quick/slow	**hurtig/langsom**	hoordee/**lahng**som
early/late	**tidlig/sen**	teedhlee/sayn
cheap/expensive	**billig/dyr**	billee/dewr
near/far	**nær/fjern**	nair/fyehrn
hot/cold	**varm/kold**	vahrm/kol
full/empty	**fuld/tom**	fool/tom
easy/difficult	**let/vanskelig**	lehd/**vahnss**gerlee
heavy/light	**tung/let**	toong/lehd
open/shut	**åben/lukket**	awbern/**loo**gerd
right/wrong	**rigtig/forkert**	rigdee/for**kayrd**
old/new	**gammel/ny**	gahmerl/new
old/young	**gammel/ung**	gahmerl/oong
beautiful/ugly	**smuk/grim**	smoog/grim
good/bad	**god/dårlig**	goadh/**dawr**lee
better/worse	**bedre/værre**	behdhrer/**veh**rer

Some prepositions and a few more useful words

at	**ved**	vaydh
on	**på**	paw
in	**i**	ee
to	**til**	til
from	**fra**	frar
inside	**indeni**	**in**nernee
outside	**udenfor**	**oo**dhernfor
up	**op**	ob
down	**ned**	naydh
before	**før**	furr
after	**efter**	**ehf**derr
with	**med**	maydh
without	**uden**	**oo**dhern
through	**gennem**	**geh**nerm
towards	**imod**	ee**moadh**
until	**indtil**	intil
during	**i løbet af**	ee **lur**berd ahf
and	**og**	o
or	**eller**	**eh**lerr
not	**ikke**	**ig**ger
nothing	**intet**	**in**derd
none	**ingen**	**ing**ern
very	**meget**	**migh**erd
also	**også**	**os**ser
soon	**snart**	snahrd
perhaps	**måske**	moss**gay**
here	**her**	hair

there	**der**	dair
now	**nu**	noo
then	**så**	saw

Arrival

Your passport, please.	**Deres pas!**	**deh**rerss pahss
Here it is.	**Værs'go.**	**vehr**sgoa
Have you anything to declare?	**Har De noget at for-tolde?**	harr dee **noa**gerd ahd for**to**ller
No, nothing at all.	**Nej, intet.**	nigh **in**derd
Porter!	**Drager!**	**drah**gerr
Can you help me with my luggage, please?	**Vil De hjælpe mig med min bagage?**	vil dee **yehl**per migh maydh meen bah**gai**sher
That's my suitcase.	**Det er min kuffert.**	day air meen **koo**ferrd
Where's the bus to the centre of town, please?	**Hvor holder bussen til centrum?**	vor **hol**lerr **boos**sern til **sehn**troam
This way, please.	**Denne vej.**	**deh**ner vigh

Changing money

| Can you change a traveller's cheque, please? | **Kan De indløse en rejsecheck?** | kahn dee **in**lursser ayn **righs**serchehg |
| Where's the nearest bank, please? | **Hvor er den nærmeste bank?** | vor air dehn **nair**mersder bahnk |

Car rental

I'd like a car.	**Jeg vil gerne leje en vogn.**	yay vil **gehr**ner **ligh**er ayn **voa**(g)ern
For how long?	**Hvor længe?**	vor **lehn**ger
A day/Four days/ A week/Two weeks.	**En dag/Fire dage/ En uge/to uger.**	ayn dai/**feer**er **dal**(g)er/ ayn **oo**(g)er/toa **oo**(g)err

Taxi

| Where can I get a taxi? | **Hvor kan jeg få en taxa?** | vor kahn yay faw ayn **tah**gsah |
| What's the fare to . . . ? | **Hvad koster det til . . . ?** | vahdh **koss**derr day til |

| Come in! The door's open. | Kom ind! Døren er åben. | kom in durrern air awbern |
| May we have breakfast in our room? | Kan vi få morgenmad på værelset? | kahn vee faw mor(g)ernmahdh paw vairaylserd |

Breakfast

I'll have ...	Jeg vil gerne have ...	yay vil gehrner hai(wer)
I'll have some fruit juice.	Jeg vil gerne have noget frugtsaft.	yay vil gehrner hai(wer) noa(g)erd froogdsahfd
a boiled egg	et kogt æg	ayd kogd ehg
a fried egg	et spejlæg	ayd sbighlehg
some bacon/some ham	noget bacon/noget skinke	noa(g)erd baykern/ noa(g)erd sginggerr
some toast	noget ristet brød	noa(g)erd risderd brurd
a pot of tea	en kande te	ayn kahner tay
a cup of tea	en kop te	ayn kob tay
some coffee	noget kaffe	noa(g)erd kahfer
some chocolate	noget chokolade	noa(g)erd shoagoalardher
more butter	mere smør	mayrer smurr
some hot water	noget varmt vand	noa(g)erd vahrmd vahn

Difficulties

The central heating doesn't work.	Centralvarmen virker ikke.	sehntrarlvahrmen veergerr igger
the light/the socket	lyset/stikkontaken	lewsserd/sdiggondahgdern
the tap/the toilet	vandhanen/toilettet	vahnharnern/toilehderd
There's no hot water.	Der er ikke noget varmt vand.	dair air igger noa(g)erd vahrmd vahn
May I see the manager, please?	Jeg vil gerne tale med direktøren.	yay vil gehrner tailer maydh direhgturrern

Telephone—Mail

There's a call for you.	Der er telefon til Dem.	dair air taylayfoan til dehm
Hold the line, please.	Et øjeblik.	ayd oierblig
Operator, I've been cut off.	Frøken, jeg er blevet afbrudt.	frurgern yay air blayverd owbrood

DANISH

Take me to this address, please.	**Kør mig til denne adresse.**	kurr migh til **deh**ner ah-**dreh**sser
I'm in a hurry.	**Jeg har travlt.**	yay harr trowlt
Could you drive more slowly, please?	**Vil De være venlig at køre lidt langsommere?**	vil dee **vai**rer **vehn**lee ahd **kur**rer let **lahng**somerrer

Hotel and other accommodation

My name is...	**Mit navn er...**	mid nown air
Have you a reservation?	**Har De reserveret?**	harr di raysehr**vai**rerd
Yes, here's the confirmation.	**Ja, her er bekræftelsen.**	yar hair air ber**krehf**derl-sern
I'd like...	**Jeg vil gerne have...**	yay vil **gehr**ner **hai**(wer)
I'd like a single room/a double room.	**Jeg vil gerne have et enkeltværelse/et dobbeltværelse.**	yay vil **gehr**ner **hai**(wer) ayd **ehng**gerldvairaylser/ ayd **do**berldvairaylser
a room with a bath/ with a shower	**et værelse med bad/med brusebad**	ayd **vai**raylser maydh bardh/maydh **broos**ser-bardh

How much?

What's the price per night/per week/per month?	**Hvor meget koster det pr. nat/pr. uge/ pr. måned?**	vor **migh**erd **koss**derr day pehr nahd/pehr **oo**(g)er/ pehr **maw**nerdh
May I see the room?	**Må jeg se værelset?**	maw yay say **vai**raylserd
I'm sorry, I don't like it.	**Jeg synes ikke om det.**	yay **sew**nerss **ig**ger om day
Yes, that's fine. I'll take it.	**Ja, det er godt. Det tager jeg.**	yar day air god day **tar**(g)err yay
What's my room number, please?	**Hvilket nummer har mit værelse?**	**vil**kerd **noo**merr harr mid **vai**raylser
Number 123.	**Nummer 123.**	**noo**merr 123

Service, please

| Who is it? | **Hvem er det?** | vehm air day |
| Just a minute. | **Et øjeblik.** | ayd **oi**erblig |

Did anyone telephone me?	**Er der blevet ringet til mig?**	air dair **blay**verd **ring**erd til migh
Is there any mail for me?	**Er der post til mig?**	air dair possd til migh
Are there any messages for me?	**Er der en besked til mig?**	air dair ayn ber**sgaydh** til migh

Checking out

May I have my bill, please?	**Må jeg bede om regningen?**	maw yay **bay**dher om **righ**ningern
We're in a great hurry.	**Vi skal skynde os.**	vee sgahl **sgur**ner oss
It's been a very enjoyable stay.	**Det har været et meget behageligt ophold.**	day harr **vai**rerd ayd **migh**erd ber**har**gerligd **obhol**

Eating out

Good evening, sir/ Good evening, madam.	**Godaften hr./ Godaften frue.**	goadh**ahf**dern hehr/ goadh**ahf**dern **froo**er
Good evening. I'd like a table for two, please.	**Godaften. Jeg vil gerne have et bord til to.**	goadh**ahf**dern. yay vil **gehr**ner **hai**(wer) ayd bord til toa
Do you have a fixed-price menu?	**Har De en "dagens middag"?**	harr dee ayn **dai**(g)ernss **middar**(g)
May I see the à la carte menu?	**Må jeg se spisekortet?**	maw yay say **sbee**serkor-derd
May we have an ashtray, please?	**Må vi få et askebæger?**	maw vee faw ayd **ahss**gerbeh(g)err
some bread	**noget brod**	**noa**(g)erd brurdh
a fork	**en gaffel**	ayn **gah**ferl
a knife	**en kniv**	ayn **kneeoo**
a spoon	**en ske**	ayn **sgay**
a plate	**en tallerken**	ayn **tah**lehrgern
a glass	**et glas**	ayd **glahss**
a napkin	**en serviet**	ayn sehr**viehd**
another chair	**en stol til**	ayn sdoal til
Where's the gentlemen's toilet (men's room)?	**Hvor er her-retoilettet?**	vor air **hehr**rer-toaahlehderd
Where's the ladies' toilet (ladies' room)?	**Hvor er dametoilettet?**	vor air **dar**mer-toaahlehderd

DANISH

Appetizers

I'd like some . . .	**Jeg vil gerne have . . .**	yay vil **gehr**ner **hai**(wer)
I'd like some assorted appetizers.	**Jeg vil gerne have forskellig hors d'oeuvre.**	yay vil **gehr**ner **hai**(wer) foss**gehl**ee or**durvr**
orange juice	**noget orangesaft**	**noa**gert oa**rahng**shersahft
ham	**skinke**	s**ging**ger
melon	**melon**	may**loan**
pâté	**postej**	poss**digh**
smoked salmon	**røget laks**	**rur**(g)ert lahgs
shrimps (shrimp)	**rejer**	**righ**er

Soup

Have you any . . . ?	**Har De . . . ?**	harr dee
Have you any chicken soup?	**Har De hønsekodssuppe?**	harr dee **hurnss**(g)ergurdssooper
vegetable soup	**grønsagssuppe**	**grurn**sar(gs)soaber
onion soup	**løgsuppe**	**lurg**soaber

Fish

I'd like some . . .	**Jeg vil gerne have . . .**	yay vil **gehr**ner **hai**(wer)
I'd like some fish.	**Jeg vil gerne have fisk.**	yay vil **gehr**ner **hai**(wer) fisg
sole	**sotunge**	**sur**doanger
trout	**orred**	**urr**erd
lobster	**hummer**	**hoa**merr
crayfish	**krebs**	**kreh**bss
prawns	**store rejer**	**stoa**rer **righ**err
I'd like it . . .	**Jeg vil gerne have den . . .**	yay vil **gehr**ner **hai**(wer) dehn
I'd like it steamed.	**Jeg vil gerne have den dampkogt.**	yay vil **gehr**ner **hai**(wer) dehn **dahmp**kogd
grilled	**grilleret**	**gri**layrerd
boiled	**kogt**	kogd
baked	**stegt i ovnen**	**sdehgd** ee **oaoo**nern
fried	**stegt**	**sdehgd**

Meat—Poultry—Game

I'd like some . . .	Jeg vil gerne have . . .	yay vil gehrner hai(wer)
I'd like some beef.	Jeg vil gerne have oksekød.	yay vil gehrner hai(wer) ogserkurd
a beef steak	en engelsk bøf	ayn ehngerlsk burf
some roast beef	roastbeef	rossdbif
a veal cutlet	en kalvekotelet	ayn kahlverkoaterlehd
mutton	fårekød	fawrerkurdh
lamb	lammekød	lahmorkurdh
a pork chop	en svinekotelet	ayn sveenerkoaterlehd
roast pork	flæskesteg	flehssgersdigh
hare	hare	harrer
chicken	kylling	kewling
roast chicken	stegt kylling	sdehgd kewling
duck	and	ahn
How do you like your meat?	Hvordan vil De gerne have Deres kød tilberedt?	vordahn vil dee gehrner hai(wer) dayrerss kurdh tilberrayd
rare	rødt	rurd
medium	medium	maydeeom
well done	gennemstegt	gehnermsdehgd

Vegetables

What vegetables have you got?	Hvilke grønsager har De?	vilger grurnsar(g)err harr dee
I'd like some . . .	Jeg vil gerne have . . .	yay vil gehrner hai(wer)
I'd like some asparagus.	Jeg vil gerne have asparges.	yay vil gehrner hai(wer) ahssrahrerss
green beans	grønne bønner	grurner burnerr
mushrooms	champignoner	shahngpinyongnerr
carrots	gulerødder	goolerrurderr
onions	løg	lurg
red cabbage	rødkål	rurdhkawl
spinach	spinat	sbinaid
rice	ris	reess
peas	ærter	airterr
tomatoes	tomater	toamaiderr
green salad	grøn salat	grurn sahlaid
potatoes	kartofler	kahrtoflerr

DANISH

Desserts

Nothing more, thanks.	**Tak, ikke mere.**	tahk igger mayrer
Just a small portion, please.	**Kun en lille portion.**	koon ayn liller porsyoan
Have you any ice-cream?	**Har De is?**	harr dee eess
fruit salad	**frugtsalat**	froagdsahlaid
fresh fruit	**frisk frugt**	frisg froogd
cheese	**ost**	oossd

Drink

What would you like to drink?	**Hvad ønsker De at drikke?**	vahdh urnskerr dee ahd drigger
I'll have a beer, please.	**Jeg vil gerne have en øl.**	yay vil gehrner hai(wer) ayn url
I'll have a whisky, please.	**Jeg vil gerne have en whisky.**	yay vil gehrner hai(wer) ayn wisskee

Wine

I'd like a bottle of wine.	**Jeg vil gerne have en flaske vin.**	yay vil gehrner hai(wer) ayn flahssger veen
red wine	**rødvin**	rurdhveen
rosé wine	**rosé-vin**	roasayveen
white wine	**hvidvin**	vidhveen
Cheers!	**Skål!**	skawl

The bill (check)

May I have the bill (check) please?	**Jeg vil gerne have regningen.**	yay vil gehrner hai(wer) righningern
Is service included?	**Er det med be-tjening?**	air day mehdh ber-tyayning
Everything's included.	**Alt er iberegnet.**	ahlt air eeberrighnert
Thank you, that was a very good meal.	**Mange tak, det smagte fortræffeligt.**	mahnger tahk day smargder fortrehferligd

Travelling

| Where's the railway station, please? | **Hvor er banegården?** | vor air bainergawr(d)ern |

Where's the ticket office, please?	Hvor er billet- kontoret?	vor air bilehdkontoarerd
I'd like a ticket to...	Jeg vil gerne have en billet til...	yay vil gehrner hai(wer) ayn bilehd til
First or second class?	Første eller anden klasse?	furrster ehlerr ahndern klahsser
First class, please.	Første klasse.	furrster klahsser
Single or return (one way or round-trip)?	Enkelt eller retur?	ehnggerld ehlerr rertoor
Do I have to change trains?	Skal jeg skifte tog?	sgahl yigh sgifder taw(g)
What platform does the train leave from?	Fra hvilken perron afgår toget?	frar vilgern pehrong ow-gawr tawgerd
Where's the nearest underground (sub-way) station?	Hvor er den nærmeste under-grundsstation?	vor air dehn nairmersder oanerrgroansssdahshoan
Where's the bus station, please?	Hvor er rutebil-stationen?	vor air rooderbeelsdah-shoanern
When's the first bus to...?	Hvornår kører den første bus til...?	vornawr kurrerr dehn fursder booss til
the last bus the next bus	den sidste bus den næste bus	dehn see(d)sder booss dehn nehsder booss
Please let me off at the next stop.	Jeg vil gerne af ved næste stoppested.	yay vil gehrner ahv vaydh nehsder sdobbersdehdh

Relaxing

What's on at the cinema (movies)?	Hvad går der i bio-grafen?	vahdh gawr dair ee bioa-grarfern
What's on at the theatre?	Hvad går der på teatret?	vahdh gawr dair paw tayaidrerd
What time does the film begin? And the play?	Hvornår begynder filmen? Og stykket?	vornawr bergewnerr fil-mern? o stewgerd
Are there any tickets for tonight?	Er der flere billetter til i aften?	air dair flayrer bilehderr til ee ahfdern
Where can we go dancing?	Hvor kan vi gå ud og danse?	vor kahn vee gaw oodh o dahnser
Would you like to dance?	Vil De danse?	vil dee dahnser

Introductions

How do you do?	**Goddag.**	goadh**dai**
How are you?	**Hvordan har De det?**	vor**dahn** harr dee day
Very well, thank you. And you?	**Godt, tak. Og De?**	god tahk. o dee
May I introduce Miss Philips?	**Må jeg præsentere Dem for frøken Philips?**	maw yigh praisern**tay**rer dehm for **frur**gern Philips
My name is...	**Mit navn er...**	mid nown air
I'm very pleased to meet you.	**Det glæder mig at træffe Dem.**	day **glai**dherr migh ahd **treh**fer dehm
How long have you been here?	**Hvor længe har De været her?**	vor **lahng**er harr dee **vai**rerd hair
It was nice meeting you.	**Det har glædet mig at træffe Dem.**	day harr **glaidh**erd migh ahd **treh**fer dehm

Dating

Would you like a cigarette?	**Må jeg byde Dem en cigaret?**	maw yay **bew**dher dehm ayn sigah**rehd**
May I get you a drink?	**Må jeg byde Dem en drink?**	maw yay **bew**dher dehm ayn drink
Do you have a light, please?	**Undskyld, kan De give mig ild?**	**oon**sgewl kahn dee **gee**ver migh il
Are you waiting for someone?	**Venter De på nogen?**	**vehn**derr dee paw **noa**gern
Are you free this evening?	**Er De ledig i aften?**	air dee **lay**dhee ee **ahf**dern
Where shall we meet?	**Hvor skal vi mødes?**	vor sgahl vee **mur**dherss
What time shall I meet you?	**Hvornår skal vi mødes?**	vor**nawr** sgahl vee **mur**dherss
May I take you home?	**Må jeg følge Dem hjem?**	maw yay **furl**ger dehm yehm
Thank you, it's been a wonderful evening.	**Tusind tak, det har været en vidunderlig aften.**	**toos**sin tahg day harr **vai**rerd ayn vid**hoa**nerrlee **ahf**dern
What's your telephone number?	**Hvad er Deres telefonnummer?**	vahdh air **day**rerss tayler-**foan**noomerr
Do you live alone?	**Bor De alene?**	**boar** dee ah**lay**ner

What time is your last train?	**Hvornår går Deres sidste tog?**	vornawr gawr **day**rerss **seess**der tawg
Good-night ...	**Godnat ...**	goadh**nahd**

Banks

Where's the nearest bank, please?	**Hvor er den nærmeste bank?**	vor air dehn **nair**mersder bahnk
Where can I cash some traveller's cheques?	**Hvor kan jeg ind-løse rejsechecks?**	vor kahn yay in**lursser righ**ssershehks
What time does the bank open/What time does it close?	**Hvornår åbner banken/Hvornår lukker den?**	vor**nawr awb**nerr **bahng**gern/vor**nawr loa**gerr dehn
I'm expecting some money from home. Has it arrived?	**Jeg venter nogle penge hjemmefra. Er de kommet?**	yay **vehn**derr no(g)ler **pehng**ger **yehm**erfrar. air dee **ko**mmerd
Can you give me some small change, please?	**Vil De give mig nogle småpenge?**	vill dee **gee**(ver) migh **no**(g)ler smaw**pehng**er

Shops, stores and services

Where is the nearest chemist's (pharmacy)?	**Hvor er det nærmeste apotek?**	vor air day **nair**mersder ahpoa**tayg**
the nearest hair-dresser's	**den nærmeste frisør**	dehn **nair**mersder fri**surr**
the photo shop	**fotoforretningen**	**foat**oaforehdningern
the jeweller's	**guldsmeden**	**gool**smaydhern
the department store	**stormagasinet**	s**doar**mahgahsseenerd
the police station	**politistationen**	poleet**ee**stahshoanern
the garage	**parkeringshuset**	pahr**kay**ringsshoosserd
How do I get there?	**Hvordan kommer jeg derhen?**	vor**dahn ko**mmerr yay **dehr**hehn
Is it within walking distance?	**Kan man nemt gå derhen?**	kahn mahn nehmd gaw **dehr**hehn

Service

Can you help me, please?	**Vil De hjælpe mig?**	vil dee **yehl**ber migh
Can you show me this? And that, too.	**Vil De vise mig den her? Og den der.**	vil dee **vee**ser migh dehn hair? o dehn dair
It's too expensive/ too big/too small.	**Den er for dyr/for stor/for lille.**	dehn air for dewr/for stoar/for **lil**ler

DANISH

DANISH

Can you show me some more?	Kan De vise mig nogle flere?	kahn dee **vee**sser migh **no(g)**ler flay**r**er
something better something cheaper	noget bedre noget billigere	noa(g)erd be**h**dhrer noa(g)erd **bi**lliggerrer
How much is this? And that?	Hvor meget koster den her? Og den der?	vor **migh**erd koss**d**err dehn hair? o dehn dair
It's not quite what I want.	Det er ikke helt det, jeg gerne vil have.	day air **i**gger hayld day yay **gehr**ner vil **hai**(wer)
I like it.	Den kan jeg lide.	dehn kahn yay **lee**(dher)

Chemist's (Pharmacy)

| I'd like something for a cold/for a cough/for travel sickness. | Jeg vil gerne have noget mod for-kølelse/mod hoste/mod køresyge. | yay vil **gehr**ner **hai**(wer) noa(g)erd moadh for**kur**-lerlser/moadh **hoass**der/ moadh **kur**rersew(g)er |
| Can you recommend something for hay-fever/for sunburn? | Kan De anbefale noget mod høfeber/mod solforbrænding? | kahn dee **ahn**berfailer noa(g)erd moadh **hur**fayberr/moadh **soal**for-brehning |

Toiletry

May I have some razor blades?	Må jeg få nogle barberblade?	maw yay faw **no(g)**ler bahr**bayr**blaidher
some shaving cream some toothpaste	noget barbercreme noget tandpasta	noa**g**erd bahr**bay**kraym noa**g**erd **tahn**pahsdah
I'd like some soap.	Jeg vil gerne have noget håndsæbe.	yay vil **gehr**ner **hai**(wer) noa(g)erd **hon**saiber
some suntan oil	noget sololie	noa(g)erd **soal**oalyer

At the barber's

I'd like a haircut, please.	Jeg vil gerne klippes.	yay vil **gehr**ner kl**i**bberss
Short/Leave it long.	Kort/Lad det være langt.	kord/lahd day **vai**rer lahngd
A razor cut, please.	Skåret med bar-berblad.	**sgaw**rerd maydh bahr-**bayr**blahdh

At the hairdresser's

I'd like a shampoo and set, please.	Jeg vil gerne have en vask og vandon-dulation.	yay vil **gehr**ner **hai**(wer) ayn vahsg o **vahn**on-doolahshoan
I'd like a bleach.	Jeg vil gerne have en blegning.	yay vil **gehr**ner **hai**(wer) ayn **bligh**ning
a permanent	en permanent	ayn pehr**mah**nehnd
a colour rinse	en skylning	ayn **sgewl**ning
a manicure	en manicure	ayn mahni**kewr**

Photography

| I'd like a film for this camera. | Jeg vil gerne have en film til dette apparat. | yay vil **gehr**ner **hai**(wer) ayn film til **deh**der ahbah**rard** |
| This camera doesn't work. | Dette apparat virker ikke. | **deh**der ahbah**rard veer**ger **ig**ger |

At the post office

| Where's the nearest post office, please? | Hvor er det nærmeste posthus? | vor air day **nair**mersder **possd**hooss |
| I'd like to send this by express (special delivery)/by air mail. | Jeg vil gerne sende dette ekspres/som luftpost. | yay vil **gehr**ner **seh**ner **deh**der ehks**brehss**/som **loofd**possd |

Service stations

Where is the nearest service station, please?	Hvor er den nærmeste service-station?	vor air dehn **nair**mersder **surr**vissssdahshoan
Fill her up, please.	Vil De fylde den op?	vil dee **few**ler dehn ob
Check the oil, please.	Vil De kontrollere oliestanden?	vil dee kontroa**lay**rer **oal**yersdahnern
Would you check the tyres?	Vil De kontrollere dækkene?	vil dee kontroa**lay**rer **deh**gerner

Street directions

| Can you show me on the map where I am? | Vil De vise mig på kortet, hvor jeg er? | vil dee **vee**ser migh paw **kor**terd vor yay air |
| You're on the wrong road. | De er ikke på den rigtige vej. | dee air **ig**ger paw dehn **rayg**di(g)er vigh |

Go back to...	**Kør tilbage til ...**	kurr tilbai(g)er til
Go straight ahead.	**Kør ligeud.**	kurr lee(g)eroodh
It's on the left/on the right.	**Det er til venstre/til højre.**	day air til **vehn**strer/til **hol**rer

Accidents

May I use your telephone?	**Må jeg låne Deres telefon?**	maw yay **law**ner **day**rerss **tay**ler**foan**
Call a doctor quickly.	**Tilkald straks en læge.**	**til**kahl sdrahgs ayn **lai**ger
Call an ambulance.	**Tilkald en ambulance.**	**til**kahl ayn ahmboo**lahng**ser
Please call the police.	**Tilkald politiet.**	**til**kahl poleetee**eerd**

Numbers

one	en	ayn
two	to	toa
three	tre	tray
four	fire	feerer
five	fem	fehm
six	seks	sehgs
seven	syv	sewoo
eight	otte	odder
nine	ni	nee
ten	ti	tee
eleven	elleve	ehlver
twelve	tolv	tol
thirteen	tretten	trehtern
fourteen	fjorten	fyortern
fifteen	femten	fehmtern
sixteen	seksten	sehgstern
seventeen	sytten	sewtern
eighteen	atten	ahtern
nineteen	nitten	nittern
twenty	tyve	tewver
twenty-one	en og tyve	ayn o tewver
thirty	tredive	trehdver
forty	fyrre	fewrer
fifty	halvtreds	hahltrayss
sixty	tres	trayss
seventy	halvfjerds	hahlfyehrss
eighty	firs	feerss
ninety	halvfems	hahlfehmss

one hundred	hundrede	hoonrerdher
one thousand	tusind	toossin
ten thousand	ti tusind	tee toossin

Days

It's Sunday.	Det er søndag.	day air surndai
Monday	mandag	mahndai
Tuesday	tirsdag	teerssdai
Wednesday	onsdag	oanssdai
Thursday	torsdag	torssdai
Friday	fredag	fraydai
Saturday	lørdag	lurrdai
yesterday	i går	ee gawr
today	i dag	ee dai
tomorrow	i morgen	ee mor(g)ern
morning/afternoon	formiddag/ eftermiddag	formiddai/ehfderrmiddai
evening/night	aften/nat	ahfdern/nahd

Months

January	januar	yahnooarr
February	februar	faybrooarr
March	marts	mahrdss
April	april	ahpreel
May	maj	migh
June	juni	yoonee
July	juli	yoolee
August	august	owgoossd
September	september	sehbtehmberr
October	oktober	ogtoaberr
November	november	noavehmberr
December	december	daysehmberr
Merry Christmas!	Glædelig jul! Godt	glaidherlee yool! goad
Happy New Year!	nytår!	newdawr

DANISH

DUTCH

Guide to Pronunciation

Letter	Approximate pronunciation	Symbol	Example	

Consonants

c, f, h, k, l, m, n, p, q, t, v, y, z	as in English			
b	as in English, but when at the end of a word, like p in cup	b p	ben heb	behn hehp
ch	1) generally like ch in Scottish loch	kh	nacht	nahkht
	2) in words of French origin like sh in shut	sh	cheque	shehk
chtj	like Dutch ch followed by Dutch j	khy	nichtje	nikhyer
d	as in English, but, when at the end of a word, like t in hit	d t	doe bed	doo beht
g	1) generally like ch in Scottish loch, but often slightly softer and voiced	ǧ	goed	ǧoot
	2) in a few words of French origin, like s in pleasure	zh	genie	zhernee
	3) like ch in Scottish loch when at the end of a word	kh	deeg	daykh

j	like y in yes	y	ja	yar
nj	like ñ in Spanish señor or like ni in onion	ñ	oranje	oarahñer
r	always trilled, either in the front or the back of the mouth	r	warm	vahrm
s	always like s in sit	s/ss	roos	roass
sj, stj	like sh in shut	sh	meisje	maysher
sch	like s followed by a Dutch ch	skh	schrijven	skhrayver(n)
th	like t	t	thee	tay
tj	like ty in hit you	ty	katje	kahtyer
w	something like v, but with the bottom lip raised a little higher	v	water	varterr

Vowels

In Dutch a vowel is *short* when followed by two consonants, or by one consonant at the end of a word. It is *long* when it is at the end of a word, or before a consonant followed by a vowel, or when written double.

a	1) when short, between a in cat and u in cut, or like o in American college	ah	kat	kaht
	2) when long, like a in cart	ar	vader	varderr
e	1) when short, like e in bed	eh	bed	beht
	2) when long, like a in late, but a pure vowel	ay	zee	zay
	3) in unstressed syllables, like a in above	er	zitten	zittern
eu	(long) like eu in French feu; approximately like u in fur, said with rounded lips	ur	deur	durr
i	1) when short, like i in bit	i	kind	kint
	2) when long (also spelt ie), like ee in bee	ee	bier	beer
	3) sometimes, in unstressed syllables, like a in above	er	monnik	monnerk
ij	sometimes, in unstressed syllables, like a in above	er	lelijk	laylerk
o	1) when short, like a very short version of aw in lawn	o	pot	pot
	2) when long, something like oa in road, but a pure vowel and with more rounded lips	oa	boot	boat
oe	(long) like oo in moon and well rounded	oo	hoe	hoo

| u | 1) when short, something like **u** in hurt, but with rounded lips | er | **bus** | berss |
| | 2) when long, like **u** in French sur or **ü** in German für; say **ee**, and without moving your tongue, round your lips. The resulting "rounded **ee**" should be the correct sound | ew | **nu** | new |

Diphthongs

ai	like **igh** in s**igh**	igh	**ai**	igh
ei, ij	like **a** in l**a**te	ay	**reis**	rayss
au, ou	Dutch short **o** followed by a weak, short **u**-sound; can sound very much like **ow** in n**ow**	ow	**koud**	kowt

The following diphthongs have a long vowel as their first element:

aai	like **a** in c**a**t followed by a short **ee** sound	aree	**draai**	draree
eeuw	like **a** in l**a**te followed by a short **oo** sound	ayoo	**leeuw**	layoo
ieuw	like **ee** in fr**ee**, followed by a short **oo** sound	eeoo	**nieuw**	neeoo
ooi	like **o** in wr**o**te followed by a short **ee** sound	oaee	**nooit**	noaeet
oei	like **oo** in s**oo**n, followed by a short **ee** sound	ooee	**roeit**	rooeet
ui	like **u** in f**u**r, followed by a short Dutch **u** sound, as described in **u** number 2)	urew	**huis**	hurewss
uw	like the sound described in **u** number 2), followed by a weak **oo** sound	ewoo	**duw**	dewoo

N.B.
1) When two consonants are next to each other, one will often influence the other even if it is not in the same word, e.g., *ziens* is pronounced **zeenss**, but in the expression *tot ziens*, it is pronounced **seenss** under the influence of the **t** before it.
2) In the **-en** ending of verbs and plural nouns, the **n** is generally dropped in everyday speech.

DUTCH

Some basic expressions

Yes.	Ja.	yar
No.	Nee.	nay
Please.	Alstublieft.	ahlsstew**bleeft**
Thank you.	Dank U.	dahngk ew
Thank you very much.	Hartelijk dank.	**hahr**terlerk dahngk
That's all right.	Niets te danken.	neets ter **dahng**kern

Greetings

Good morning.	Goedemorgen.	ġooder**mor**ġern
Good afternoon.	Goedemiddag.	ġooder**mid**dahkh
Good evening.	Goedenavond.	ġoode**nar**vernt
Good night.	Goedenacht.	ġoode**nahkht**
Good-bye.	Tot ziens.	tot seenss
See you later.	Tot straks.	tot strahks
This is Mr....	Dit is Mijnheer...	dit iss mer**nayr**
This is Mrs....	Dit is Mevrouw...	dit iss mer**vrow**
This is Miss...	Dit is Juffrouw...	dit iss **yer**frow
I'm very pleased to meet you.	Aangenaam kennis te maken.	**arn**ġernarm **keh**nerss ter **mar**kern
How are you?	Hoe gaat het?	hoo **ġar**tert
Very well, thank you.	Heel goed, dank U.	hayl ġoot dahngk ew
And you?	En U?	ehn ew
Fine.	Uitstekend.	urewt**stay**kernt
Excuse me.	Neemt U me niet kwalijk.	naymt ew mer neet **kvar**lerk

Questions

Where?	Waar?	varr
Where is...?	Waar is...?	varr iss
Where are...?	Waar zijn...?	varr zayn
When?	Wanneer?	vahn**nayr**
What?	Wat?	vaht
How?	Hoe?	hoo
How much?	Hoeveel?	hoo**vayl**
How many?	Hoeveel?	hoo**vayl**

DUTCH

Who?	**Wie?**	vee
Why?	**Waarom?**	**var**rom
Which?	**Welk/Welke?**	vehlk/**vehl**ker
What do you call this?	**Hoe noemt U dit?**	hoo noomt ew dit
What do you call that?	**Hoe noemt U dat?**	hoo noomt ew daht
What does this mean?	**Wat betekent dit?**	vaht ber**tay**kernt dit
What does that mean?	**Wat betekent dat?**	vaht ber**tay**kernt daht

Do you speak . . . ?

Do you speak English?	**Spreekt U Engels?**	spraykt ew **ehng**erlss
Do you speak German?	**Spreekt U Duits?**	spraykt ew durewts
Do you speak French?	**Spreekt U Frans?**	spraykt ew frahnss
Do you speak Spanish?	**Spreekt U Spaans?**	spraykt ew sparnss
Do you speak Italian?	**Spreekt U Italiaans?**	spraykt ew itahli**arnss**
Could you speak more slowly, please?	**Kunt U wat langzamer spreken, alstublieft?**	kernt ew vaht **lahng**zar-merr **spray**kern ahlsstew**bleeft**
Please point to the phrase in the book.	**Wijs me de zin aan in het boek, alstublieft.**	vayss mer der zin arn in heht book ahlsstew**bleeft**
Just a minute. I'll see if I can find it in this book.	**Een ogenblik. Ik zal proberen het in dit boek op te zoeken.**	een oa**ğ**ernblik. ik zahl proa**bay**rern heht in dit book op te **zoo**kern
I understand.	**Ik begrijp het.**	ik ber**ğrayp**heht
I don't understand.	**Ik begrijp het niet.**	ik ber**ğrayp**heht neet

Can . . . ?

| Can I have . . . ? | **Mag ik . . . hebben?** | mahkh ik . . . **heh**bern |
| Can we have . . . ? | **Mogen wij . . . hebben?** | moa**ğ**ern vay . . . **heh**bern |

DUTCH

Can you show me . . . ?	**Kunt U me . . . tonen?**	kernt ew mer . . . **toa**nern
Can you tell me . . . ?	**Kunt U mij zeggen . . . ?**	kernt ew may **zeh**gern
Can you help me, please?	**Kunt U mij helpen, alstublieft?**	kernt ew may **hehl**pern ahlsstew**bleeft**

Wanting

I'd like . . .	**Ik wil graag . . .**	ik vil ġrarkh
We'd like . . .	**Wij willen graag . . .**	vay **vil**lern ġrarkh
Please give me . . .	**Geeft ew . . . , alstublieft.**	ġayft ew mer . . . ahlsstee**bleeft**
Give it to me, please.	**Geeft U het me, alstublieft.**	ġayft ew heht mer ahlsstew**bleeft**
Please bring me . . .	**Brengt U me . . . , alstublieft.**	brehngt ew mer . . . ahlsstew**bleeft**
Bring it to me, please.	**Brengt U het me, alstublieft.**	brehngt ew heht mer ahlsstew**bleeft**
I'm hungry.	**Ik heb honger.**	ik hehp **hong**err
I'm thirsty.	**Ik heb dorst.**	ik hehp dorst
I'm tired.	**Ik ben moe.**	ik behn moo
I'm lost.	**Ik ben verdwaald.**	ik behn verr**dvarlt**
It's important.	**Het is belangrijk.**	heht iss berlahngrayk
It's urgent.	**Het is dringend.**	heht iss **dring**ernt
Hurry up!	**Vlug!**	vlerkh

It is/There is . . .

It is/It's . . .	**Het is . . .**	heht iss
Is it . . . ?	**Is het . . . ?**	iss heht
It isn't . . .	**Het is niet . . .**	heht iss neet
There is/There are . . .	**Er is/Er zijn . . .**	ehr iss/ehr zayn
Is there/Are there . . . ?	**Is er/Zijn er . . . ?**	iss ehr/zayn ehr
There isn't/There aren't . . .	**Er is geen/Er zijn geen . . .**	ehr iss ġayn/ehr zayn ġayn
There isn't any/ There aren't any.	**Er is er geen/Er zijn er geen.**	ehr iss ehr ġayn/ehr zayn ehr ġayn

DUTCH

A few common words

big/small	**groot/klein**	ǧroat/klayn
quick/slow	**snel/langzaam**	snehl/**lahng**zarm
early/late	**vroeg/laat**	vrookh/lart
cheap/expensive	**goedkoop/duur**	ǧoot**koap**/dewr
near/far	**dichtbij/ver**	dikht**bay** vehr
hot/cold	**warm/koud**	vahrm/kowt
full/empty	**vol/leeg**	vol/laykh
easy/difficult	**gemakkelijk/moeilijk**	ǧer**mah**kerlerk/**mooee**lerk
heavy/light	**zwaar/licht**	zvarr/likht
open/shut	**open/dicht**	**oa**pern/dikht
right/wrong	**juist/verkeerd**	yurewst/ver**kayrt**
old/new	**oud/nieuw**	owt/neeoo
old/young	**oud/jong**	owt/yong
beautiful/ugly	**mooi/lelijk**	moaae/**lay**lerk
good/bad	**goed/slecht**	ǧoot/slehkht
better/worse	**beter/slechter**	**bay**ter/**slehkh**terr

Some prepositions and a few more useful words

at	**te**	ter
on	**op**	op
in	**in**	in
to	**naar**	narr
from	**van**	vahn
inside	**binnen**	**bin**nern
outside	**buiten**	**burew**tern
up	**op**	op
down	**neer**	nayr
before	**voor**	voar
after	**na**	nar
with	**met**	meht
without	**zonder**	**zon**derr
through	**door**	doar
towards	**naar**	narr
until	**tot**	tot
during	**tijdens**	**tay**dernss
and	**en**	ehn
or	**of**	off
not	**niet**	neet
nothing	**niets**	neets
none	**geen**	ǧayn
very	**zeer**	zayr
also	**ook**	oak
soon	**spoedig**	**spoo**derkh
perhaps	**misschien**	miss**kheen**

here	**hier**	heer
there	**daar**	darr
now	**nu**	new
then	**dan**	dahn

Arrival

Your passport, please.	**Uw paspoort, alstublieft.**	ewoo **pahss**poart ahlsstew**bleeft**
Here it is.	**Alstublieft.**	ahlsstew**bleeft**
Have you anything to declare?	**Hebt U iets aan te geven?**	hehpt ew eets arn ter **ĝay**vern
No, nothing at all.	**Nee, helemaal niets.**	nay **hay**lermarl neets
Porter!	**Kruier!**	**kru**rewer
Can you help me with my luggage, please?	**Kunt U me met mijn bagage helpen, alstublieft?**	kernt ew mer meht mayn bah**ĝar**zher **hehl**pern ahlsstew**bleeft**
That's my suitcase.	**Dat is mijn koffer.**	daht iss mayn **koff**err
Where's the bus to the centre of town, please?	**Waar is de bus naar het centrum, alstublieft?**	varr iss der berss narr heht **sehn**trerm ahlsstew-**bleeft**
This way, please.	**Hierlangs, alstublieft.**	**heer**lahngss ahlsstew-**bleeft**

Changing money

| Can you change a traveller's cheque, please? | **Kunt U een traveller's cheque wisselen, alstublieft?** | kernt ew ern "traveller's cheque" **vi**serlern ahlsstew**bleeft** |
| Where's the nearest bank, please? | **Waar is de dichtst-bijzijnde bank, alstublieft?** | varr iss der **dikhtst**bayzaynder bahngk ahlsstew**bleeft** |

Car rental

I'd like a car.	**Ik wil graag een auto huren.**	ik vil **ĝrarkh** ern **ow**toa **hew**rern
For how long?	**Voor hoe lang?**	voar hoo lahng
A day/Four days/A week/Two weeks.	**Een dag/Vier dagen/Een week/Twee weken.**	ayn dahkh/veer **dah**ĝer(n)/ayn vayk/tvay **vay**kern

Taxi

Where can I get a taxi?	Waar kan ik een taxi krijgen?	varr kahn ik ern **tak**see **kray**ğern
What's the fare to...?	Wat kost het naar...?	vaht kost heht narr
Take me to this address, please.	Breng me naar dit adres, alstublieft.	brehng mer narr dit ah-**drehss** ahlsstew**bleeft**
I'm in a hurry.	Ik heb haast.	ik hehp harst
Could you drive more slowly, please?	Wilt U wat langzamer rijden, alstublieft?	vilt ew vaht **lahng**zarmerr **ray**dern ahlsstew**bleeft**

Hotel and other accommodation

My name is...	Mijn naam is...	mayn narm iss
Have you a reservation?	Hebt U gereserveerd?	hehpt ew ğerrayserr**vayrt**
Yes, here's the confirmation.	Ja, hier is de bevestiging.	yar heer iss der ber-**vehss**stiğing
I'd like...	Ik wil graag...	ik vil ğrarkh
I'd like a single room/a double room.	Ik wil graag een éénpersoonskamer/een tweepersoons kamer.	ik vil ğrarkh een **ayn**perrsoansskarmerr/ern **tvay**perrsoansskarmerr
a room with a bath/with a shower	een kamer met bad/met douche	ern **kar**merr meht baht/meht **doo**sher

How much?

What's the price per night/per week/per month?	Hoeveel is het per nacht/per week/per maand?	hoo**vayl** iss heht pehr nahkht/pehr vayk/pehr marnt
May I see the room?	Mag ik de kamer zien?	mahkh ik der **kar**merr zeen
I'm sorry, I don't like it.	Het spijt me, hij bevalt me niet.	heht spayt mer hay ber-**vahlt** mer neet
Yes, that's fine. I'll take it.	Ja, dat is goed. Die neem ik.	yar daht iss ğoot. dee naym ik
What's my room number, please?	Wat is mijn kamernummer, alstublieft?	vaht iss mayn **kar**merrnermerr ahlsstew**bleeft**
Number 123.	Nummer 123.	**ner**merr 123.

DUTCH

Service, please

Who is it?	**Wie is daar?**	vee iss darr
Just a minute.	**Een ogenblikje.**	ern oağernblikyer
Come in! The door's open.	**Binnen! De deur is open.**	binern. der durr iss oapern
May we have breakfast in our room?	**Kunnen we in onze kamer ontbijten?**	kernern ver in onzer karmerr ontbaytern

Breakfast

I'll have ...	**Ik neem ...**	ik naym
I'll have some fruit juice.	**Ik neem vruchtensap.**	ik naym vrerkhternsahp
a boiled egg	**een gekookt ei**	ern ğerkoakt ay
a fried egg	**een gebakken ei**	ern ğerbahkern ay
some bacon/some ham	**spek/ham**	spehk/hahm
some toast	**toast**	toast
a pot of tea	**een kannetje thee**	ern kahnertyer tay
a cup of tea	**een kopje thee**	ern kopyer tay
some coffee	**koffie**	kofee
some chocolate	**chocola**	shoakoalar
more butter	**nog wat boter**	nokh vaht boaterr
some hot water	**wat warm water**	vaht vahrm varterr

Difficulties

The central heating doesn't work.	**De centrale verwarming werkt niet.**	der sehntrarler verrvahrming vehrkt neet
the light/the socket	**het licht/het stopcontact**	heht likht/heht stopkontahkt
the tap/the toilet	**de kraan/het toilet**	der krarn/heht tvahleht
There's no hot water.	**Er is geen warm water.**	ehr iss ğayn vahrm varterr
May I see the manager, please?	**Mag ik de direkteur spreken, alstublieft?**	mahkk ik der deererkturr spraykern ahlsstewbleeft

Telephone—Mail

| There's a call for you. | **Er is telefoon voor U.** | ehr iss taylerfoan voar ew |
| Hold the line, please. | **Blijft U aan het toestel, alstublieft.** | blayft ew arn heht toosterl ahlsstewbleeft |

Operator, I've been cut off.	**Juffrouw, mijn gesprek is verbroken.**	yerfrow mayn ğersprehk iss verrbroakern
Did anyone telephone me?	**Heeft er iemand voor mij opgebeld?**	hayft ehr eemahnt voar may opğerbehlt
Is there any mail for me?	**Is er post voor mij?**	iss ehr post voar may
Are there any messages for me?	**Heeft iemand een boodschap voor mij achtergelaten?**	hayft eemahnt ern boatskhahp voar may ahkhterrğerlartern

Checking out

May I have my bill, please?	**Mag ik de rekening, alstublieft?**	mahkh ik der raykerning ahlsstewbleeft
We're in a great hurry.	**Wij hebben erge haast.**	vay hehbern ehrğer harst
It's been a very enjoyable stay.	**Wij hebben het hier erg prettig gehad.**	vay hehbern het heer ehrkh prehterkh ğerhaht

Eating out

Good evening, sir/Good evening, madam.	**Goedenavond, Mijnheer/Goedenavond Mevrouw.**	ğoodernarvernt mernayr ğoodernarvernt mervrow
Good evening. I'd like a table for two, please.	**Goedenavond. Ik wil graag een tafel voor twee personen.**	ğoodernarvernt. ik vil ğrarkh ern tarferl voar tvay perrsoanern
Do you have a fixed-price menu?	**Hebt U een menu à prix fixe?**	hehpt ew ern mernewah pree feeks
May I see the à la carte menu?	**Mag ik het menu à la carte?**	mahkh ik heht mernew ah lah kahrt
May we have an ashtray, please?	**Kunt U ons een asbak brengen, alstublieft?**	kernt ew onss ern ahssbahk brehngern ahlsstewbleeft
some bread	**wat brood**	vat broat
a fork	**een vork**	ern vork
a knife	**een mes**	ern mehss
a spoon	**een lepel**	ern layperl
a plate	**een bord**	ern bort
a glass	**een glas**	ern ğlahss
a napkin	**een servet**	ern sehrveht
another chair	**nog een stoel**	nokh ern stool

DUTCH

| Where s the gentlemen's toilet (men's room)? | **Waar is het heren-toilet?** | varr iss heht **hay**rern-tvahleht |
| Where's the ladies' toilet (ladies' room)? | **Waar is het dames-toilet?** | varr iss heht **darmers**s-tvahleht |

Appetizers

I'd like some . . .	**Ik wil graag . . .**	ik vil ǵrarkh
I'd like some assorted appetizers.	**Ik wil graag hors-d'oeuvre varié.**	ik vil ǵrarkh or durvr vahree**ay**
orange juice	**sinaasappelsap**	**see**narsahperlsahp
ham	**ham**	hahm
melon	**meloen**	mer**loon**
pâté	**paté**	pah**tay**
smoked salmon	**gerookte zalm**	ǵer**roak**ter zahlm
shrimps (shrimp)	**garnalen**	ǵahr**nar**lern

Soup

Have you any . . . ?	**Hebt U . . . ?**	hehpt ew
Have you any chicken soup?	**Hebt U kippesoep?**	hehpt ew **ki**persoop
vegetable soup	**groentesoep**	**ǵroon**tersoop
onion soup	**uiensoep**	**urew**ernsoop

Fish

I'd like some . . .	**Ik wil graag . . .**	ik vil ǵrarkh
I'd like some fish.	**Ik wil graag vis.**	ik vil ǵrarkh viss
sole	**zeetong**	**zay**tong
trout	**forel**	foa**rehl**
lobster	**kreeft**	krayft
crayfish	**rivierkreeft**	ree**veer**krayft
prawns	**steurgarnalen**	**sturr**ǵahrnarlern
I'd like it . . .	**Ik heb hem graag . . .**	ik hehp hehm ǵrarkh
I'd like it steamed.	**Ik heb hem graag gestoomd.**	ik hehp hehm ǵrarkh ǵer**stoamt**
grilled	**gegrilleerd**	ǵer**ǵri**layrt
boiled	**gekookt**	ǵer**koakt**
baked	**in de oven ge-bakken**	in der **oa**vern ǵer**bah**kern
fried	**gebakken**	ǵer**bah**kern

DUTCH

Meat—Poultry—Game

I'd like some . . .	Ik wil graag . . .	ik vil ğrarkh
I'd like some beef.	Ik wil graag rundvlees.	ik vil ğrarkh rerntvlayss
a beef steak	een biefstuk	ern beefsterk
some roast beef	rosbief	rossbeef
a veal cutlet	een kalfskotelet	ern kahlfskoaterleht
mutton	schapevlees	skhahpervlayss
lamb	lamsvlees	lahmssvlayss
a pork chop	een varkenskotelet	ayn vahrkernsskoaterleht
roast pork	varkensfricandeau	vahrkernssfreekahndoa
hare	haas	harss
chicken	kip	kip
roast chicken	gebraden kip	ğerbrardern kip
duck	eend	aynt
How do you like your meat?	Hoe wenst U het vlees?	hoo vehnst ew heht vlayss
rare	rood	roat
medium	lichtgebakken	likhtğerbahkern
well done	doorgebakken	doarğerbahkern

Vegetables

What vegetables have you got?	Wat voor groenten hebt U?	vaht voar ğroontern hehpt ew
I'd like some . . .	Ik wil graag . . .	ik vil ğrarkh
I'd like some asparagus.	Il wil graag asperges.	ik vil ğrarkh ahsspehrzherss
green beans	sperziebonen	spehrzeeboanern
mushrooms	champignons	shahmpeeñongss
carrots	worteltjes	vorterltyehss
onions	uien	urewern
red cabbage	rode kool	roader koal
spinach	spinazie	speenarzee
rice	rijst	rayst
peas	doperwtjes	dopehrtyerss
tomatoes	tomaten	toamartern
green salad	sla	slar
potatoes	aardappelen	arrdahperlern

Desserts

Nothing more, thanks.	Niets meer, dank U.	neets mayr dangk ew

·

DUTCH

DUTCH

Just a small portion, please.	**Een kleine portie, alstublieft.**	ern **klay**ner **por**see ahlsstew**bleeft**
Have you any ice-cream?	**Hebt U ijs?**	hehpt ew ayss
fruit salad	**vruchtensla**	**vrerkh**ternslar
fresh fruit	**vers fruit**	vehrss frurewt
cheese	**kaas**	karss

Drink

What would you like to drink?	**Wat wilt U drinken?**	vaht vilt ew **dring**kern
I'll have a beer, please.	**Een pils, alstublieft.**	ern pilss ahlsstew**bleeft**
I'll have a whisky, please.	**Een whisky, alstublieft.**	ern **viss**kee ahlsstew**bleeft**

Wine

I'd like a bottle of wine.	**Ik wil graag een fles wijn.**	ik vil ĝrarkh ern flehss vayn
red wine	**rode wijn**	**roa**der vayn
rosé wine	**rosé**	**roa**zay
white wine	**witte wijn**	**vit**er vayn
Cheers!	**Proost!**	proast

The bill (check)

May I have the bill (check) please?	**Mag ik de rekening, alstublieft?**	mahkh ik der **ray**kerning ahlsstew**bleeft**
Is service included?	**Is de bediening inbegrepen?**	iss der ber**dee**ning inber**ĝray**pern
Everything's included.	**Alles inclusief.**	**ah**lerss inklew**zeef**
Thank you, that was a very good meal.	**Dank U, het was een uitstekende maaltijd.**	dangk ew heht vahss ern **urewt**staykernder **marl**tayt

Travelling

| Where's the railway station, please? | **Waar is het station, alstublieft?** | varr iss heht stah**shon** ahlsstew**bleeft** |
| Where's the ticket office, please? | **Waar is het loket, alstublieft?** | varr iss heht loa**keht** ahlsstew**bleeft** |

I'd like a ticket to ...	**Ik wil graag een kaartje naar ...**	ik vil ǵrarkh ern **karr**tyer narr
First or second class?	**Eerste of tweede klas?**	**ayr**ster off **tvay**der klahss
First class, please.	**Eerste klas, alstublieft.**	**ayr**ster klahss ahlsstew**bleeft**
Single or return (one way or round-trip)?	**Enkele reis of retour?**	**ehng**kerler rayss off rer**toor**
Do I have to change trains?	**Moet ik overstappen?**	moot ik **oa**verrstahpern
What platform does the train leave from?	**Van welk perron vertrekt de trein?**	vahn vehlk peh**ron** verr**trehkt** der trayn
Where's the nearest underground (subway) station?	**Waar is het dichtstbijzijnde metrostation?**	varr iss hert **dikhtst**bayzaynder **meh**troastah**shon**
Where's the bus station, please?	**Waar is het busstation, alstublieft?**	varr iss heht **berss**stahshon ahlsstew**bleeft**
When's the first bus to ...?	**Om hoe laat vertrekt de eerste bus naar ...?**	om hoo lart verr**trehkt** der **ayr**ster berss narr
the last bus the next bus	**de laatste bus de volgende bus**	der **lart**ster berss der **vol**ǵernde berss
Please let me off at the next stop.	**Wilt U me bij de volgende halte laten uitstappen?**	vilt ew mer bay der **vol**ǵernder **hahl**ter lar**tern** **urewt**stahpern

Relaxing

What's on at the cinema (movies)?	**Wat wordt er in de bioscoop gegeven?**	vaht vort ehr in der bee**o**skoap ǵer**ǵay**vern
What's on at the theatre?	**Wat wordt er in de schouwburg gegeven?**	vahr vort ehr in der **skhow**berkh ǵer**ǵay**vern
What time does the film begin? And the play?	**Om hoe laat begint de film? En het toneelstuk?**	om hoo lart ber**ǵint** der film? ehn hert toa**nayl**sterk
Are there any tickets for tonight?	**Zijn er nog plaatsen vrij voor vanavond?**	zayn ehr nokh **plart**sern vray voar vahn**ar**vont
Where can we go dancing?	**Waar kunnen we gaan dansen?**	varr **ker**nern ver ǵarn **dahn**sern
Would you like to dance?	**Mag ik deze dans van U?**	mahkh ik **day**zer dahnss vahn ew

DUTCH

DUTCH

Introductions

How do you do?	**Hoe maakt U het?**	hoo markt ew heht
How are you?	**Hoe gaat het?**	hoo ğart heht
Very well, thank you. And you?	**Uitstekend, dank U. En U?**	urewt**stay**kernt dahngk ew. ehn ew
May I introduce Miss Philips?	**Mag ik U Juffrouw Philips voorstellen?**	mahkh ik ew **yer**frow Philips **voor**stehlern
My name is...	**Mijn naam is...**	mayn narm iss
I'm very pleased to meet you.	**Prettig kennis met U te maken.**	**preh**terkh **keh**nerss meht ew ter **mar**kern
How long have you been here?	**Hoelang bent U al hier?**	**hoo**lahng behnt ew ahl heer
It was nice meeting you.	**Het was mij een genoegen.**	heht vahss may ayn ğer**noo**ğern

Dating

Would you like a cigarette?	**Mag ik U een sigaret aanbieden?**	mahkh ik ew ern seeğar**reht arn**beedern
May I get you a drink?	**Mag ik U iets te drinken aanbieden?**	mahkh ik ew eets ter **dring**kern **arn**beedern
Do you have a light, please?	**Hebt U een vuurtje, alstublieft?**	hehpt ew ern **vewrt**yer ahlsstew**bleeft**
Are you waiting for someone?	**Wacht U op iemand?**	vahkht ew op **ee**mahnt
Are you free this evening?	**Bent U vanavond vrij?**	behnt ew vahn**arvont** vray
Where shall we meet?	**Waar spreken we af?**	varr **spray**kern ver ahf
What time shall I meet you?	**Hoe laat spreken we af?**	hoo lart **spray**kern ver ahf
May I take you home?	**Mag ik U naar huis brengen?**	mahkh ik ew narr hurewss **brehng**ern
Thank you, it's been a wonderful evening.	**Dank U, het was een heerlijke avond.**	dahngk ew heht vahss ern **hayr**lerker **arvernt**
What's your telephone number?	**Wat is uw telefoon-nummer?**	vaht iss ewoo tayler**foan**nermerr
Do you live alone?	**Woont U alleen?**	voant ew ah**leen**
What time is your last train?	**Om hoe laat gaat uw laatste trein?**	om hoo lart ğart ewoo **lart**ster trayn
Good-night...	**Tot ziens...**	tot seenss

Banks

Where's the nearest bank, please?	**Waar is de dichtstbijzijnde bank, alstublieft?**	varr iss der **dikhtst**bayzaynder bahngk ahlsstew**bleeft**
Where can I cash some traveller's cheques?	**Waar kan ik traveller's cheques inwisselen?**	varr kahn ik "traveller's cheques" **in**viserlern
What time does the bank open? What time does it close?	**Om hoe laat gaat de bank open? Om hoe laat gaat hij dicht?**	om hoo lart ġart der bahngk **oa**pern? om hoo lart ġart hay dikht
I'm expecting some money from home. Has it arrived?	**Ik verwacht geld van thuis. Is het aangekomen?**	ik verr**vahkht** ġehlt vahn turewss. iss heht **arn**ġerkoamern
Can you give me some small change, please?	**Kunt U me wat kleingeld geven, alstublieft?**	kernt ew mer vaht **klayn**ġehlt **ġay**vern ahlsstew**bleeft**

Shops, stores and services

Where is the nearest chemist's (pharmacy)?	**Waar is de dichtstbijzijnde apotheek?**	varr iss der **dikhtst**bayzaynder arpoa**tayk**
the nearest hairdresser's	**de dichtstbijzijnde kapper**	der **dikhtst**bayzaynder **kah**perr
the photo shop	**de fotowinkel**	der **foa**toavingkerl
the jeweller's	**de juwelier**	der yewver**leer**
the department store	**het warenhuis**	heht **var**trrnhurewss
the police station	**het politiebureau**	heht polee(t)seebewroa
the garage	**de garage**	der ġah**rar**zher
How do I get there?	**Hoe kom ik daar?**	hoo kom ik darr
Is it within walking distance?	**Is het te lopen?**	iss heht ter **loa**pern

Service

Can you help me, please?	**Kunt U mij helpen, alstublieft?**	kernt ew may **hehl**pern ahlsstew**bleeft**
Can you show me this? And that, too.	**Kunt U me dit laten zien? En dat ook.**	kernt ew mer dit **lar**tern zeen ehn dat oak
It's too expensive/ too big/too small.	**Het is te duur/te groot/te klein.**	heht iss ter dewr/ter ġroat/ter klayn

Can you show me some more?	Kunt U me er nog wat laten zien?	kernt ew mer ehr mokh vaht lartern zeen
something better	iets beters	eets bayterrss
something cheaper	iets goedkopers	eets ğootkoaperss
How much is this? And that?	Hoeveel is dit? En dat?	hoovayl iss dit? ehn daht
It's not quite what I want.	Het is niet precies wat ik zoek.	heht iss neet prerseess vaht ik zook
I like it.	Het bevalt me.	heht bervahlt mer

Chemist's (Pharmacy)

| I'd like something for a cold/for a cough/for travel sickness. | Ik wil graag iets tegen een verkoudheid/tegen hoesten/tegen misselijkheid. | ik vil ğrarkh eets tayğern ern verkowthayt/tayğern hoostern/tayğern miserlerkhayt |
| Can you recommend something for hay-fever/for sunburn? | Kunt U mij iets tegen hooikoorts aanbevelen/tegen zonnebrand? | kernt ew may eets tayğern hoaeekoarts arnbervaylern/tayğern zonerbrahnt |

Toiletry

May I have some razor blades?	Mag ik scheer-mesjes?	mahkh ik skhayrmeh-sherss
some shaving cream	scheercrème	skhayrkraim
some toothpaste	tandpasta	tahntpahstarr
I'd like some soap.	Ik wil graag zeep.	ik vil ğrarkh zayp
some suntan oil	zonne-olie	zoneroalee

At the barber's

I'd like a haircut, please.	Knippen, alstublieft.	knipern ahlsstewbleeft
Short/Leave it long.	Kort/Laat het lang.	kort/lart heht lahng
A razor cut, please.	Met het mes, alstublieft.	meht heht mehss ahlsstewbleeft

At the hairdresser's

| I'd like a shampoo and set, please. | Wassen en water-golven, alstublieft. | vahsern ehn varterrğolvern ahlsstewbleeft |

I'd like a bleach.	**Ik wil het laten bleken.**	ik vil heht lar**tern blay**kern
a permanent	**een permanent**	ern pehrmar**nehnt**
a colour rinse	**een kleurspoeling**	ern **klurr**spooling
a manicure	**een manicure**	ern marnee**kew**rer

Photography

| I'd like a film for this camera. | **Ik wil graag een film voor dit toestel.** | ik vil ĝrarkh ern film voar dit **toos**terl |
| This camera doesn't work. | **Deze camera doet het niet.** | **day**zer **kar**merrah doot heht neet |

At the post office

| Where's the nearest post office, please? | **Waar is het dichtstbijzijnde postkantoor, alstublieft?** | varr iss heht **dikhtst**-bayzaynder **post**kahn-toar ahlstew**bleeft** |
| I'd like to send this by express (special delivery)/by air mail. | **Ik wil dit per ex-press versturen/per luchtpost.** | ik vil pehr ehks**prehss** verstewrern/pehr **lerkht**post |

Service stations

Where is the nearest service station, please?	**Waar is het dichtstbijzijnde ben-zinestation, alstu-blieft?**	varr iss heht **dikhtst**-bayzaynder behn-**zee**nerstahshon ahlstew**bleeft**
Fill her up, please.	**Vol, alstublieft.**	vol ahlstew**bleeft**
Check the oil, please.	**Wilt U de olie con-troleren, alstublieft?**	vilt ew der **oa**lee kon-troa**lay**rern ahlstew**bleeft**
Would you check the tyres?	**Wilt U de banden controleren?**	vilt ew der **bahn**dern kon-troa**lay**rern

Street directions

Can you show me on the map where I am?	**Kunt U mij op de kaart aanwijzen waar ik ben?**	kern ew may op der karrt **arn**vayzern varr ik behn
You're on the wrong road.	**U bent verkeerd gereden.**	ew behnt verr**kayrt** ĝer-**ray**dern
Go back to ...	**Rijd terug naar ...**	rayt ter**rerkh** narr

DUTCH

Go straight ahead.	**Rijd rechtuit.**	rayt **rehkh**turewt
It's on the left/on the right.	**Het is aan de linkerkant/aan de rechterkant.**	heht iss arn der **ling**kerkahnt/arn der **rehkh**terkahnt

Accidents

May I use your telephone?	**Mag ik van uw telefoon gebruik maken?**	mahkh ik vahn ewoo tayler**foan** ğer**brurewk** **mar**kern
Call a doctor quickly.	**Roep vlug een dokter.**	roop vlerkh ern **dok**terr
Call an ambulance.	**Roep een ambulance.**	roop ern ahmbew**lahn**ser
Please call the police.	**Roep de politie, alstublieft.**	roop de po**lee**(t)see ahlsstew**bleeft**

Numbers

<table>
<tr><td>one</td><td>een</td><td>ayn</td></tr>
<tr><td>two</td><td>twee</td><td>tvay</td></tr>
<tr><td>three</td><td>drie</td><td>dree</td></tr>
<tr><td>four</td><td>vier</td><td>veer</td></tr>
<tr><td>five</td><td>vijf</td><td>vayf</td></tr>
<tr><td>six</td><td>zes</td><td>zehss</td></tr>
<tr><td>seven</td><td>zeven</td><td>zayvern</td></tr>
<tr><td>eight</td><td>acht</td><td>ahkht</td></tr>
<tr><td>nine</td><td>negen</td><td>nayğern</td></tr>
<tr><td>ten</td><td>tien</td><td>teen</td></tr>
<tr><td>eleven</td><td>elf</td><td>ehlf</td></tr>
<tr><td>twelve</td><td>twaalf</td><td>tvarlf</td></tr>
<tr><td>thirteen</td><td>dertien</td><td>dehrteen</td></tr>
<tr><td>fourteen</td><td>veertien</td><td>vayrteen</td></tr>
<tr><td>fifteen</td><td>vijftien</td><td>vayfteen</td></tr>
<tr><td>sixteen</td><td>zestien</td><td>zehssteen</td></tr>
<tr><td>seventeen</td><td>zeventien</td><td>zayvernteen</td></tr>
<tr><td>eighteen</td><td>achttien</td><td>ahkhteen</td></tr>
<tr><td>nineteen</td><td>negentien</td><td>nayğernteen</td></tr>
<tr><td>twenty</td><td>twintig</td><td>tvinterkh</td></tr>
<tr><td>twenty-one</td><td>eenentwintig</td><td>aynerntvinterkh</td></tr>
<tr><td>thirty</td><td>dertig</td><td>dehrterkh</td></tr>
<tr><td>forty</td><td>veertig</td><td>vayrterkh</td></tr>
<tr><td>fifty</td><td>vijftig</td><td>vayfterkh</td></tr>
<tr><td>sixty</td><td>zestig</td><td>zehssterkh</td></tr>
<tr><td>seventy</td><td>zeventig</td><td>zayvernterkh</td></tr>
<tr><td>eighty</td><td>tachtig</td><td>tahkhterkh</td></tr>
<tr><td>ninety</td><td>negentig</td><td>nayğernterkh</td></tr>
</table>

one hundred	**honderd**	hon**derrt**
one thousand	**duizend**	**durew**zernt
ten thousand	**tienduizend**	**teen**durewzernt

Days

| It's Sunday. | **Het is zondag.** | heht iss **zon**dahkh |

Monday	**maandag**	**marn**dahkh
Tuesday	**dinsdag**	**dinss**dahkh
Wednesday	**woensdag**	**voonss**dahkh
Thursday	**donderdag**	**don**derrdahkh
Friday	**vrijdag**	**vray**dahkh
Saturday	**zaterdag**	**zar**terrdahkh

yesterday	**gisteren**	**ġi**sterrern
today	**vandaag**	vahn**darkh**
tomorrow	**morgen**	**mor**ġern
morning/afternoon	**ochtend/namiddag**	**okh**ternt/**nar**midankh
evening/night	**avond/nacht**	**ar**vernt/**nah**kht

Months

January	**januari**	yahne**war**ree
February	**februari**	fehvre**war**ree
March	**maart**	marrt
April	**april**	ah**pril**
May	**mei**	may
June	**juni**	**yew**nee
July	**juli**	**yew**lee
August	**augustus**	ow**ġers**sterss
September	**september**	sehp**tehm**berr
October	**oktober**	ok**toa**berr
November	**november**	noa**vehm**berr
December	**december**	day**sehm**berr

| Merry Christmas! | **Prettig Kerstfeest!** | **preh**terkh **kehrst**fayst! |
| Happy New Year! | **Gelukkig Nieuwjaar!** | er-lerkerkh **neeooy**arr |

FINNISH

Guide to Pronunciation

Letter	Approximate pronunciation	Symbol	Example	

Consonants

k, m, n, p, t, v	as in English			
d	as in rea**d**y, but sometimes very weak	d	**taide**	tigh**d**ay
g	only found after **n**; **ng** is pronounced as in si**ng**er	ng	sa**ng**en	sah**ng**ayn
h	as in **h**ot, whatever its position in the word	h	**Lahti**	la**hh**ti
j	like **y** in **y**ou	y	**ja**	yah
l	as in **l**et	l	ta**l**o	tah**l**oa
r	always rolled	r	**raha**	**r**ah**h**ah
s	always as in **s**et	s/ss	si**ll**ä	si**ll**æ
			kiitos	**kee**toass

Vowels

a	like a in car, but shorter	ah	matala	mahtahlah
e	like a in late	ay	kolme	koalmay
i	like i in pin	i	takki	tahkki
o	like aw in law, but shorter	oa	olla	oallah
u	like u in pull	oo	hupsu	hoopsoo
y	like u in French sur or ü in German über; say ee as in see and round your lips while still trying to pronounce ee	ew	yksi	ewksi
ä	like a in hat	æ	äkkiä	ækkiæ
ö	like ur in fur, but with the lips rounded	ur	tyttö	tewttur

N.B. The letters b, c, f, q, š, sh, x, z, ż and å are only found in words borrowed from foreign languages, and they are pronounced as in the language of origin.

Diphthongs

In Finnish, diphthongs occur only in the first syllable of a word, except for those ending in -i, which can occur anywhere. They should be pronounced as a combination of the two vowel sounds represented by the spelling. The first vowel is pronounced louder in the following diphthongs: ai, ei, oi, ui, yi, äi, öi, au, eu, ou, ey, äy, öy, iu; the second vowel is louder in: ie, uo, yö.

Double letters

Remember that in Finnish *every* letter is pronounced, therefore a letter written double is pronounced long. Thus, the kk in kukka should be pronounced like the two k-sounds in the words thick coat. Similarly, the aa in kaatua should be pronounced long (like a in English car). These distinctions are important, not least because kuka has a different meaning from kukka and katua a different meaning from kaatua.

Stress

A strong stress always falls on the first syllable of a word.

Some basic expressions

Yes.	Kyllä.	kewllæ
No.	Ei.	ay
Please.	Olkaa hyvä.	oalkar hewvæ
Thank you.	Kiitos.	keetoass
Thank you very much.	Kiitoksia paljon.	keetoaksiah pahlyoan
That's all right.	Ei kestä.	ay kaysstæ

Greetings

Good morning.	Hyvää huomenta.	hewvææ hoooamayntah
Good afternoon.	Hyvää päivää.	hewvææ pæivææ
Good evening.	Hyvää iltaa.	hewvææ iltar
Good night.	Hyvää yötä.	hewvææ ewurtæ
Good-bye.	Näkemiin.	nækaymeen
See you later.	Pikaisiin näkemiin.	pikighsseen nækaymeen
This is Mr....	Tämä on herra...	tæmæ oan hayrrah
This is Mrs....	Tämä on rouva...	tæmæ oan roavah
This is Miss...	Tämä on neiti...	tæmæ oan nayti
I'm very pleased to meet you.	Hauska tutustua.	howsskah tootoosstooah
How are you?	Mitä kuuluu?	mitæ kooloo
Very well, thank you.	Erittäin hyvää, kiitos.	ayrittæin hewvææ keetoass
And you?	Entä teille?	ayntæ tayllay
Fine.	Kiitos hyvää.	keetoass hewvææ
Excuse me.	Anteeksi.	ahntayksi

Questions

Where?	Missä?	misssæ
Where is...?	Missä on...?	misssæ oan
Where are...?	Missä ovat...?	misssæ oavaht
When?	Milloin?	milloyn
What?	Mikä?	mikæ
How?	Kuinka?	kooingkah
How much?	Kuinka paljon?	kooingkah pahlyoan

How many?	**Kuinka monta?**	kooingkah moantah
Who?	**Kuka?**	kookah
Why?	**Miksi?**	miksi
Which?	**Mikä?**	mikæ
What do you call this?	**Miksi tätä kutsu-taan?**	miksi tætæ kootsootarn
What do you call that?	**Miksi tuota kutsu-taan?**	miksi toooatah koot-sootarn
What does this mean?	**Mitä tämä tar-koittaa?**	mitæ tæmæ tahrkoyttar
What does that mean?	**Mitä tuo tarkoittaa?**	mitæ toooa tahrkoyttar

Do you speak ... ?

Do you speak English?	**Puhutteko en-glantia?**	poohoottaykoa aynglahn-tiah
Do you speak German?	**Puhutteko saksaa?**	poohoottaykoa sahksah
Do you speak French?	**Puhutteko ranskaa?**	poohoottaykoa rahnskar
Do you speak Spanish?	**Puhutteko es-panjaa?**	poohoottaykoa aysspahnyar
Do you speak Italian?	**Puhutteko italiaa?**	poohoottaykoa italiar
Could you speak more slowly, please?	**Voisitteko puhua hitaammin?**	voysittaykoa poohooah hitarmmin
Please point to the phrase in the book.	**Olkaa hyvä ja näyt-täkää lause kirjasta.**	oalkar hewvæ yah næewttækææ lowsay kiryahsstah
Just a minute. I'll see if I can find it in this book.	**Hetkinen. Katson löydänkö sen tästä kirjasta.**	haytkinayn. kahtsoan lurewdængkur sayn tæsstæ kiryahsstah
I understand.	**Ymmärrän.**	ewmmærræn
I don't understand.	**En ymmärrä.**	ayn ewmmærræ

Can ... ?

Can I have ... ?	**Voinko saada ... ?**	voyngkoa sardah
Can we have ... ?	**Voimmeko saada ... ?**	voymmaykoa sardah
Can you show me ... ?	**Voitteko näyttää minulle ... ?**	voyttaykoa næewttææ minoollay

Can you tell me ... ?	**Voitteko sanoa minulle ... ?**	**voyt**taykoa **sah**noaah minoollay
Can you help me, please?	**Voitteko auttaa minua?**	**voyt**taykoa **owt**tar minooah

Wanting

I'd like ...	**Haluaisin ...**	**hah**looighssin
We'd like ...	**Haluaisimme ...**	**hah**looighssimmay
Please give me ...	**Olkaa hyvä ja antakaa minulle ...**	**oal**kar hewvæ yah **ahn**tahkar minoollay
Give it to me, please.	**Antakaa se minulle.**	**ahn**tahkar say minoollay
Please bring me ...	**Tuokaa minulle ...**	**tooo**akar minoollay
Bring it to me, please.	**Tuokaa se minulle.**	**tooo**akar say minoollay
I'm hungry.	**Minun on nälkä.**	minoon oan **næl**kæ
I'm thirsty.	**Minun on jano.**	minoon oan **yah**noa
I'm tired.	**Olen väsynyt.**	**oa**layn **væ**sewnewt
I'm lost.	**Olen eksyksissä.**	**oa**layn **ayk**sewksisssæ
It's important.	**Se on tärkeää.**	say oan **tær**kayæ
It's urgent.	**Sillä on kiire.**	**sil**læ oan **kee**ray
Hurry up!	**Pitäkää kiirettä!**	**pitæ**kæ **kee**rayttæ

It is/There is ...

It is/It's ...	**Se on ...**	say oan
Is it ... ?	**Onko se ... ?**	**oang**koa say
It isn't ...	**Se ei ole ...**	say ay **oa**lay
There is/There are ...	**Siellä on ...**	**siayl**læ oan
Is there/Are there ... ?	**Onko siellä ... ?**	**oang**koa **siayl**læ
There isn't/There aren't ...	**Siellä ei ole ...**	**siayl**læ ay **oa**lay
There isn't any/There aren't any.	**Ei ole yhtään.**	ay **oa**lay **ewh**tææn

A few common words

big/small	**suuri/pieni**	**soo**ri/**pee**ayni
quick/slow	**nopea/hidas**	**noa**payah/**hi**dahss
early/late	**aikaisin/myöhään**	**igh**kighssin/**mewurh**ææn

cheap/expensive	**halpa/kallis**	hahlpah/**kahl**liss
near/far	**lähellä/kaukana**	**læ**hayllæ/**kow**kahnah
hot/cold	**kuuma/kylmä**	**koo**mah/**kewl**mæ
full/empty	**täysi/tyhjä**	**tæew**si/**tewh**yæ
easy/difficult	**helppo/vaikea**	**hayl**ppoa/**vigh**kayah
heavy/light	**painava/kevyt**	**pigh**nahvah/**kay**vewt
open/shut	**avoin/suljettu**	**ah**voyn/**sool**yayttoo
right/wrong	**oikea/väärä**	**oy**kayah/**væ**æræ
old/new	**vanha/uusi**	**vahn**nah/**oo**si
old/young	**vanha/nuori**	**vahn**nah/**nooo**ari
beautiful/ugly	**kaunis/ruma**	**kow**niss/**roo**mah
good/bad	**hyvä/huono**	**hew**væ/**hooo**anoa
better/worse	**parempi/huonompi**	**pah**raympi/**hooo**anoampi

Some prepositions and a few more useful words

at	**-lla, -llä**	-llah, -llæ
on	**päällä**	**pæ**ællæ
in	**-ssa, -ssä**	-ssah, -ssæ
to	**-lle**	-llay
from	**-sta, -stä**	-stah, -stæ
inside	**sisällä**	**si**sællæ
outside	**ulkopuolella**	**ool**kaopoooalayllah
up	**ylos**	**ew**lurss
down	**alas**	**ah**lahss
before	**ennen**	**ayn**nayn
after	**jälkeen**	**yæl**kayn
with	**kanssa**	**kahns**sah
without	**ilman**	**il**mahn
through	**läpi**	**læ**pi
towards	**kohti**	**koah**ti
until	**asti**	**ahss**ti
during	**aikana**	**igh**kahnah
and	**ja**	yah
or	**tai**	tigh
not	**ei**	ay
nothing	**ei mitään**	ay **mi**tææn
none	**ei yhtään**	ay **ewht**æææn
very	**erittäin**	**ayr**ittæin
also	**myös**	**mew**urss
soon	**pian**	**pi**ahn
perhaps	**ehkä**	**ayh**kæ
here	**tässä**	**tæss**sæ
there	**tuossa**	**tooo**asssah
now	**nyt**	newt
then	**sitten**	**sit**tayn

Arrival

Your passport, please.	Passinne, olkaa hyvä.	pahsssinnay oalkar hewvæ
Here it is.	Tässä.	tæsssæ
Have you anything to declare?	Onko teillä mitään tullattavaa?	oangkoa tayllä mitææn toollahttahvar
No, nothing at all.	Ei, ei mitään.	ay ay mitææn
Porter!	Kantaja!	kahntahyah
Can you help me with my luggage, please?	Voitteko auttaa minua kantamaan matkatavarani?	voyttaykoa owttar minooah kahntahmarn mahtkahtahvahrahni
That's my suitcase.	Tuo on minun matkalaukkuni.	toooa oan minoon matkahlowkkooni
Where's the bus to the centre of town, please?	Mistä lähtee bussi keskikaupungille?	misstæ læhtay boosssi kaysskikowpoonggillay
This way, please.	Tätä tietä, olkaa hyvä.	tætæ tiaytæ oalkar hewvæ

Changing money

Can you change a traveller's cheque, please?	Voitteko vaihtaa matkašekin?	voyttaykoa vighhtar mahtkahshaykin
Where's the nearest bank, please?	Missä on lähin pankki?	misssæ oan læhin pahnkki

Car rental

I'd like a car.	Haluaisin auton.	hahlooighsin owtoan
For how long?	Kuinka pitkäksi aikaa?	kooingkah pitkæksi ighkar
A day/Four days/ A week/Two weeks.	Päiväksi/Neljäksi päiväksi/Viikoksi/ Kahdeksi viikoksi.	pæivæksi/naylyæksi pæivæksi/veekoaksi/ kahhdayksi veekoaksi

Taxi

Where can I get a taxi?	Mistä voin saada taksin?	misstæ voyn sardah tahksin
What's the fare to...?	Paljonko se maksaa...n?	pahlyoangkoa say mahksar...n

Take me to this address, please.	**Viekää minut tähän osoitteeseen.**	**via**ykææ **mi**noot tæhæn **oa**soyttayssayn
I'm in a hurry.	**Minulla on kiire.**	**mi**noollah oan **kee**ray
Could you drive more slowly, please?	**Voisitteko ajaa hitaammin?**	**voy**sittaykoa ahyar hitarmmin

Hotel and other accommodation

My name is . . .	**Nimeni on . . .**	**ni**mayni oan
Have you a reservation?	**Onko teillä varaus?**	**oang**koa tayllæ vahrahooss
Yes, here's the confirmation.	**Kyllä, tässä on vahvistus.**	**kewl**læ **tæss**sæ oan vahhvisstooss
I'd like . . .	**Haluaisin . . .**	**hah**looighsin
I'd like a single room/a double room.	**Haluaisin yhden hengen huoneen/ kahden hengen huoneen.**	**hah**looighssin **ewh**dayn **hayng**ayn **hoooa**nayn/ **kahh**dayn **hayng**ayn **hoooa**nayn
a room with a bath/with a shower	**huoneen jossa on kylpy/jossa on suihku**	**hoooa**nayn **yoass**sah oan **kewl**pew/**yoass**sah oan **sooih**koo

How much?

What's the price per night/per week/per month?	**Paljonko hinta on yöltä/viikolta/ kuukaudelta?**	**pahl**yoangkoa **hin**tah oan **ewurl**tæ/**vee**koaltah/ **koo**kowdayltah
May I see the room?	**Saanko nähdä huoneen?**	**sarng**koa **næh**dæ **hoooa**nayn
I'm sorry, I don't like it.	**Valitan mutta en pidä siitä.**	**vah**litahn **moot**tah ayn **pi**dæ **see**tæ
Yes, that's fine. I'll take it.	**Kyllä, se sopii mainiosti. Otan sen.**	**kewl**læ say **soa**pee **migh**nioassti. **oa**tahn sayn
What's my room number, please?	**Mikä on huoneeni numero?**	**mi**kæ oan **hoooa**nayni **noo**mayroa
Number 123.	**Numero 123.**	**noo**mayroa 123

Service, please

Who is it?	**Kuka siellä?**	**koo**kah **si**ayllæ
Just a minute.	**Hetkinen.**	**hayt**kinayn
Come in! The door's open.	**Sisään! Ovi on auki.**	**si**ssæææn! **oa**vi oan owki
May we have breakfast in our room?	**Voimmeko saada varhaisaamiaisen huoneeseemme?**	**voym**maykoa **sar**dah **vahr**highssarmiighssayn **hoooa**nayssaymmay

Breakfast

I'll have ...	Haluaisin ...	hahlooighssin
I'll have some fruit juice.	Haluaisin hedelmätuoremehua.	hahlooighssin haydaylmætoooaraymayhooah
a boiled egg	keitetyn munan	kaytaytewn moonahn
a fried egg	paistetun munan	pighsstaytoon moonahn
some bacon/some ham	pekonia/kinkkua	paykoaniah/kinkkooah
some toast	paahtoleipää	parhtoalaypææ
a pot of tea	annoksen teetä	ahnnoaksayn taytæ
a cup of tea	kupin teetä	koopin taytæ
some coffee	kahvia	kahhviah
some chocolate	kaakaota	karkahoatah
more butter	lisää voita	lisææ voytah
some hot water	kuumaa vettä	koomar vayttæ

Difficulties

The central heating doesn't work.	Keskuslämmitys ei toimi.	kaysskoosslæmmitewss ay toymi
the light/the socket the tap/the toilet	valo/pistorasia hana/wc	vahloa/pisstoarahssiah hahnah/vay say
There's no hot water.	Kuumaa vettä ei tule.	koomar vayttæ ay toolay
May I see the manager, please?	Haluaisin tavata johtajan.	hahlooighssin tahvahtah yoahtahyahn

Telephone—Mail

There's a call for you.	Teille on puhelu.	tayllay oan poohayloo
Hold the line, please.	Hetkinen, olkaa hyvä.	haytkinayn oalkar hewvæ
Operator, I've been cut off.	Keskus, puhelu katkesi.	kaysskooss poohayloo kahtkayssi
Did anyone telephone me?	Onko kukaan soittanut minulle?	oangkoa kookarn soyttahnoot minoollay
Is there any mail for me?	Onko minulle mitään postia?	oangkoa minoollay mitææn poasstiah
Are there any messages for me?	Onko minulle mitään viestejä?	oangkoa minoollay mitææn viaysstayyæ

Checking out

May I have my bill, please?	**Saisinko laskuni?**	sighsingkoa lahsskooni
We're in a great hurry.	**Meillä on kova kiire.**	mayllæ oan koavah keeray
It's been a very enjoyable stay.	**Nautimme kovasti oleskelustamme.**	nowtimmay koavahsti oalaysskayloosstahmmay

Eating out

Good evening, sir/ Good evening, madam.	**Hyvää iltaa.**	hewvææ iltar
Good evening. I'd like a table for two, please.	**Hyvää iltaa. Haluaisin pöydän kahdelle.**	hewvææ iltar. hahlooighsin purewdæn kahhdayllay
Do you have a fixed-price menu?	**Onko teillä päivän ateriaa?**	oangkoa tayllæ pæivæn ahtayriar
May I see the à la carte menu?	**Saanko à la carte ruokalistan?**	sarngkoa ah lah kahrt roooakahlisstahn
May we have an ashtray, please?	**Saisimmeko tuhkakupin?**	sighsimmaykoa toohkahkoopin
some bread	**leipää**	laypææ
a fork	**haarukan**	harrookahn
a knife	**veitsen**	vaytsayn
a spoon	**lusikan**	loosikahn
a plate	**lautasen**	lowtahsayn
a glass	**lasin**	lahsin
a napkin	**lautasliinan**	lowtahsleenahn
another chair	**vielä yhden tuolin**	viaylay ewhdayn toooalin
Where's the gentlemen's toilet (men's room)?	**Missä on miestenhuone?**	misssæ oan miaystaynhoooanay
Where's the ladies' toilet (ladies' room)?	**Missä on naistenhuone?**	misssæ oan nighstaynhoooanay

Appetizers

I'd like some ...	**Haluaisin ...**	hahlooighssin
I'd like some assorted appetizers.	**Haluaisin alkupala-valikoiman.**	hahlooighssin ahlkoopahlahvahlikoymahn
orange juice	**appelsiinimehun**	ahppaylseenimayhoon
ham	**kinkkua**	kinkkooah

FINNISH

melon	melonia	**may**loaniah
pâté	tahnaa	tahhnar
smoked salmon	savustettua lohta	sahvoosstayttooah loahtah
shrimps (shrimp)	katkarapuja	kahtkahrahpooyah

Soup

Have you any . . . ?	**Onko teillä . . . ?**	oangkoa tayllæ
Have you any chicken soup?	**Onko teillä kanakeittoa?**	oangkoa tayllæ kahnah-kayttooah
vegetable soup	**vihanneskeittoa**	vihahnnaysskayttooaah
onion soup	**sipulikeittoa**	sipoolikayttoaah

Fish

I'd like some . . .	**Haluaisin . . .**	hahlooighssin
I'd like some fish.	**Haluaisin kalaa.**	hahlooighssin kahlar
sole	**kampelaa**	kahmpaylar
trout	**taimenta**	tighmayntah
lobster	**hummeria**	hoommayiah
crayfish	**rapuja**	rahpooyah
prawns	**isoja katkarapuja**	isoayah kahtkahrah-pooyah
I'd like it . . .	**Haluaisin sen . . .**	hahlooighssin sayn
I'd like it steamed.	**Haluaisin sen höyrytettynä.**	hahlooighssin sayn hurew-rewtayttewnæ
grilled	**pariloituna**	pahriloytoonah
boiled	**keitettynä**	kayttayttewnæ
baked	**uunissa paistettuna**	oonisssah pighsstayt-toonah
fried	**paistettuna**	pighsstayttoonah

Meat—Poultry—Game

I'd like some . . .	**Haluaisin . . .**	hahlooighssin
I'd like some beef.	**Haluaisin naudan-lihaa.**	hahlooighssin nowdahn-lihar
a beef steak	**pihvin**	pihvin
some roast beef	**paahtopaistia**	parhtoapighsstiah
a veal cutlet	**vasikanleikkeen**	vahsikahnlaykkayn
mutton	**lammasta**	lahmmahsstah
lamb	**nuorta lammasta**	noooartah lahmmahsstah
a pork chop	**porsaankyljyksen**	porsarngkewlyewksayn

roast pork	porsaanpaistia	porsaanpighsstiah
hare	jäniksenlihaa	yæniksaynlihar
chicken	kanaa	kahnar
roast chicken	kanapaistia	kahnahpighsstiah
duck	ankkaa	ahnkkar

How do you like your meat?	Miten valmistettuna haluatte lihan?	mitayn vahlmisstayttoonah hahlooahttay lihahn
rare	verisenä	vayrissaynæ
medium	puolikypsänä	poooalikewpsænæ
well done	hyvin paistettuna	hewvin pighsstayttoonah

Vegetables

What vegetables have you got?	Mitä vihanneksia teillä on?	mitæ vihahnnayksiah tayllah oan
I'd like some...	Haluaisin...	hahlooighssin
I'd like some asparagus.	Haluaisin parsaa.	hahlooighssin pahrsar

green beans	vihreitä papuja	vihraytæ pahpooyah
mushrooms	sieniä	siayniæ
carrots	porkkanaa	porkkahnar
onions	sipulia	sipooliah
red cabbage	punakaalia	poonahkarliah
spinach	pinaattia	pinarttiah
rice	riisiä	reesiæ
peas	herneitä	hayrnaytæ
tomatoes	tomaatteja	toamarttayyah
green salad	vihreätä sekasalaattia	vihrayætæ saykahssahlarttiah
potatoes	perunoita	payroonoitah

Desserts

Nothing more, thanks.	Ei muuta, kiitos.	ay mootah keetoass
Just a small portion, please.	Vain pieni annos.	vighn piayni ahnnoass
Have you any ice-cream?	Onko teillä jäätelöä?	oangkoa tayllæ yææ-tayluræ
fruit salad	hedelmäsalaattia	haydaylmæsahlarttiah
fresh fruit	tuoreita hedelmiä	toooaraytah haydaylmiæ
cheese	juustoa	yoosstoa

Drink

What would you like to drink?	**Mitä haluaisitte juoda?**	mitæ **hah**looighssittay **jooo**adah
I'll have a beer, please.	**Haluaisin oluen.**	**hah**looighssin **oa**looayn
I'll have a whisky, please.	**Haluaisin viskin.**	**hah**looighssin **viss**kin

Wine

I'd like a bottle of wine.	**Haluaisin pullon viiniä.**	**hah**looighssin **pool**loan **vee**niæ
red wine	**punaviiniä**	**poo**nahveeniæ
rosé wine	**rosé-viiniä**	**ro**asayveeniæ
white wine	**valkoviiniä**	**vahl**koaveeniæ
Cheers!	**Terveydeksenne!**	**tayr**vayewdayksaynnay

The bill (check)

May I have the bill (check) please?	**Saisinko laskun?**	**sigh**singkoa **lahss**koon
Is service included?	**Sisältyykö siihen palvelu?**	**si**sæltewkur **see**hayn **pahl**vayloo
Everything's included.	**Kaikki on mukana.**	**kighk**ki oan **moo**kahnah
Thank you, that was a very good meal.	**Kiitoksia, se oli erittäin hyvä ateria.**	**kee**toaksiah say **oa**li **ay**rittæin **hew**væ **ah**tayriah

Travelling

Where's the railway station, please?	**Missä on rautatieasema?**	**miss**sæ oan **row**tahtiay-**ahs**saymah
Where's the ticket office, please?	**Missä on lipun-myynti?**	**miss**sæ oan **li**poonmewnti
I'd like a ticket to ...	**Haluaisin lipun ... n.**	**hah**looighssin **li**poon ... n
First or second class?	**Ensimmäinen vai toinen luokka?**	**ayn**simmæinayn vigh **toy**nayn **looo**akkah
First class, please.	**Ensimmäinen.**	**ayn**simmæinayn
Single or return (one way or round-trip)?	**Yhdensuuntainen vai edestakainen?**	**ewh**daynsoontighnayn vigh **ay**dayssstahkighnayn

64

Do I have to change trains?	**Täytyykö minun vaih-taa junaa?**	tæewtewkur minoon vighhtar yoonar
What platform does the train leave from?	**Miltä laiturilta juna lähtee?**	miltæ lightooriltah yoonah læhtay
Where's the nearest underground (sub-way) station?	**Missä on lähin maanalaisen asema?**	misssæ oan læhin marnhahlighssayn ahsaymah
Where's the bus station, please?	**Missä on linja-autoasema?**	misssæ oan linyah owtoa-ahssaymah
When's the first bus to . . . ?	**Milloin lähtee en-simmäinen bussi . . . n?**	milloyn læhtay aynsim-mæinayn boosssi . . . n
the last bus the next bus	**viimeinen bussi/ seuraava bussi**	veemaynayn boosssi/ sayoorarvah boosssi
Please let me off at the next stop.	**Päästäisitteko minut pois seuraavalla pysäkillä?**	pææsstæissittaykur minoot poyss sayoo-rarvahllah pewsækillæ

Relaxing

What's on at the cinema (movies)?	**Mitä elokuvissa esitetään?**	mitæ ayloakoovisssah aysitaytæœn
What's on at the theatre?	**Mitä teatterissa esitetään?**	mitæ tayahttayrisssah aysitaytæœn
What time does the film begin? And the play?	**Mihin aikaan elokuva alkaa? Entä näytelmä?**	mihin ighkarn ayloakoovah ahlkarr? ayntæ næewtaylmæ
Are there any tickets for tonight?	**Onko täksi illaksi vielä lippuja?**	oangkoa tæksi illaksi viayæ lippooyah
Where can we go dancing?	**Mihin voimme mennä tanssimaan?**	mihin voymmay maynnæ tahnsssimarn
Would you like to dance?	**Haluaisitteko tanssia?**	hahlooighssittaykoa tahnsssiah

Introductions

How do you do?	**Hyvää päivää.**	hewvæœ pæivæœ
How are you?	**Mitä kuuluu?**	mitæ kooloo
Very well, thank you. And you?	**Kiitos, erittäin hyvää. Entä teille?**	keetoass ayrrittæin hewvæœ. ayntæ tayllay
May I introduce Miss Philips?	**Saanko esitellä neiti Philipsin?**	sarngkoa aysitayllæ nayti filipsin

64

My name is ...	**Minun nimeni on ...**	minoon nimayni oan
I'm very pleased to meet you.	**Hauska tavata.**	howsskah tahvahtah
How long have you been here?	**Kauanko olette ollut täällä?**	kowahngkoa oalayttay oalloot tæællæ
It was nice meeting you.	**Oli hauska tavata.**	oali howsskah tahvahtah

Dating

Would you like a cigarette?	**Haluaisitteko savukkeen?**	hahlooighssittaykoa savookkayn
May I get you a drink?	**Saanko tarjota teille lasillisen?**	sarngkoa tahryoatah tayllay lahsillissayn
Do you have a light, please?	**Onko teillä tulta?**	oangkoa tayllæ tooltah
Are you waiting for someone?	**Odotatteko jotakuta?**	oadoatahttaykoa yoatahkootah
Are you free this evening?	**Oletteko vapaa tänä iltana?**	oalayttaykoa vahpar tænæ iltahnah
Where shall we meet?	**Missä tapaamme?**	misssæ tahparmmay
What time shall I meet you?	**Mihin aikaan tapaan teidät?**	mihin ighkarn tahparn taydæt
May I take you home?	**Saanko saattaa teidät kotiin?**	sarngkoa sarttar taydæt koateen
Thank you, it's been a wonderful evening.	**Kiitos, oli ihana ilta.**	keetoass oali ihahnah iltah
What's your telephone number?	**Mikä on puhelinnumeronne?**	mikæ oan poohaylinnoomayroannay
Do you live alone?	**Asutteko yksin?**	ahsoottaykoa ewksin
What time is your last train?	**Mihin aikaa viimeinen junanne lähtee?**	mihin ighkar veemaynayn yoonahnnay læhtay
Good-night ...	**Hyvää yötä ...**	hewvææ ewurtæ

Banks

Where's the nearest bank, please?	**Missä on lähin pankki?**	misssæ oan læhin pahnkki
Where can I cash some traveller's cheques?	**Missä voin vaihtaa matkašekkejä?**	misssæ voyn vighhtar mahtkahshaykkayyæ

What time does the bank open? What time does it close?	**Mihin aikaan pankki avataan? Mihin aikaan se suljetaan?**	mihin **igh**karn **pahnkki ahv**ahtarn? mihin **igh**karn say **sool**yaytarn
I'm expecting some money from home. Has it arrived?	**Odotan rahaa kotoa. Onkohan se jo tullut?**	**oad**oatahn **rah**har **ko**atoaah. **oangk**oahahn say yoa **tool**loot
Can you give me some small change, please?	**Voitteko antaa minulle hiukan vaihtorahaa?**	**voyt**taykoa **ah**ntar minoollay **hio**okahn **vighh**toarahhar

Shops, stores and services

Where is the nearest chemist's (pharmacy)?	**Missä on lähin apteekki?**	**misss**æ oan **læ**hin **ahp**taykki
the nearest hairdresser's	**lähin kampaamo**	**læ**hin **kahm**parmoa
the photo shop	**valokuvausliike**	**vah**loakoovahoossleekay
the jeweller's	**kultaseppä**	**kool**tassayppæ
the department store	**tavaratalo**	**tah**vahrahtahloa
the police station	**poliisiasema**	**poa**leessiahssaymah
the garage	**pysäköintitalo**	**pews**ækurintitahloa
How do I get there?	**Miten sinne pääsee?**	**mi**tayn **sin**nay **pææ**say
Is it within walking distance?	**Onko se kävelymatkan päässä?**	**oangk**oa say **kæ**vaylew- mahtkahn **pææsss**æ

Service

Can you help me, please?	**Voitteko auttaa minua?**	**voyt**taykoa **owt**taa **min**ooah
Can you show me this? And that, too.	**Voitteko näyttää minulle tätä? Ja myös tuota.**	**voyt**taykoa **næ**ewttæœ minoollay **tæt**æ? yah mewurss **tooo**atah
It's too expensive/ too big/too small.	**Se on liian kallis/ liian suuri/liian pieni.**	say oan **lee**ahn **kahl**lis/ **lee**ahn **soor**i/**lee**ahn **piay**ni
Can you show me some more?	**Voitteko näyttää minulle vielä joitakin muita?**	**voyt**taykoa **næ**ewttiæœ minoollay **viay**læ **yoy**tahkin **mooi**tah
something better	**jotakin parempaa**	**yoa**tahkin **pah**raympar
something cheaper	**jotakin halvempaa**	**yoa**tahkin **hahl**vaympar

How much is this? And that?	Paljonko tämä maksaa? Entä tuo?	pahlyoangkoa tæmæ mahksar? ayntæ toooa
It's not quite what I want.	Se ei ole aivan sitä mitä haluan.	say ay oalay ighvahn sitæ mitæ hahlooahn
I like it.	Pidän siitä.	pidæn seetæ

Chemist's (Pharmacy)

I'd like something for a cold/for a cough/for travel sickness.	Haluaisin jotakin vilustumiseen/yskään/matkapahoinvointiin.	hahlooighssin yoatahkin viloosstoomissayn/ewsskææn/mahtkahpahhoynvoynteen
Can you recommend something for hay-fever/for sunburn?	Voitteko suositella jotakin heinänuhaan/auringonpolttamaan?	voyttaykoa soooasitayllah yoatahkin haynænooharn/owringoanpoalttahmarn

Toiletry

May I have some razor blades?	Saisinko parranajokoneenteriä?	sighsingkoa pahrrahnahyoakoanayntayriæ
some shaving cream some toothpaste	partavaahdoketta hammastahnaa	pahrtahvarhdoakayttah hahmmahsstahhnar
I'd like some soap. some suntan oil	Haluaisin saippuaa. aurinköölyjä	hahlooighssin sighppooar owringkoaurlyewæ

At the barber's

I'd like a haircut, please.	Haluaisin hiustenleikkuun.	hahlooighssin hioosstaynlaykkoon
Short/Leave it long.	Lyhyiksi/Jättäkää ne pitkiksi.	lewhewiksi/yættækææ nay pitkiksi
A razor cut, please.	Veitsellä, olkaa hyvä.	vaytsayllæ oalkar hewvæ

At the hairdresser's

I'd like a shampoo and set, please.	Haluaisin pesun ja kampauksen.	hahlooighssin paysoon yah kahmpahooksayn
I'd like a bleach.	Haluaisin vaalennuksen.	hahlooighssin varlaynnook sayn
a permanent a colour rinse a manicure	permanentin värihuuhtelun käsienhoidon	payrmahnayntin værihoohtayloon kæsiaynhoydoan

Photography

I'd like a film for this camera.	**Haluaisin filmin tähän kameraan.**	hahlooighssin filmin tæhæn kahmayrarn
This camera doesn't work.	**Tämä kamera ei toimi.**	tæmæ kahmayrah ay toymi

At the post office

Where's the nearest post office, please?	**Missä on lähin postitoimisto?**	misssæ oan læhin poasstitoymisstoa
I'd like to send this by express (special delivery)/by air mail.	**Haluaisin lähettää tämän pikakirjeenä/lentopostitse.**	hahlooighssin læhayttææ tæmæn pikahkiryaynæ/layntoapoasstitsay

Service stations

Where is the nearest service station, please?	**Missä on lähin huoltoasema?**	misssæ oan læhin hoooaltoaahssaymah
Fill her up, please.	**Täyteen, olkaa hyvä.**	tæewtayn oalkar hewvæ
Check the oil, please.	**Tarkistakaa öljy.**	tahrkisstahkar urlyew
Would you check the tyres?	**Tarkistaisitteko renkaat?**	tahrkisstighssittaykoa rayngkart

Street directions

Can you show me on the map where I am?	**Voitteko näyttää minulle kartalta missä olen?**	voyttaykoa næewttææ minoollay kahrtahltah misssæ oalayn
You're on the wrong road.	**Olette väärällä tiellä.**	oalayttay væærællæ teeayllæ
Go back to ...	**Menkää takaisin ...**	mayngkææ tahkighssin
Go straight ahead.	**Ajakaa suoraan eteenpäin.**	ahyahkar soooaraan aytaynpæin
It's on the left/on the right.	**Se on vasemmalla/oikealla.**	say oan vahsaymmahllah/oykayahllah

Accidents

May I use your telephone?	**Saanko käyttää puhelintanne?**	sarngkoa kæewttææ poohaylintahnnay
Call a doctor quickly.	**Kutsukaa nopeasti lääkäri.**	kootsookar noapayahssti læækæri

| Call an ambulance. | **Kutsukaa ambulanssi.** | kootsookar ahmboolahnsssi |
| Please call the police. | **Olkaa hyvä ja kutsukaa poliisi.** | oalkar hewvæ yah kootsookar poaleessi |

Numbers

one	**yksi**	ewksi
two	**kaksi**	kahksi
three	**kolme**	koalmay
four	**neljä**	naylyæ
five	**viisi**	veesi
six	**kuusi**	koosi
seven	**seitsemän**	saytsaymæn
eight	**kahdeksan**	kahhdayksahn
nine	**yhdeksän**	ewhdayksæn
ten	**kymmenen**	kewmmaynayn
eleven	**yksitoista**	ewksitoysstah
twelve	**kaksitoista**	kahksitoysstah
thirteen	**kolmetoista**	koalmaytoysstah
fourteen	**neljätoista**	naylyætoysstah
fifteen	**viisitoista**	veesitoysstah
sixteen	**kuusitoista**	koositoysstah
seventeen	**seitsemäntoista**	saytsaymæntoysstah
eighteen	**kahdeksantoista**	kahhdayksahntoysstah
nineteen	**yhdeksäntoista**	ewhdayksæntoysstah
twenty	**kaksikymmentä**	kahksikewmmayntæ
twenty-one	**kaksikymmentäyksi**	kahksikewmmayntæewksi
thirty	**kolmekymmentä**	koalmaykewmmayntæ
forty	**neljäkymmentä** .	naylyækewmmayntæ
fifty	**viisikymmentä**	veesikewmmayntæ
sixty	**kuusikymmentä**	koosikewmmayntæ
seventy	**seitsemänkymmentä**	saytsaymængkewmmayntæ
eighty	**kahdeksankymmentä**	kahhdayksahngkewmmayntæ
ninety	**yhdeksänkymmentä**	ewhdayksængkewmmayntæ
one hundred	**sata**	sahtah
one thousand	**tuhat**	toohat
ten thousand	**kymmenentuhatta**	kewmmaynayntoohahttah

Days

It's Sunday.	**On sunnuntai.**	oan soonnoontigh
Monday	**maanantai**	marnahntigh
Tuesday	**tiistai**	teesstigh
Wednesday	**keskiviikko**	kaysskiveekkoa

Thursday	torstai	toarsstigh
Friday	perjantai	payryayntigh
Saturday	lauantai	lowahntigh
yesterday	eilen	aylayn
today	tänään	tænææn
tomorrow	huomenna	hoooamaynnah
morning/afternoon	aamupäivä/iltapäivä	armoopæivæ/iltahpæivæ
evening/night	ilta/yö	iltah/ewur

Months

January	tammikuu	tahmmikoo
February	helmikuu	haylmikoo
March	maaliskuu	marlisskoo
April	huhtikuu	hoohtikoo
May	toukokuu	toaookoakoo
June	kesäkuu	kaysækoo
July	heinäkuu	haynækoo
August	elokuu	ayloakoo
September	syyskuu	sewsskoo
October	lokakuu	loakahkoo
November	marraskuu	mahrrahsskoo
December	joulukuu	yoaoolookoo
Merry Christmas!	Hyvää joulua!	hewvææ yoaoolooah!
Happy New Year!	Onnellista uutta vuotta!	oannayllisstah oottah vooattah

FRENCH

Guide to Pronunciation

Letter	Approximate pronunciation	Symbol	Example	

Consonants

b, c, d, f, k, as in English
l, m, n, p, s,
t, v, x, z

ch	like **sh** in **sh**ut	sh	**ch**er**ch**er	shehrshay
ç	like **s** in **s**it	s	**ç**a	sah
g	1) before **e, i, y**, like **s** in plea**s**ure	zh	man**g**er	mahngzhay
	2) before **a, o, u**, like **g** in **g**o	g	**g**arçon	gahrsawng
gn	like **ni** in o**ni**on	ñ	li**gn**e	leeñ
h	always silent		**h**omme	om
j	like **s** in plea**s**ure	zh	**j**amais	zhahmeh
qu	like **k** in **k**ill	k	**qu**i	kee
r	rolled in the back of the mouth, rather like gargling	r	**r**ouge	roozh
w	usually like **v** in **v**oice	v	**w**agon	vahgawng

FRENCH

Vowels

a, à or â	between the a in hat and the a in father	ah	**mari**	mahree
é, er, et, e	like a in late	ay	**enchanté**	ahngshahngtay
è, ê, e + most consonants	like e in get	eh	**même**	mehm
e	sometimes (when at the end of a syllable or of a one-syllable word), like er in other (quite short)	er	**me**	mer
i	like ee in meet	ee	**il**	eel
o	generally like o in hot but sometimes like o in wrote	o	**donner**	donay
ô	like o in wrote	oa	**Rhône**	roan
u	no equivalent in English. Round your lips and try to say ee; this should sound more or less correct	ew	**cru**	krew

Sounds spelt with two or more letters

ai, ay	can be pronounced as a in late	ay	**j'ai**	zhay
aient, ais, ait, aî	like e in get	eh	**chaîne**	shehn
(e)au	similar to o in wrote	oa	**chaud**	shoa
ei	like e in get	eh	**peine**	pehn
eu	like ur in fur, but with lips rounded, not spread	ur	**peu**	pur
oi	like w followed by the a in hat	wah	**moi**	mwah
ou	like oo in look	oo	**nouveau**	noovoa
ui	approximately like wee in between	wee	**traduire**	trahdweer

Nasal sounds

The following sounds are pronounced through the mouth and the nose at the same time, very much like the twang found in speech in some parts of America or Britain.

an	something like arn in tarnish	ahng	**tante**	tahngt
en	generally like the previous sound	ahng	**enchanté**	ahngshahngtay
ien	sounds like yan in yank	yang	**bien**	byang
(a)in	approximately like ang in rang	ang	**instant**	angstahng
on	approximately like orn in corn	awng	**maison**	mayzawng
un	approximately like ang in rang	ang	**brun**	brang

Liaison

Normally, the final consonants are not pronounced in French. However, when a word ending in a consonant is followed by one beginning with a vowel, they are often run together, and the consonant is pronounced as if it began the following word. For instance, **nous** (*we*) is pronounced **noo**, but, in the sentence **"Nous avons un enfant"** (*We have a child*), the **s** of **nous** is pronounced, and the sentence sounds something like: **noozahvawngzangnahngfahng**. Another example: **"comment"** is pronounced **komahng**, but the **t** is pronounced in **"Comment allez-vous?"** (*How are you*), which sounds something like: **komahngtahlay voo**.

FRENCH

Some basic expressions

Yes.	Oui.	wee
No.	Non.	nawng
Please.	S'il vous plaît.	seel voo play
Thank you.	Merci.	mehrsee
Thank you very much.	Merci beaucoup.	mehrsee boakoo
That's all right.	Il n'y a pas de quoi.	eel nee ah pah der kwah

Greetings

Good morning.	Bonjour.	bawngzhoor
Good afternoon.	Bonjour.	bawngzhoor
Good evening.	Bonsoir.	bawngswahr
Good night.	Bonne nuit.	bon nwee
Good-bye.	Au revoir.	oa rervwahr
See you later.	A bientôt.	ah byangtoa
This is Mr....	Voici Monsieur...	vwahssee merssyur
This is Mrs....	Voici Madame...	vwahssee mahdahm
This is Miss...	Voici Mademoiselle...	vwahssee mahdmwahzehl
I'm very pleased to meet you.	Enchanté.	ahngshahngtay
How are you?	Comment allez-vous?	komahngtahlayvoo
Very well, thank you. And you?	Très bien, merci. Et vous?	treh byang mehrsee. ay voo
Fine.	Bien.	byang
Excuse me.	Excusez-moi.	ehkskewzaymwah

Questions

Where?	Où?	oo
Where is...?	Où se trouve...?	oo ser troov
Where are...?	Où se trouvent...?	oo ser troov
When?	Quand?	kahng

What?	**Quoi?**	kwah
How?	**Comment?**	komahng
How much?	**Combien?**	kawngbyang
How many?	**Combien?**	kawngbyang
Who?	**Qui?**	kee
Why?	**Pourquoi?**	poorkwah
Which?	**Lequel/Laquelle?**	lerkehl/lahkehl
What do you call this?	**Comment appelez-vous ceci?**	komahng ahperlayvoo serssee
What do you call that?	**Comment appelez-vous cela?**	komahng ahperlayvoo serlah
What does this mean?	**Que veut dire ceci?**	ker vur deer serssee
What does that mean?	**Que veut dire cela?**	ker vur deer serlah

Do you speak . . . ?

Do you speak English?	**Parlez-vous anglais?**	pahrlayvoo ahngglay
Do you speak German?	**Parlez-vous allemand?**	pahrlayvoo ahlmahng
Do you speak French?	**Parlez-vous français?**	pahrlayvoo frahngsay
Do you speak Spanish?	**Parlez-vous espagnol?**	pahrlayvoo ehspahñol
Do you speak Italian?	**Parlez-vous italien?**	pahrlayvoo eetahlyang
Could you speak more slowly, please?	**Pourriez-vous parler plus lentement, s'il vous plaît?**	pooreeayvoo pahrlay plew lahngtermahng seel-vooplay
Please point to the phrase in the book.	**Montrez-moi la phrase dans le livre, s'il vous plaît.**	mawngtraymwah lah frahz dahng ler leevr seelvooplay
Just a minute. I'll see if I can find it in this book.	**Un instant. Je vais voir si je la trouve dans ce livre.**	angnangstahng. zher vay vwahr see zher lah troov dahng ser leevr
I understand.	**Je comprends.**	zher kawngprahng
I don't understand.	**Je ne comprends pas.**	zher ner kawngprahng pah

FRENCH

FRENCH

Can...?

Can I have...?	**Puis-je avoir...?**	pweezh ahvwahr
Can we have...?	**Pouvons-nous avoir...?**	poovawngnoo ahvwahr
Can you show me...?	**Pouvez-vous m'indiquer...?**	poovayvoo mangdeekay
Can you tell me...?	**Pouvez-vous me dire...?**	poovayvoo mer deer
Can you help me, please?	**Pouvez-vous m'aider, s'il vous plaît?**	poovayvoo mayday seelvooplay

Wanting

I'd like...	**Je voudrais...**	zher voodray
We'd like...	**Nous voudrions...**	noo voodreeawng
Please give me...	**S'il vous plaît, donnez-moi...**	seelvooplay donaymwah
Give it to me, please.	**Donnez-le moi, s'il vous plaît.**	donaylermwah seelvooplay
Please bring me...	**S'il vous plaît, apportez-moi...**	seelvooplay ahportaymwah
Bring it to me, please.	**Apportez-le moi, s'il vous plaît.**	ahportayler mwah seelvooplay
I'm hungry.	**J'ai faim.**	zhay fang
I'm thirsty.	**J'ai soif.**	zhay swahf
I'm tired.	**Je suis fatigué.**	zher swee fahteegay
I'm lost.	**Je me suis perdu.**	zher mer swee pehrdew
It's important.	**C'est important.**	saytangportahng
It's urgent.	**C'est urgent.**	saytewrzhahng
Hurry up!	**Dépêchez-vous!**	daypayshayvoo

It is/There is...

It is/It's...	**C'est...**	say
Is it...?	**Est-ce...?**	ehss
It isn't...	**Ce n'est pas...**	ser nay pah

There is/There are . . .	**Il y a . . .**	eel ee ah
Is there/Are there . . . ?	**Y a-t-il . . . ?**	ee ahteel
There isn't/There aren't . . .	**Il n'y a pas . . .**	eel nee ah pah
There isn't any/ There aren't any.	**Il n'y en a pas.**	eel nee ahngnah pah

A few common words

big/small	**grand/petit**	grahng/pertee
quick/slow	**rapide/lent**	rahpeed/lahng
early/late	**tôt/tard**	toa/tahr
cheap/expensive	**bon marché/cher**	bawng mahrshay/shehr . . .
near/far	**près/loin**	pray/lwang
hot/cold	**chaud/froid**	shoa/frwah
full/empty	**plein/vide**	plang/veed
easy/difficult	**facile/difficile**	fahsseel/deefeesseel
heavy/light	**lourd/léger**	loor/layzhay
open/shut	**ouvert/fermé**	oovair/fehrmay
right/wrong	**juste/faux**	zhewst/foa
old/new	**ancien/nouveau**	ahngsyang/noovoa
old/young	**vieux/jeune**	vyur/zhurn
beautiful/ugly	**beau/laid**	boa/lay
good/bad	**bon/mauvais**	bawng/movay
better/worse	**meilleur/pire**	mayyurr/peer

Some prepositions and a few more useful words

at	**à**	ah
on	**sur**	sewr
in	**dans**	dahng
to	**à**	ah
from	**de**	der
inside	**dedans**	derdahng
outside	**dehors**	derawr
up	**en haut**	ahng oa
down	**en bas**	ahng bah
before	**avant**	ahvahng
after	**après**	ahpray
with	**avec**	ahvehk
without	**sans**	sahng
through	**à travers**	ah trahvehr
towards	**vers**	vehr
until	**jusqu'à**	zhewskah
during	**pendant**	pahngdahng
and	**et**	ay

FRENCH

FRENCH

or	ou	oo
not	ne . . . pas	ner . . . pah
nothing	rien	ryang
none	aucun	oakang
very	très	tray
also	aussi	oasee
soon	bientôt	byangtoa
perhaps	peut-être	purtehtr
here	ici	eesee
there	là	lah
now	maintenant	mangternahng
then	alors	ahlawr

Arrival

Your passport, please.	Votre passeport, s'il vous plaît.	votr pahsspawr seel-vooplay
Here it is.	Le voici.	lervwahsee
Have you anything to declare?	Avez-vous quelque chose à déclarer?	ahvayvoo kehlkershoaz ah dayklahray
No, nothing at all.	Non, rien du tout.	nawng ryang dew too
Porter!	Porteur!	porturr
Can you help me with my luggage, please?	Pouvez-vous prendre mes bagages, s'il vous plaît?	poovayvoo prahngdr may bahgahzh seelvooplay
That's my suitcase.	C'est ma valise.	say mah vahleez
Where's the bus to the centre of town, please?	Où est le bus qui va en ville, s'il vous plaît?	oo ay ler bewss kee vah ahng veel seelvooplay
This way, please.	Par ici, s'il vous plaît.	pahr eessee seelvooplay

Changing money

| Can you change a traveller's cheque, please? | Pouvez-vous changer un chèque de voyage, s'il vous plaît? | poovayvoo shanhngzhay ang shekh der vwahyahzh seelvooplay |
| Where's the nearest bank, please? | Où est la banque la plus proche, s'il vous plaît? | oo ay lah bahngk lah plew prosh seelvooplay |

Car rental

I'd like a car.	Je voudrais une voiture.	zher voodray ewn vwahtewr
For how long?	Pour combien de temps?	poor kawngbyang der tahng
A day/Four days/ A week/Two weeks.	Un jour/Quatre jours/ Une semaine/Deux semaines.	ang zhoor/kahtr zhoor/ewn sermehn/dur sermehn

Taxi

Where can I get a taxi?	Où puis-je avoir un taxi?	oo pweezh ahvwahr ang tahksee
What's the fare to...?	Quel est le tarif pour...?	kehl ay ler tahreef poor
Take me to this address, please.	Conduisez-moi à cette adresse, s'il vous plaît.	kawngdweezaymwah ah seht ahdrehss seelvooplay
I'm in a hurry.	Je suis pressé.	zher swee prehssay
Could you drive more slowly, please?	Pourriez-vous conduire plus lentement, s'il vous plaît?	pooreeayvoo kawngdweer plew lahngtermahng seelvooplay

Hotel and other accommodation

My name is...	Je m'appelle...	zher mahpehl
Have you a reservation?	Avez-vous fait réserver?	ahvayvoo fay rayzehrvay
Yes, here's the confirmation.	Oui, voici la confirmation.	wee, vwahsee lah kawngfeermahsyawng
I'd like...	J'aimerais...	zhehmerray
I'd like a single room/a double room.	J'aimerais une chambre pour une personne/pour deux personnes.	zhehmerray ewn shahngbr poor ewn pehrson/poor dur pehrson
a room with a bath/with a shower	une chambre avec bain/avec douche	ewn shahngbr ahvehk bang/ahvehk doosh

FRENCH

How much?

What's the price per night/per week/per month?	**Quel est le prix pour une nuit/pour une semaine/pour un mois?**	kehl ay ler pree poor ewn nwee/poor ewn sermehn/poor ang mwah
May I see the room?	**Puis-je voir la chambre?**	pweezh vwahr lah shahngbr
I'm sorry, I don't like it.	**Je regrette, elle ne me plaît pas.**	zher rergreht ehl ner mer play pah
Yes, that's fine. I'll take it.	**Oui, c'est bien. Je la prends.**	wee say byang. zher lah prahng
What's my room number, please?	**Quel est le numéro de ma chambre, s'il vous plaît?**	kehl ay ler newmayroa der mah shahngbr seel-vooplay
Number 123.	**Numéro 123.**	newmayroa 123.

Service, please

Who is it?	**Qui est-ce?**	kee ehss
Just a minute.	**Un instant, s'il vous plaît.**	angnangstahng seel-vooplay
Come in! The door's open.	**Entrez! La porte est ouverte.**	ahngtray! lah port aytoovairt
May we have breakfast in our room?	**Pouvons-nous prendre le petit déjeuner dans notre chambre?**	poovawngnoo prahngdr le pertee dayzhurnay dahng notr shahngbr

Breakfast

I'll have ...	**Je voudrais ...**	zher voodray
I'll have some fruit juice.	**Je voudrais un jus de fruit.**	zher voodray ang zhew der frwee
a boiled egg	**un œuf à la coque**	angnurf ah lah kok
a fried egg	**un œuf sur le plat**	angnurf sewr ler plah
some bacon/some ham	**du bacon/du jambon**	dew baykern/dew zhahngbawng
some toast	**des toasts**	day toast
a pot of tea	**du thé**	dew tay
a cup of tea	**une tasse de thé**	ewn tahss der tay
some coffee	**du café**	dew kahfay
some chocolate	**du chocolat**	dew shokolah
more butter	**davantage de beurre**	dahvahngtahzh der burr
some hot water	**de l'eau chaude**	der loa shoad

Difficulties

The central heating doesn't work.	**Le chauffage central ne marche pas.**	ler shoafahzh sahngtrahl ner mahrsh pah
the light/the socket the tap/the toilet	**la lumière/la prise le robinet/les toilettes**	lah lewmyair/lah preez ler robeenay/lay twahleht
There's no hot water.	**Il n'y a pas d'eau chaude.**	eel nee ah pah doa shoad
May I see the manager, please?	**Puis-je voir le directeur, s'il vous plaît?**	pweezh vwahr ler deerehkturr seelvooplay

Telephone—Mail

There's a call for you.	**Il y a un appel pour vous.**	eel ee ah angnahpehl poor voo
Hold the line, please.	**Ne quittez pas, s'il vous plaît.**	ner keetay pah seelvooplay
Operator, I've been cut off.	**Mademoiselle, la communication a été coupée.**	mahdmwahzehl lah komewneekahsyawng ah aytay koopay
Did anyone telephone me?	**Est-ce qu'on m'a appelé?**	ehss kawng mah ahperlay
Is there any mail for me?	**Y a-t-il du courrier pour moi?**	ee ahteel dew kooreeay poor mwah
Are there any messages for me?	**Y a-t-il un message pour moi?**	ee ahteel ang mehssahzh poor mwah

Checking out

May I have my bill, please?	**Puis-je avoir ma note, s'il vous plaît?**	pweezh ahvwahr mah not seelvooplay
We're in a great hurry.	**Nous sommes très pressés.**	noh som tray prehssay
It's been a very enjoyable stay.	**Le séjour a été très agréable.**	ler sayzhoor ah aytay trayzahgrayahbl

Eating out

Good evening, sir/ Good evening, madam.	**Bonsoir, Monsieur/ Bonsoir, Madame.**	bawngswahr mersyur/ bawngswahr mahdahm

FRENCH

Good evening, I'd like a table for two, please.	Bonsoir. Je voudrais une table pour deux personnes, s'il vous plaît.	bawngswahr. zher voodray ewn tahbl poor dur pehrson seelvooplay
Do you have a fixed-price menu?	Avez-vous un menu?	ahvayvoo ang mernew
May I see the à la carte menu?	Puis-je voir la carte?	pweezh vwahr lah kahrt
May we have an ashtray, please?	Pouvons-nous avoir un cendrier, s'il vous plaît?	poovawngnoo ahvwahr ang sahngdreeay seelvooplay
some bread	du pain	dew pang
a fork	une fourchette	ewn foorsheht
a knife	un couteau	ang kootoa
a spoon	une cuillère	ewn kweeyair
a plate	une assiette	ewn ahssyeht
a glass	un verre	ang vair
a napkin	une serviette	ewn sehrvyeht
another chair	une autre chaise	ewn oatr shaiz
Where's the gentlemen's toilet (men's room)?	Où sont les toilettes pour messieurs?	oo sawng lay twahleht poor maysyur
Where's the ladies' toilet (ladies' room)?	Où sont les toilettes pour dames?	oo sawng lay twahleht poor dahm

Appetizers

I'd like some ...	Je voudrais ...	zher voodray
I'd like some assorted appetizers.	Je voudrais des hors-d'œuvre variés.	zher voodray day ordurvr vahreeay
orange juice	un jus d'orange	ang zhew dorahngzh
ham	du jambon	dew zhahngbawng
melon	du melon	der merlawng
pâté	du pâté	dew pahtay
smoked salmon	du saumon fumé	dew soamawng fewmay
shrimps (shrimp)	des crevettes	day krerveht

Soup

Have you any ... ?	Avez-vous ... ?	ahvayvoo
Have you any chicken soup?	Avez-vous du potage au poulet?	ahvayvoo dew potahzh oa poolay
vegetable soup	une soupe de légumes	ewn soop der laygewm
onion soup	de la soupe à l'oignon	der lah soop ah loñawng

Fish

I'd like some . . .	**J'aimerais . . .**	zhehmerray
I'd like some fish.	**J'aimerais du poisson.**	zhehmerray dew pwahssawng
sole	**de la sole**	der lah sol
trout	**de la truite**	der lah trweet
lobster	**du homard**	dew omahr
crayfish	**des écrevisses**	day aykrerveess
prawns	**des langoustines**	day lahnggoosteen
I'd like it . . .	**Je l'aimerais . . .**	zher lehmerray
I'd like it steamed.	**Je l'aimerais cuit à la vapeur.**	zher lehmerray kwee ah lah vahpurr
grilled	**grillé**	greeyay
boiled	**au court-bouillon**	oa koor booyawng
baked	**cuit au four**	kwee oa foor
fried	**frit**	free

Meat—Poultry—Game

I'd like some . . .	**Je voudrais . . .**	zher voodray
I'd like some beef.	**Je voudrais du bœuf.**	zher voodray dew burf
a beef steak	**un bifteck**	ang beeftehk
some roast beef	**du rosbif**	dew roazbeef
a veal cutlet	**une côtelette de veau**	ewn koatleht de voa
mutton	**du mouton**	dew mootawng
lamb	**de l'agneau**	der lahñoa
a pork chop	**une côtelette de porc**	ewn koatleht der pawr
roast pork	**du rôti de porc**	dew roatee der pawr
hare	**du lièvre**	dew lyehvr
chicken	**du poulet**	dew poolay
roast chicken	**du poulet rôti**	dew poolay roatee
duck	**du canard**	dew kahnahr
How do you like your meat?	**Comment désirez-vous la viande?**	komahng dayzeerayvoo lah vyahngd
rare	**saignante**	sehñahngt
medium	**à point**	ah pwang
well done	**bien cuite**	byang kweet

FRENCH

Vegetables

What vegetables have you got?	Quels légumes servez-vous?	kehl laygewm sehrvayvoo
I'd like some . . .	Je voudrais . . .	zher voodray
I'd like some asparagus.	Je voudrais des asperges.	zher voodray dayzahspehrzh

green beans	des haricots verts	day ahreekoa vair
mushrooms	des champignons	day shahngpeeñawng
carrots	des carottes	day kahrot
onions	des oignons	dayzoñawng
red cabbage	du chou rouge	dew shoo roozh
spinach	des épinards	dayzaypeenahr
rice	du riz	dew ree
peas	des petits pois	day pertee pwah
tomatoes	des tomates	day tomaht
green salad	de la salade verte	der lah sahlahd vairt
potatoes	des pommes de terre	day pom der tair

Desserts

Nothing more, thanks.	Je ne veux plus rien, merci.	zher ner vur plew ryang mehrsee
Just a small portion, please.	Juste une petite portion, s'il vous plaît.	zhewst ewn perteet porsyawng seelvooplay
Have you any ice-cream?	Avez-vous des glaces?	ahvayvoo day glahss
fruit salad	une salade de fruits	ewn sahlahd der frwee
fresh fruit	des fruits frais	day frwee fray
cheese	du fromage	dew fromahzh

Drink

What would you like to drink?	Qu'aimeriez-vous boire?	kehmerreeayvoo bwahr
I'll have a beer, please.	J'aimerais une bière, s'il vous plaît.	zhehmerray ewn byair seelvooplay
I'll have a whisky, please.	Je voudrais un whisky, s'il vous plaît.	zher voodray ang weeskee seelvooplay

Wine

I'd like a bottle of wine.	**Je voudrais une bouteille de vin.**	zher voodray ewn bootay der vang
red wine	**vin rouge**	vang roozh
rosé wine	**vin rosé**	vang roazay
white wine	**vin blanc**	vang blahng
Cheers!	**A votre santé!**	ah votr sahngtay

The bill (check)

May I have the bill (check) please?	**Puis-je avoir l'addition, s'il vous plaît?**	pweezh ahvwahr lahdee-ssyawng seelvooplay
Is service included?	**Le service est-il compris?**	ler sehrveess ayteel kawngpree
Everything's included.	**Tout est compris.**	tootay kawngpree
Thank you, that was a very good meal.	**Merci, c'était très bon.**	mehrsee saytay tray bawng

Travelling

Where's the railway station, please?	**Où se trouve la gare, s'il vous plaît?**	oo ser troov lah gahr seelvooplay
Where's the ticket office, please?	**Où est le guichet, s'il vous plaît?**	oo ay ler geeshay seelvooplay
I'd like a ticket to ...	**J'aimerais un billet pour ...**	zhehmerray ang beeyay poor
First or second class?	**Première ou deuxième classe?**	prermyair oo durzyehm klahss
First class, please.	**Première classe, s'il vous plaît.**	prermyair klahss seelvooplay
Single or return (one way or round-trip)?	**Aller simple ou aller et retour?**	ahlay sangpl oo ahlay ay rertoor
Do I have to change trains?	**Est-ce que je dois changer de train?**	ehss ker zher dwah shahngzhay der trang
What platform does the train leave from?	**De quel quai le train part-il?**	der kehl kay ler trang pahrteel
Where's the nearest underground (subway) station?	**Où est la station de métro la plus proche?**	oo ay lah stahsyawng der maytroa la plew prosh
Where's the bus station, please?	**Où est la gare routière, s'il vous plaît?**	oo ay lah gahr rootyair seelvooplay

FRENCH

When's the first bus to . . . ?	**A quelle heure est le premier autobus pour . . .?**	ah kehl urr ay ler prer-myayroatoabewss poor
the last bus	**le dernier autobus**	ler dehrnyayroatoabewss
the next bus	**le prochain autobus**	ler proshehnoatoabewss
Please let me off at the next stop.	**S'il vous plaît, déposez-moi au prochain arrêt.**	seelvooplay daypoazay-mwah oa proshehnahray

Relaxing

What's on at the cinema (movies)?	**Que donne-t-on au cinéma?**	ker dontawng oa see-naymah
What's on at the theatre?	**Que joue-t-on au théâtre?**	ker zhootawng oa tayahtr
What time does the film begin?	**A quelle heure commence le film?**	ah kehl urr komahngss ler feelm
And the play?	**Et la pièce?**	ay lah pyehss
Are there any tickets for tonight?	**Reste-t-il encore des places pour ce soir?**	rehstteel ahngkawr day plahss poor ser swahr
Where can we go dancing?	**Où pouvons-nous aller danser?**	oo poovawngnoo ahlay dahngsay
Would you like to dance?	**Voulez-vous danser?**	voolayvoo dahngsay

Introductions

How do you do?	**Bonjour.**	bawngzhoor
How are you?	**Comment allez-vous?**	komahngtahlayvoo
Very well, thank you. And you?	**Très bien, merci. Et vous?**	tray byang mehrsee. ay voo
May I introduce Miss Philips?	**Puis-je vous présenter Mademoiselle Philips?**	pweezh voo prayzahngtay mahdmwahzehl feeleeps
My name is . . .	**Je m'appelle . . .**	zher mahpehl
I'm very pleased to meet you.	**Je suis ravi de vous connaître.**	zher swee rahvee der voo konaitr

FRENCH

How long have you been here?	**Depuis combien de temps êtes-vous ici?**	derpwee kawngbyang der tahng ehtvoo eesee
It was nice meeting you.	**Enchanté d'avoir fait votre connaissance.**	ahngshahngtay dahvwahr fay votr konaysahngss

Dating

Would you like a cigarette?	**Voulez-vous une cigarette?**	voolayvoo ewn seegahreht
May I get you a drink?	**Puis-je vous offrir un verre?**	pweezh vooz offreer ang vair
Do you have a light, please?	**Avez-vous du feu, s'il vous plaît?**	ahvayvoo dew fur seelvooplay
Are you waiting for someone?	**Attendez-vous quelqu'un?**	ahtahngdayvoo kehlkang
Are you free this evening?	**Etes-vous libre ce soir?**	ehtvoo leebr ser swahr
Where shall we meet?	**Où nous retrouverons-nous?**	oo noo rertrooverrawngnoo
What time shall I meet you?	**A quelle heure vous verrai-je?**	ah kehl urr voo vairayzh
May I take you home?	**Puis-je vous ramener chez vous?**	pweezh voo rahmnay shay voo
Thank you, it's been a wonderful evening.	**Merci pour cette merveilleuse soirée.**	mehrsee poor seht mehrvayyurz swahray
What's your telephone number?	**Quel est votre numéro de téléphone?**	kehl ay votr newmayroa der taylayfon
Do you live alone?	**Habitez-vous seule?**	ahbeetayvoo surl
What time is your last train?	**A quelle heure est votre dernier train?**	ah kehl urr ay votr dairnyay trang
Good-night...	**Bonne nuit...**	bon nwee

Banks

Where's the nearest bank, please?	**Où se trouve la banque la plus proche, s'il vous plaît?**	oo ser troov lah bahngk lah plew prosh seelvooplay
Where can I cash some traveller's cheques?	**Où puis-je toucher des chèques de voyage?**	oo pweezh tooshay day shehk der vwahyahzh

FRENCH

What time does the bank open?	A quelle heure la banque ouvre-t-elle?	ah kehl urr lah bahngk oovrertehl
What time does it close?	A quelle heure ferme-t-elle?	ah kehl urr fairmtehl
I'm expecting some money from home. Has it arrived?	J'attends de l'argent de la maison. Est-il arrivé?	zhahtahng der lahrzhahng der lah mayzawng ayteel ahreevay
Can you give me some small change, please?	Pouvez-vous me donner de la monnaie, s'il vous plaît?	poovayvoo mer donay der lah monay seelvooplay

Shops, stores and services

Where is the nearest chemist's (pharmacy)?	Où est la pharmacie la plus proche?	oo ay lah fahrmahssee lah plew prosh
the nearest hairdresser's	le coiffeur le plus proche	le kwahfurr ler plew prosh
the photo shop	le magasin de photographie	le mahgahzang der foatoagrahfee
the jeweller's	la bijouterie	lah beezhooterree
the department store	le grand magasin	ler grahng mahgahzang
the police station	le poste de police	ler post der poleess
the garage	le garage	ler gahrahzh
How do I get there?	Comment puis-je m'y rendre?	komahng pweezh mee rahngdr
Is it within walking distance?	Est-il possible d'y aller à pied?	ayteel posseebl dee ahlay ah pyay

Service

Can you help me, please?	Pouvez-vous m'aider, s'il vous plaît?	poovayvoo mayday seelvooplay
Can you show me this? And that, too.	Pouvez-vous me montrer ceci? Et cela aussi.	poovayvoo mer mawngtray serssee? ay serlah oasee
It's too expensive/too big/too small.	C'est trop cher/trop grand/trop petit.	say troa shair/troa grahng/troa pertee
Can you show me some more?	Pouvez-vous me montrer un plus grand choix?	poovayvoo mer mawngtray ang plew grahng shwah
something better	quelque chose de mieux	kehlker shoaz der myur
something cheaper	quelque chose de meilleur marché	kehlker shoaz der mayyurr mahrshay

How much is this? And that?	**Combien coûte ceci? Et cela?**	kawngbyang koot sersee ay serlah
It's not quite what I want.	**Ce n'est pas exactement ce que je désire.**	ser nay pah ehgzahktermahng ser ker zher dayzeer
I like it.	**Cela me plaît.**	serlah mer play

Chemist's (Pharmacy)

| I'd like something for a cold/for a cough/for travel sickness. | **J'aimerais quelque chose contre le rhume/contre la toux/contre le mal de coeur.** | zhehmerray kehlkershoaz kawngtr ler rewm/kawngtr lah too/kawngtr ler mahl der kurr |
| Can you recommend something for hayfever/for sunburn? | **Pouvez-vous m'indiquer quelque chose contre le rhume des foins/contre un coup de soleil?** | poovayvoo mangdeekay kehlker shoaz kawngtr ler rewm day fwang/kawngtr ang koo der solay |

Toiletry

May I have some razor blades?	**Puis-je avoir des lames de rasoir?**	pweezh ahvwahr day lahm de rahzwahr
some shaving cream	**de la crème à raser**	der lah krehm ah rahzay
some toothpaste	**du dentifrice**	dew dahngteefreess
I'd like some soap.	**Je voudrais du savon.**	zher voodray dew sahvawng
some suntan oil	**de l'huile solaire**	der lweel solair

At the barber's

I'd like a haircut, please.	**Je voudrais me faire couper les cheveux, s'il vous plaît.**	zher voodray mer fair koopay lay shervur seelvooplay
Short/Leave it long.	**Courts/Laissez-les longs.**	koor/layssaylay lawng
A razor cut, please.	**Une coupe au rasoir, s'il vous plaît.**	ewn koop oa rahzwahr seelvooplay

At the hairdresser's

| I'd like a shampoo and set, please. | **J'aimerais un shampooing-mise en plis, s'il vous plaît.** | zhehmerray ang shahngpwangmeezahng plee seelvooplay |

FRENCH

I'd like a bleach.	Je voudrais une dé-coloration.	zher voodray ewn daykolorahsyawng
a permanent	une permanente	ewn pehrmahnahngt
a colour rinse	un rinçage	ang rangsahzh
a manicure	une manucure	ewn mahnewkewr

Photography

| I'd like a film for this camera. | J'aimerais un film pour cet appareil. | zhehmerray ang feelm poor seht ahpahray |
| This camera doesn't work. | Cet appareil ne marche pas. | seht ahpahray ner mahrsh pah |

At the post office

| Where's the nearest post office, please? | Où est le bureau de poste le plus proche, s'il vous plaît? | oo ay ler bewroa der post ler plew prosh seelvooplay |
| I'd like to send this by express (special delivery)/by air mail. | J'aimerais envoyer ceci par express/par avion. | zhehmerray ahngvvwahyay serssee pahr ehksprehss/pahr ahvyawng |

Service stations

Where is the nearest service station, please?	Où est la station-service la plus proche, s'il vous plaît?	oo ay lah stahs-syawngsehrveess lah plew prosh seelvooplay
Fill her up, please.	Le plein, s'il vous plaît.	ler plang seelvooplay
Check the oil, please.	Contrôlez l'huile, s'il vous plaît.	kawngtroalay lweel seelvooplay
Would you check the tyres?	Voudriez-vous véri-fier les pneus?	voodreeayvoo vayreefeeay lay pnur

Street directions

Can you show me on the map where I am?	Pouvez-vous me montrer sur la carte où je me trouve?	poovayvoo mer mawngtray sewr lah kahrt oo zher mer troov
You're on the wrong road.	Vous n'êtes pas sur la bonne route.	voo neht pah sewr lah bon root
Go back to ...	Retournez à ...	rertoornay ah

| Go straight ahead. | **Continuez tout droit.** | kawngteeneway too drwah |
| It's on the left/on the right. | **C'est à gauche/à droite.** | saytah goash/ah drwaht |

Accidents

May I use your telephone?	**Puis-je utiliser votre téléphone?**	pweezh ewteeleezay votr taylayfon
Call a doctor quickly.	**Appelez vite un docteur.**	ahperlay veet ang dokturr
Call an ambulance.	**Appelez une ambulance.**	ahperlay ewn ahngbewlahngss
Please call the police.	**Appelez la police, s'il vous plaît.**	ahperlay lah poleess seel-vooplay

Numbers

one	**un**	ang
two	**deux**	dur
three	**trois**	trwah
four	**quatre**	kahtr
five	**cinq**	sangk
six	**six**	seess
seven	**sept**	seht
eight	**huit**	weet
nine	**neuf**	nurf
ten	**dix**	deess
eleven	**onze**	awngz
twelve	**douze**	dooz
thirteen	**treize**	traiz
fourteen	**quatorze**	kahtorz
fifteen	**quinze**	kangz
sixteen	**seize**	saiz
seventeen	**dix-sept**	deess-seht
eighteen	**dix-huit**	deez-weet
nineteen	**dix-neuf**	deez-nurf
twenty	**vingt**	vangt
twenty-one	**vingt et un**	vang-tay-ang
thirty	**trente**	trahngt
forty	**quarante**	kahrahngt
fifty	**cinquante**	sangkahngt
sixty	**soixante**	swahsahngt
seventy	**soixante-dix**	swahsahngtdeess
eighty	**quatre vingts**	kahtrervang
ninety	**quatre-vingt-dix**	kahtrervangdeess
one hundred	**cent**	sahng
one thousand	**mille**	meel
ten thousand	**dix mille**	dee meel

FRENCH

FRENCH

Days

It's Sunday.	C'est dimanche.	say deemahngsh
Monday	lundi	langdee
Tuesday	mardi	mahrdee
Wednesday	mercredi	mehrkrerdee
Thursday	jeudi	zhurdee
Friday	vendredi	vahngdrerdee
Saturday	samedi	sahmdee
yesterday	hier	eeair
today	aujourd'hui	oazhoordwee
tomorrow	demain	dermang
morning/afternoon	matin/après-midi	mahtang/ahpraymeedee
evening/night	soir/nuit	swahr/nwee

Months

January	janvier	zhahngveeay
February	février	fayvreeay
March	mars	mahrss
April	avril	ahvreel
May	mai	may
June	juin	zhwang
July	juillet	zhweeyay
August	août	oot
September	septembre	sehptahngbr
October	octobre	oktobr
November	novembre	novahngbr
December	décembre	daysahngbr
Merry Christmas!	Joyeux Noël! Bonne	zhwahyur noaehl! bon
Happy New Year!	Année!	ahnay

GERMAN

Guide to Pronunciation

Letter	Approximate pronunciation	Symbol	Example	

Consonants

f, h, k, l, m, n, p, t, x	normally pronounced as in English			
b	1) at the end of a word, or between a vowel and a consonant, like **p** in u**p**	p	**ab**	ahp
	2) elsewhere as in English	b	**bis**	biss
c	1) before **e**, **i**, **ö**, and **ä**, like **ts** in hi**ts**	ts	**Celsius**	**ts**ehlzeeuss
	2) elsewhere like **c** in cat	k	**Café**	kahfay
ch	like **ch** in Scottish lo**ch**	kh	**ich**	i**kh**
d	1) at the end of a word, or between a vowel and a consonant, like **t** in ea**t**	t	**Rad**	rart
	2) elsewhere, like **d** in **d**o	d	**durstig**	**d**urstikh
g	1) always hard as in **g**o, but, at the end of a word, often more like **ck** in ta**ck**	g	**gehen**	**g**ayern
		k	**weg**	vehk
	2) when preceded by **i** at the end of a word, like Scottish lo**ch**	kh	**billig**	b**l**ikh
j	like **y** in **y**es	y	**ja**	yar
qu	like **k** followed by **v** in **v**at	kv	**Quark**	kvahrk
r	generally rolled in the back of the mouth	r	**warum**	vahrum

GERMAN

s	1) before or between vowels like **z** in **z**oo	z	**sie**	zee
	2) before **p** and **t**, at the beginning of a syllable like **sh** in **sh**ut	sh	**spät**	shpait
	3) elsewhere, like **s** in s**i**t	s/ss	**es ist**	ehss ist
ß	always like **s** in sit	ss	**heiß**	highss
sch	like **sh** in **sh**ut	sh	**schnell**	shnehl
tsch	like **ch** in **ch**ip	ch	**deutsch**	doych
tz	like **ts** in hi**ts**	ts	**Platz**	plahts
v	like **f** in **f**or	f	**vier**	feer
w	like **v** in **v**ice	v	**wie**	vee
z	like **ts** in hi**ts**	ts	**zeigen**	tsighgern

Vowels

N.B. In German, vowels are generally long when followed by **h** or by one consonant and short when followed by two or more consonants.

a	1) short, like **u** in c**u**t	ah	**hat**	haht
	2) long, like **a** in c**a**r	ar	**Abend**	arbernt
ä	1) short, like **e** in l**e**t	eh	**nächst**	nehkhst
	2) long, like **ai** in h**ai**r	ai	**spät**	sphait
e	1) short, like **e** in l**e**t	eh	**sprechen**	shprehkhern
	2) long, like **a** in l**a**te	ay	**gehen**	gayern
	3) in unstressed syllables, it is generally pronounced like **a** in about	er	**bitte**	biter
			geben	gaybern
i	1) short, like **i** in h**i**t	i	**bis**	biss
	2) long, like **ee** in m**ee**t	ee	**ihm**	eem
ie	like **ee** in b**ee**	ee	**hier**	heer
o	1) short, like **o** in g**o**t	o	**voll**	fol
	2) long, like **o** in n**o**te	oa	**ohne**	oaner
ö	like **ur** in f**ur** (long or short)	ur	**können**	kurnern
u	1) short, like **oo** in f**oo**t	u	**Nuß**	nuss
	2) long, like **oo** in m**oo**n	oo	**gut**	goot
ü	like French **u** in une; no English equivalent. Round your lips and try to say **ea** as in m**ea**n (long or short)	ew	**über**	ewberr
y	like German **ü**	ew	**Symphonie**	zewmfoanee

Diphthongs

ai, ay, ei, ey	like **igh** in h**igh**	igh	**mein**	mighn
au	like **ow** in n**ow**	ow	**auf**	owf
äu, eu	like **oy** in b**oy**	oy	**neu**	noy

Some basic expressions

Yes.	**Ja.**	yar
No.	**Nein.**	nighn
Please.	**Bitte.**	biter
Thank you.	**Danke.**	**dahng**ker
Thank you very much.	**Vielen Dank.**	**fee**lern dahngk
That's all right.	**Gern geschehen.**	gairn ger**shay**ern

Greetings

Good morning.	**Guten Morgen.**	**goo**tern **mor**gern
Good afternoon.	**Guten Tag.**	**goo**tern targ
Good evening.	**Guten Abend.**	**goo**tern **ar**bernt
Good night.	**Gute Nacht.**	**goo**ter nahkht
Good-bye.	**Auf Wiedersehen.**	owf **vee**derrzayern
See you later.	**Auf bald.**	owf bahlt
This is Mr. . . .	**Das ist Herr . . .**	dahss ist hair
This is Mrs. . . .	**Das ist Frau . . .**	dahss ist frow
This is Miss . . .	**Das ist Fräulein . . .**	dahss ist **froy**lighn
I'm very pleased to meet you.	**Sehr erfreut.**	zair ehr**froyt**
How are you?	**Wie geht es Ihnen?**	vee gayt ehss **ee**nern
Very well, thank you. And you?	**Sehr gut, danke. Und Ihnen?**	zair goot **dahng**ker. unt **ee**nern
Fine.	**Gut.**	goot
Excuse me.	**Verzeihung.**	fehr**tsigh**ung

Questions

Where?	**Wo?**	voa
Where is . . . ?	**Wo ist . . . ?**	voa ist
Where are . . . ?	**Wo sind . . . ?**	voa zint
When?	**Wann?**	vahn
What?	**Was?**	vahss
How?	**Wie?**	vee
How much?	**Wieviel?**	vee**feel**
How many?	**Wie viele?**	vee**fee**ler

Who?	**Wer?**	vair
Why?	**Warum?**	vah**rum**
Which?	**Welcher/Welche/Welches?**	**vehl**kherr/**vehl**kher/**vehl**kherss
What do you call this?	**Wie heißt dies?**	vee highst deess
What do you call that?	**Wie heißt das?**	vee highst dahss
What does this mean?	**Was bedeutet dies?**	vahss ber**doy**tert deess
What does that mean?	**Was bedeutet das?**	vahss ber**doy**tert dahss

Do you speak...?

Do you speak English?	**Sprechen Sie Englisch?**	**shpreh**khern zee **ehng**lish
Do you speak German?	**Sprechen Sie Deutsch?**	**shpreh**khern zee doych
Do you speak French?	**Sprechen Sie Französisch?**	**shpreh**khern zee frahn**tsur**zish
Do you speak Spanish?	**Sprechen Sie Spanisch?**	**shpreh**khern zee **shpar**nish
Do you speak Italian?	**Sprechen Sie Italienisch?**	**shpreh**khern zee ital**yay**nish
Could you speak more slowly, please?	**Könnten Sie bitte langsamer sprechen?**	**kurn**tern zee **b**iter **lahng**zarmerr **shpreh**khern
Please point to the phrase in the book.	**Bitte zeigen Sie mir den Satz im Buch.**	**b**iter **tsigh**gern zee meer dayn zahts im book**h**
Just a minute. I'll see if I can find it in this book.	**Einen Augenblick, ich sehe mal nach, ob ich es in diesem Buch finde.**	**igh**nern **ow**gernblik ikh zayer mahl nahk**h** op ikh ehss in **dee**zerm book**h** finder
I understand.	**Ich verstehe.**	ikh fehr**shtay**er
I don't understand.	**Ich verstehe nicht.**	ikh fehr**shtay**er nikht

Can...?

| Can I have...? | **Kann ich...haben?** | kahn ikh...**har**bern |
| Can we have...? | **Können wir...haben?** | **kur**nern veer...**har**bern |

Can you show me...?	**Können Sie mir...zeigen?**	kurnern zee meer...tsighgern
Can you tell me...?	**Können Sie mir sagen...?**	kurnern zee meer zargern
Can you help me, please?	**Können Sie mir bitte helfen?**	kurnern zee meer biter hehlfern

Wanting

I'd like...	**Ich hätte gern...**	ikh hehter gairn
We'd like...	**Wir hätten gern...**	veer hehtern gairn
Please give me...	**Geben Sie mir bitte...**	gaybern zee meer biter
Give it to me, please.	**Bitte geben Sie es mir.**	biter gaybern zee ehss meer
Please bring me...	**Bringen Sie mir bitte...**	bringern zee meer biter
Bring it to me, please.	**Bitte bringen Sie es mir.**	biter bringern zee ehss meer
I'm hungry.	**Ich habe Hunger.**	ikh harber hunger
I'm thirsty.	**Ich habe Durst.**	ikh harber durst
I'm tired.	**Ich bin müde.**	ikh bin mewder
I'm lost.	**Ich habe mich verirrt.**	ikh harber mikh fehrirt
It's important.	**Es ist wichtig.**	ehss ist vikhtikh
It's urgent.	**Es ist dringend.**	ehss ist dringernt
Hurry up!	**Beeilen Sie sich!**	berighlern zee zikh

It is/There is...

It is/It's...	**Es ist...**	ehss ist
Is it...?	**Ist es...?**	ist ehss
It isn't...	**Es ist nicht...**	ehss ist nikht
There is/There are...	**Es gibt...**	ehss gibt
Is there/Are there...?	**Gibt es...?**	gibt ehss
There isn't/There aren't...	**Es gibt keinen/Es gibt keine/Es gibt kein...**	ehss gibt kighnern/ehss gibt kighner/ehss gibt kighn

GERMAN

| There isn't any/
There aren't any. | **Es gibt keinen/Es gibt keine/Es gibt keins.** | ehss gibt **kigh**nern/ehss gibt **kigh**ner/ehss gibt kighnss |

A few common words

big/small	**groß/klein**	groass/klighn
quick/slow	**schnell/langsam**	shnehl/**lahng**zarm
early/late	**früh/spät**	frew/shpait
cheap/expensive	**billig/teuer**	**b**lllikh/**to**yerr
near/far	**nah/weit**	nar/vight
hot/cold	**heiß/kalt**	highss/kahlt
full/empty	**voll/leer**	fol/layr
easy/difficult	**leicht/schwierig**	lighkht/**shvee**rikh
heavy/light	**schwer/leicht**	shvair/lighkht
open/shut	**offen/geschlossen**	**o**fern/ger**shloss**ern
right/wrong	**richtig/falsch**	**rikh**tikh/fahlsh
old/new	**alt/neu**	ahlt/noy
old/young	**alt/jung**	ahlt/yung
beautiful/ugly	**schön/häßlich**	shurn/**hehss**likh
good/bad	**gut/schlecht**	goot/shlehkht
better/worse	**besser/schlechter**	**behss**err/**shleh**terr

Some prepositions and a few more useful words

at	**an**	ahn
on	**auf**	owf
in	**in**	in
to	**zu**	tsoo
from	**von**	fon
inside	**drinnen**	**dri**nern
outside	**draußen**	**drow**ssern
up	**hinauf**	hinowf
down	**hinunter**	hinunter
before	**vor**	fawr
after	**nach**	nahkh
with	**mit**	mit
without	**ohne**	**oa**ner
through	**durch**	doorkh
towards	**gegen**	**gay**gern
until	**bis**	biss
during	**während**	**vai**rernt
and	**und**	unt
or	**oder**	**oa**derr
not	**nicht**	nikht
nothing	**nichts**	nikhts
none	**kein**	kighn

GERMAN

very	**sehr**	zair
also	**auch**	owkh
soon	**bald**	bahlt
perhaps	**vielleicht**	feelighkht
here	**hier**	heer
there	**dort**	dort
now	**jetzt**	yehtst
then	**dann**	dahn

Arrival

Your passport, please.	**Ihren Paß, bitte.**	eerern pahss biter
Here it is.	**Hier, bitte.**	heer biter
Have you anything to declare?	**Haben Sie etwas zu vorzollen?**	harbern zee ehtvahss tsoo fehrtsolern
No, nothing at all.	**Nein, gar nichts.**	nighn garr nikhts
Porter!	**Gepäckträger!**	gerpehktraigerr
Can you help me with my luggage, please?	**Können Sie mir mit meinem Gepäck helfen, bitte?**	kurnern zee meer mit mighnerm gerpehk hehlfern biter
That's my suitcase.	**Das ist mein Koffer.**	dahss ist mighn koferr
Where's the bus to the centre of town, please?	**Wo ist der Bus zum Stadtzentrum, bitte?**	voa ist dehr buss tsum shtahttsehntrum biter
This way, please.	**Hier durch, bitte.**	heer doorkh biter

Changing money

| Can you change a traveller's cheque, please? | **Können Sie einen Reisescheck ein- lösen, bitte?** | kurnern zee ighnern righzershehk ighnlurzern biter |
| Where's the nearest bank, please? | **Wo ist die nächste Bank, bitte?** | voa ist dee nehkhster bahngk biter |

Car rental

I'd like a car.	**Ich möchte einen Wagen.**	ikh murkhter ighnern vargern
For how long?	**Für wie lange?**	fewr vee lahnger
A day/Four days/ A week/Two weeks.	**Einen Tag/Vier Tage/Eine Woche/ Zwei Wochen.**	ighnern targ/feer targer/ighner vokher/ tsvigh vokhern

GERMAN

GERMAN

Taxi

Where can I get a taxi?	Wo finde ich ein Taxi?	voa finder ikh ighn tahksee
What's the fare to...?	Was kostet es bis...?	vahss kosstert ehss biss
Take me to this address, please.	Fahren Sie mich bitte zu dieser Adresse.	farrern zee mikh biter tsoo deezerr ahdrehsser
I'm in a hurry.	Ich habe es eilig.	ikh harber ehss ighlikh
Could you drive more slowly, please?	Können Sie bitte langsamer fahren?	kurntern zee biter lahngzarmerr farrern

Hotel and other accommodation

My name is...	Mein Name ist...	mighn narmer ist
Have you a reservation?	Haben Sie vorbestellt?	harbern zee forbershtehlt
Yes, here's the confirmation.	Ja, hier ist die Bestätigung.	yar heer ist dee bershtaitigung
I'd like...	Ich hätte gern...	ikh hehter gairn
I'd like a single room/a double room.	Ich hätte gern ein Einzelzimmer/ein Doppelzimmer.	ikh hehter gairn ighn ighntserltsimerr/ighn doperltsimerr
a room with a bath/with a shower	ein Zimmer mit Bad/mit Dusche	ighn tsimerr mit bart/mit dusher

How much?

What's the price per night/per week/per month?	Wieviel kostet es pro Nacht/pro Woche/pro Monat?	veefeel kosstert ehss proa nahkht/proa vokher/proa moanart
May I see the room?	Kann ich das Zimmer sehen?	kahn ikh dahss tsimerr zayern
I'm sorry, I don't like it.	Bedaure, es gefällt mir nicht.	berdowrer ehss gerfehlt meer nikht
Yes, that's fine. I'll take it.	Ja, sehr gut. Ich nehme es.	yar zair goot. ikh naymer ehss
What's my room number, please?	Welche Zimmernummer habe ich, bitte?	vehlkher tsimerrnumerr harber ikh biter
Number 123.	Nummer 123.	numerr 123

Service, please

Who is it?	**Wer ist da?**	vair ist dar
Just a minute.	**Einen Augenblick, bitte.**	**igh**nern **ow**gernblik **bi**ter
Come in! The door's open.	**Herein! Die Tür ist offen.**	hair**ighn**! dee tewr ist **o**fern
May we have breakfast in our room?	**Können wir in unserem Zimmer frühstücken?**	**kur**nern veer in **un**zerrerm **tsi**merr **frew**shtewkern

Breakfast

I'll have . . .	**Ich möchte . . .**	ikh **murkh**ter
I'll have some fruit juice.	**Ich möchte einen Fruchtsaft.**	ikh **murkh**ter **igh**nern **frookht**zahft
a boiled egg	**ein gekochtes Ei**	ighn ger**kokh**terss igh
a fried egg	**ein Spiegelei**	ighn **shpee**gerligh
some bacon/some ham	**Speck/Schinken**	shpehk/**shing**kern
some toast	**Toast**	toast
a pot of tea	**ein Kännchen Tee**	ighn **kehn**khern tay
a cup of tea	**eine Tasse Tee**	**igh**ner **tah**sser tay
some coffee	**Kaffee**	**kah**fay
some chocolate	**Schokolade**	shoakoa**lar**der
more butter	**noch etwas Butter**	nokh **eht**vahss **bu**terr
some hot water	**etwas heißes Wasser**	**eht**vahss **high**sserss **vah**sserr

Difficulties

The central heating doesn't work.	**Die Zentralheizung funktioniert nicht.**	dee tsehn**trarl**hightsung fungktseeoa**neert** nikht
the light/the socket	**das Licht/die Steckdose**	dahss likht/dee **shtehk**doazer
the tap/the toilet	**der Wasserhahn/die Toilette**	dair **vah**sserrharn/dee toy**leh**ter
There's no hot water.	**Es kommt kein warmes Wasser.**	ehss komt kighn **vahr**merss **vah**sserr
May I see the manager, please?	**Kann ich bitte den Direktor sprechen?**	kahn ikh **bi**ter dayn dee**rehk**tawr **shpreh**khern

Telephone—Mail

There's a call for you.	**Hier ist ein Anruf für Sie.**	heer ist ighn **ahn**roof fewr zee

GERMAN

Hold the line, please.	**Bitte bleiben Sie am Apparat.**	biter **bligh**bern zee ahm ahpah**rart**
Operator, I've been cut off.	**Fräulein, ich bin unterbrochen worden.**	**froy**lighn ikh bin unterr**brokh**ern **vor**dern
Did anyone telephone me?	**Hat mich jemand angerufen?**	haht mikh **yay**mahnt **ahn**gerroofern
Is there any mail for me?	**Ist Post für mich da?**	ist post fewr mikh dar
Are there any messages for me?	**Hat jemand eine Nachricht für mich hinterlassen?**	haht **yay**mahnt **igh**ner **nahkh**rikht fewr mikh hin-terlah**ssern**

Checking out

May I have my bill, please?	**Kann ich bitte meine Rechnung haben?**	kahn ikh biter **migh**ner **rehkh**nung **har**bern
We're in a great hurry.	**Wir haben es sehr eilig.**	veer **har**bern ehss **igh**likh
It's been a very enjoyable stay.	**Der Aufenthalt war sehr angenehm.**	dair **owf**ehnthahlt varr zair **ahn**gernaym

Eating out

Good evening, sir/ Good evening, madam.	**Guten Abend, mein Herr/Guten Abend, gnädige Frau.**	**goo**tern **ar**bernt mighn hair/**goo**tern **ar**bernt **gnai**diger frow
Good evening. I'd like a table for two, please.	**Guten Abend. Ich hätte gern einen Tisch für zwei Personen, bitte.**	**goo**tern **ar**bernt. ikh **heh**ter gairn **igh**nern tish fewr tsvigh pehr**zoa**nern biter
Do you have a fixed-price menu?	**Haben Sie ein Menü?**	**har**bern zee ighn meh**new**
May I see the à la carte menu?	**Kann ich die Speisekarte sehen?**	kahn ikh dee **shpigh**zer-kahrter **zay**ern
May we have an ashtray, please?	**Können wir bitte einen Aschen-becher haben?**	**kur**nern veer biter **igh**nern **ah**shernbehkher **har**bern
some bread	**etwas Brot**	**eht**vahss broat
a fork	**eine Gabel**	**igh**ner **gar**berl
a knife	**ein Messer**	ighn **mehs**serr
a spoon	**einen Löffel**	**igh**nern **lur**ferl
a plate	**einen Teller**	**igh**nern **tehl**err

a glass	**ein Glas**	ighn glahss
a napkin	**eine Serviette**	**igh**ner zairvee**eh**ter
another chair	**noch einen Stuhl**	nokh **igh**nern shtool

| Where's the gentle-men's toilet (men's room)? | **Wo ist die Herren-toilette?** | voa ist dee **heh**rern-twahlehter |

| Where's the ladies' toilet (ladies' room)? | **Wo ist die Damen-toilette?** | voa ist dee **dar**mern-twahlehter |

Appetizers

| I'd like some ... | **Ich hätte gern ...** | ikh **heh**ter gairn |

| I'd like some assorted appetizers. | **Ich hätte gern gemischte Vor-speisen.** | ikh **heh**ter gairn ger**mish**-ter **fawr**shpighzern |

orange juice	**Orangensaft**	oa**rahng**zhernzahft
ham	**Schinken**	**shing**kern
melon	**Melone**	may**loa**ner
pâté	**Pastete**	pahs**stay**ter
smoked salmon	**geräucherten Lachs**	ger**roy**kherrtern lahks
shrimps (shrimp)	**Krevetten**	krer**veh**tern

Soup

| Have you any ... ? | **Haben Sie ... ?** | **har**bern zee |

| Have you any chicken soup? | **Haben Sie Hühner-suppe?** | **har**bern zee **hew**nerrzuper |

| vegetable soup | **Gemüsesuppe** | ger**mew**zerzuper |
| onion soup | **Zwiebelsuppe** | **tsvee**berlzuper |

Fish

| I'd like some ... | **Ich hätte gern ...** | ikh **heh**ter gairn |

| I'd like some fish. | **Ich hätte gern Fisch.** | ikh **heh**ter gairn fish |

sole	**Seezunge**	**zay**tsunger
trout	**Forelle**	fo**reh**ler
lobster	**Hummer**	**hum**err
crayfish	**Krebs**	krayps
prawns	**Garnelen**	gahr**nay**lern

| I'd like it ... | **Ich hätte es gern ...** | ikh **heh**ter ehss gairn |

| I'd like it steamed. | **Ich hätte es gern gedämpft.** | ikh **heh**ter ehss gairn ger**dehmpft** |

| grilled | **gegrillt** | ger**grillt** |
| boiled | **gekocht** | ger**kokht** |

GERMAN

104

| baked | **gebacken** | gerbahkern |
| fried | **in der Pfanne gebraten** | in dair pfahner gerbrartern |

Meat—Poultry—Game

I'd like some ...	**Ich hätte gern ...**	ikh hehter gairn
I'd like some beef.	**Ich hätte gern Rindfleisch.**	ikh hehter gairn rintflighsh
a beef steak	**ein Beefsteak**	ighn beefstayk
some roast beef	**Roastbeef**	rostbeef
a veal cutlet	**ein Kalbskotelett**	ighn kahlpskaoterleht
mutton	**Hammelfleisch**	hahmerlflighsh
lamb	**Lammfleisch**	lahmflighsh
a pork chop	**ein Schweins- kotelett**	ighn shvighnskoaterleht
roast pork	**Schweinebraten**	shvighnerbrartern
hare	**Hase**	harzer
chicken	**Huhn**	hoon
roast chicken	**Brathühnchen**	brarthewnkhern
duck	**Ente**	ehnter
How do you like your meat?	**Wie möchten Sie Ihr Fleisch?**	vee murkhtern zee eer flighsh
rare	**halbroh**	hahlproa
medium	**mittel**	miterl
well done	**durchgebraten**	doorkhgerbrartern

Vegetables

What vegetables have you got?	**Was für Gemüse haben Sie?**	vahss fewr germewzer harbern zee
I'd like some ...	**Ich hätte gern ...**	ikh hehter gairn
I'd like some asparagus.	**Ich hätte gern Spargeln.**	ikh hehter gairn shparrgerln
green beans	**grüne Bohnen**	grewner boanern
mushrooms	**Pilze**	piltser
carrots	**Karotten**	kahrotern
onions	**Zwiebeln**	tsveeberln
red cabbage	**Rotkohl**	roatkoal
spinach	**Spinat**	shpinart
rice	**Reis**	righss
peas	**Erbsen**	airpsern
tomatoes	**Tomaten**	toamartern
green salad	**grünen Salat**	grewnern zahlart
potatoes	**Kartoffeln**	kahrtofferln

GERMAN

Desserts

Nothing more, thanks.	**Nein danke, nichts mehr.**	nighn **dahng**ker nikhts mair
Just a small portion, please.	**Nur eine kleine Portion, bitte.**	noor **igh**ner **kligh**ner portsee**oan** biter
Have you any ice-cream?	**Haben Sie Eis?**	**har**bern zee ighss
fruit salad	**Obstsalat**	**oapst**zahlart
fresh fruit	**frisches Obst**	**frish**erss oapst
cheese	**Käse**	**kai**zer

Drink

What would you like to drink?	**Was möchten Sie gern trinken?**	vahss **murkh**tern zee gairn **tring**kern
I'll have a beer, please.	**Ich nehme ein Bier, bitte.**	ikh **nay**mer ighn beer **bi**ter
I'll have a whisky, please.	**Ich möchte einen Whisky, bitte.**	ikh **murkh**te **igh**nern **viss**kee **bi**ter

Wine

I'd like a bottle of wine.	**Ich möchte eine Flasche Wein.**	ikh **murkh**ter **igh**ner **flah**sher vighn
red wine	**Rotwein**	**roat**vighn
rosé wine	**Roséwein**	roa**zay**vighn
white wine	**Weißwein**	**vighss**vighn
Cheers!	**Zum Wohl!**	tsum voal

The bill (check)

May I have the bill (check) please?	**Die Rechnung, bitte.**	dee **rehkh**nung **bi**ter
Is service included?	**Ist Bedienung inbegriffen?**	ist ber**dee**nung in**ber**grifern
Everything's included.	**Alles ist inbegriffen.**	**ah**lerss ist in**ber**grifern
Thank you, that was a very good meal.	**Danke, das Essen war sehr gut.**	**dang**ker dahss **eh**ssern varr zair goot

GERMAN

Travelling

Where's the railway station, please?	**Wo ist der Bahnhof, bitte?**	voa ist dair **barn**hoaf **bit**er
Where's the ticket office, please?	**Wo ist der Fahrkartenschalter, bitte?**	voa ist dair **farr**kahrternshahlterr **bit**er
I'd like a ticket to...	**Ich möchte eine Fahrkarte nach...**	ikh **murkh**ter **igh**ner **farr**kahrter nahkh
First or second class?	**Erste oder zweite Klasse?**	**airs**ter **oa**derr **tsvigh**ter **klahs**ser
First class, please.	**Erste Klasse, bitte.**	**airs**ter **klahs**ser **bit**er
Single or return (one way or round-trip)?	**Einfach oder hin und zurück?**	**ighn**fahkh **oa**derr hin unt tsu**rewk**
Do I have to change trains?	**Muß ich umsteigen?**	muss ikh **um**shtighern
What platform does the train leave from?	**Auf welchem Bahnsteig fährt der Zug ab?**	owf **vehl**kherm **barn**shtighg fairt dair tsoog ahp
Where's the nearest underground (subway) station?	**Wo ist die nächste U-Bahnstation?**	voa ist dee **nehkh**ster **oo**barnshtahtsioan
Where's the bus station, please?	**Wo ist der Busbahnhof, bitte?**	voa ist dair **buss**barnhoaf **bit**er
When's the first bus to...?	**Wann fährt der erste Bus nach...?**	vahn fairt dair **ehr**ster buss nahkh
the last bus	**der letzte Bus**	dair **leht**ster buss
the next bus	**der nächste Bus**	der **nehkh**ster buss
Please let me off at the next stop.	**Bitte lassen Sie mich an der nächsten Haltestelle aussteigen.**	**bit**er **lahs**sern zee mikh ahn dair **nehkh**stern **hahl**tershtehler **owss**shtighern

Relaxing

What's on at the cinema (movies)?	**Was gibt es im Kino zu sehen?**	vahss gibt ehss im **keen**oa tsoo **zay**ern
What's on at the theatre?	**Was gibt es im Theater?**	vahss gibt ehss im tay**ar**terr
What time does the film begin? And the play?	**Wann beginnt der Film? Und das Stück?**	vahn ber**gint** dair film? unt dahss shtewk

Are there any tickets for tonight?	Gibt es noch Karten für heute abend?	gibt ehss nokh **kahr**tern fewr **hoy**ter **ar**bernt
Where can we go dancing?	Wohin können wir tanzen gehen?	voahin **kur**nern veer **tahnt**sern **gay**ern
Would you like to dance?	Darf ich bitten?	dahrf ikh **bi**tern

Introductions

How do you do?	Guten Tag.	**goo**tern targ
How are you?	Wie geht es Ihnen?	vee gayt ehss **ee**nern
Very well, thank you. And you?	Sehr gut, danke. Und Ihnen?	zair goot **dahng**ker. unt **ee**nern
May I introduce Miss Philips?	Darf ich Fräulein Philips vorstellen?	dahrf ikh **froy**lighn filips **for**shtehlern
My name is...	Ich heiße...	ikh **high**sser
I'm very pleased to meet you.	Sehr erfreut.	zair ehr**froyt**
How long have you been here?	Wie lange sind Sie schon hier?	vee **lahng**er zint zee shoan heer
It was nice meeting you.	Es war mir ein Vergnügen.	ehss varr meer ighn fehr**gnew**gern

Dating

Would you like a cigarette?	Möchten Sie eine Zigarette?	**murkh**tern zee **igh**ner tsigah**reh**ter
May I get you a drink?	Darf ich Ihnen etwas zu trinken bestellen?	dahrf ikh **ee**nern **eht**vahss tsoo **tring**kern ber-**shteh**lern
Do you have a light, please?	Haben Sie Feuer, bitte?	**har**bern zee **foy**err **bi**ter
Are you waiting for someone?	Warten Sie auf jemanden?	**vahr**tern zee owf **yay**mahndern
Are you free this evening?	Sind Sie heute abend frei?	zint zee **hoy**ter **ar**bernt frigh
Where shall we meet?	Wo treffen wir uns?	voa **treh**fern veer unss
What time shall I meet you?	Wann treffe ich Sie?	vahn **treh**fer ikh zee
May I take you home?	Darf ich Sie nach Hause bringen?	dahrf ikh zee nahkh **how**zer **bring**ern

GERMAN

GERMAN

Thank you, it's been a wonderful evening.	**Danke, es war ein wunderbarer Abend.**	dahngker ehss varr ighn vunderrbarrerr arbernt
What's your telephone number?	**Wie ist Ihre Telephonnummer?**	vee ist eerer tailaifoan-numerr
Do you live alone?	**Wohnen Sie alleine?**	voanern zee ahlighn
What time is your last train?	**Wann fährt Ihr letzter Zug?**	vahn fairt eer lehtsterr tsoog
Good-night...	**Gute Nacht...**	gooter nahkht

Banks

Where's the nearest bank, please?	**Wo ist die nächste Bank, bitte?**	voa ist dee nehkster bahngk biter
Where can I cash some traveller's cheques?	**Wo kann ich Reiseschecks ein-lösen?**	voa kahn ikh righzer-shehks ighnlurzern
What time does the bank open? What time does it close?	**Wann öffnet die Bank? Wann schließt sie?**	vahn urfnert dee bahngk? vahn shleest zee
I'm expecting some money from home. Has it arrived?	**Ich erwarte Geld von zu Hause. Ist es eingetroffen?**	ikh airvahrter gehlt fon tsoo howzer. ist ehss ighngertrofern
Can you give me some small change, please?	**Können Sie mir bitte Kleingeld geben?**	kurnern zee meer biter klighngehlt gaybern

Shops, stores and services

Where is the nearest chemist's (pharmacy)?	**Wo ist die nächste Apotheke?**	voa ist dee nehkster ahpoatayker
the nearest hair-dresser's	**der nächste Friseur**	dair nehkster frizurr
the photo shop	**das Photogeschäft**	dahss foatoagershehft
the jeweller's	**der Juwelier**	dair yooverleer
the department store	**das Warenhaus**	dahss varrenhowss
the police station	**die Polizeiwache**	dee poaltsighvahkher
the garage	**die Garage**	dee gahrarzher
How do I get there?	**Wie komme ich dorthin?**	vee komer ikh dorthin
Is it within walking distance?	**Kann man zu Fuß gehen?**	kahn mahn tsoo fooss gayern

Service

Can you help me, please?	**Können Sie mir helfen, bitte?**	kurnern zee meer **hehl**fern biter
Can you show me this? And that, too.	**Können Sie mir dies zeigen? Und das ebenfalls.**	kurnern zee meer deess **tsigh**gern? unt dahss **ay**bernfahlss
It's too expensive/ too big/too small.	**Es ist zu teuer/zu groß/zu klein.**	ehss ist tsoo **toy**err/tsoo groass/tsoo klighn
Can you show me some more?	**Können Sie mir noch mehr zeigen?**	kurnern zee meer nokh mair **tsigh**gern
something better something cheaper	**etwas Besseres etwas Billigeres**	**eht**vahss **behss**errerss **eht**vahss **bil**igerrerss
How much is this? And that?	**Wieviel kostet dies? Und das?**	**vee**feel **koss**tert deess? unt dahss
It's not quite what I want.	**Es ist nicht ganz das, was ich möchte.**	ehss ist nikht gahnts dahss vahss ikh **murkh**ter
I like it.	**Es gefällt mir.**	ehss ger**fehlt** meer

Chemist's (Pharmacy)

| I'd like something for a cold/for a cough/for travel sickness. | **Ich möchte etwas gegen eine Erkältung/gegen Husten/gegen Reisekrankheit.** | ikh **murkh**ter **eht**vahss **gay**gern **igh**ner ehr**kehl**tung/**gay**gern **hoos**stern/**gay**gern **righ**zerkrahngkhight |
| Can you recommend something for hay-fever/for sunburn? | **Können Sie mir etwas gegen Heufieber/gegen Sonnenbrand empfehlen?** | kurnern zee meer **eht**vahss **gay**gern **hoy**feeberr/**gay**gern **zon**ernbrahnt ehmp**fay**lern |

Toiletry

May I have some razor blades?	**Kann ich Rasierklingen haben?**	kahn ikh rah**zeer**klingern **har**bern
some shaving cream some toothpaste	**Rasiercreme Zahnpasta**	ra**zeer**kraym **tsarn**pahstah
I'd like some soap.	**Ich hätte gern Seife.**	ikh **heh**ter gairn **zigh**fer
some suntan oil	**Sonnenöl**	**zon**ernurl

At the barber's

| I'd like a haircut, please. | **Ich möchte mir das Haar schneiden lassen, bitte.** | ikh **murkh**ter meer dahss harr **shnigh**dern **lahss**ern |

| Short/Leave it long. | **Kurz/Lassen Sie es lang.** | koorts/**lah**ssern zee ehss lahng |
| A razor cut, please. | **Einen Messer-schnitt, bitte.** | **igh**nern **meh**sserrshnit **bi**ter |

At the hairdresser's

I'd like a shampoo and set, please.	**Waschen und legen, bitte.**	**vah**shern unt **lay**gern **bi**ter
I'd like a bleach.	**Ich möchte eine Aufhellung.**	ikh **murkh**ter **igh**ner **owf**hehlung
a permanent	**eine Dauerwelle**	**igh**ner **dow**errvehler
a colour rinse	**eine Farbspülung**	**igh**ner **fahrp**shpewlung
a manicure	**eine Maniküre**	**igh**ner mahni**kew**rer

Photography

| I'd like a film for this camera. | **Ich möchte einen Film für diese Kamera.** | ikh **murkh**ter **igh**nern film fewr **dee**zer **kah**merrah |
| This camera doesn't work. | **Diese Kamera ist defekt.** | **dee**zer **kah**merrah ist dai**fehkt** |

At the post office

| Where's the nearest post office, please? | **Wo ist das nächste Postamt, bitte?** | voa ist dahss **nehkh**ster **post**ahmt **bi**ter |
| I'd like to send this by express (special delivery)/by air mail. | **Ich möchte dies durch Eilboten/ mit Luftpost Schicken.** | ikh **murkh**ter deess doorkh **ighl**boatern/ mit **luft**post **shi**kern |

Service stations

Where is the nearest service station, please?	**Wo ist die nächste Tankstelle, bitte?**	voa ist dee **nehkh**ster **tahngk**shtehler **bi**ter
Fill her up, please.	**Voll, bitte.**	fol **bi**ter
Check the oil, please.	**Kontrollieren Sie bitte das Ölstand.**	kontro**lee**rern zee **bi**ter dayn **url**shtahnt
Would you check the tyres?	**Würden Sie bitte die Reifen prüfen?**	**vewr**dern zee **bi**ter dee **righ**fern **prew**fern

GERMAN

Street directions

Can you show me on the map where I am?	**Können Sie mir auf der Karte zeigen, wo ich bin?**	kurnern zee meer owf dair kahrter tsighgern voa ikh bin
You're on the wrong road.	**Sie sind auf der falschen Straße.**	zee zint owf dair fahlshern shtrarsser
Go back to . . .	**Fahren Sie zurück nach . . .**	farrern zee tsoorewk nahkh
Go straight ahead.	**Fahren Sie geradeaus.**	farrern zee gerrarderowss
It's on the left/on the right.	**Es ist linker Hand/rechter Hand.**	ehss ist lingkerr hahnt/rehkhterr hahnt

Accidents

May I use your telephone?	**Darf ich Ihr Telephon benutzen?**	dahrf ikh eer tailaifoan bernewtsern
Call a doctor quickly.	**Rufen Sie schnell einen Arzt.**	roofern zee shnehl ighnern ahrtst
Call an ambulance.	**Rufen Sie einen Krankenwagen.**	roofen zee ighnern krahngkernvargern
Please call the police.	**Rufen Sie bitte die Polizei.**	roofen zee biter dee poalitsigh

Numbers

one	**eins**	ighnss
two	**zwei**	tsvigh
three	**drei**	drigh
four	**vier**	feer
five	**fünf**	fewnf
six	**sechs**	zehks
seven	**sieben**	zeebern
eight	**acht**	ahkht
nine	**neun**	noyn
ten	**zehn**	tsayn
eleven	**elf**	ehlf
twelve	**zwölf**	tsvurlf
thirteen	**dreizehn**	drightsayn
fourteen	**vierzehn**	feertsayn
fifteen	**fünfzehn**	fewnftsayn
sixteen	**sechzehn**	zehkhtsayn
seventeen	**siebzehn**	zeeptsayn
eighteen	**achtzehn**	ahkhtsayn
nineteen	**neunzehn**	noyntsayn

GERMAN

GERMAN

twenty	**zwanzig**	tsvahntsikh
twenty-one	**einundzwanzig**	ighnunttsvahntsikh
thirty	**dreißig**	drighssikh
forty	**vierzig**	feertsikh
fifty	**fünfzig**	fewnftsikh
sixty	**sechzig**	zehkhtsikh
seventy	**siebzig**	zeeptsikh
eighty	**achtzig**	ahkhtsikh
ninety	**neunzig**	noyntsikh
one hundred	**hundert**	hunderrt
one thousand	**tausend**	towzernt
ten thousand	**zehntausend**	tsayntowzernt

Days

It's Sunday.	**Es ist Sonntag.**	ehss ist zontark
Monday	**Montag**	moantark
Tuesday	**Dienstag**	deensstark
Wednesday	**Mittwoch**	mitvokh
Thursday	**Donnerstag**	donerrsstark
Friday	**Freitag**	frightark
Saturday	**Sonnabend**	zonarbernt
yesterday	**gestern**	gehssterrn
today	**heute**	hoyter
tomorrow	**morgen**	morgern
morning/afternoon	**Vormittag/Nach-mittag**	formitark/nahkhmitark
evening/night	**Abend/Nacht**	arbernt/nahkht

Months

January	**Januar**	yahnooarr
February	**Februar**	faybrooarr
March	**März**	mairts
April	**April**	ahpril
May	**Mai**	migh
June	**Juni**	yoonee
July	**Juli**	yoolee
August	**August**	owgust
September	**September**	zehptehmberr
October	**Oktober**	oktoaberr
November	**November**	noavehmberr
December	**Dezember**	daytsehmberr
Merry Christmas!	**Fröhliche Weihnach-ten! Glückliches Neues Jahr!**	frurlikher vighnahkhtern!
Happy New Year!		glewklikherss noyerss yarr

GREEK

Guide to Pronunciation

Letter	Approximate pronunciation	Symbol	Example	
Vowels				
α	like the vowel in car, but pronounced further forward in the mouth	ah	αρωμα	**ah**romah
ε	like **e** in s**e**ll	eh	μέρα	**meh**rah
η, ι, υ	like **ee** in m**ee**t	ee	κύριος	**kee**reeoss
ο, ω	like **o** in g**o**t	o	παρακαλώ	pahrahkah**lo**
Consonants				
β	like **v** in **v**ine	v	βιβλίο	vee**vlee**o
γ	1) before α, ο, ω, ου, and consonants, a voiced version of the **ch** sound in Scottish loch	ĝ	μεγάλος	meh**ĝah**loss
	2) before ε, αι, η, ι, υ, ει, οι, like **y** in **y**et	y	γεμάτος	yeh**mah**toss
δ	like **th** in **th**is	dh	δέν	dhehn
ζ	like **z** in **z**oo	z	ζεστός	zhe**stoss**
θ	like **th** in **th**ing	th	θά	thah
κ	like **k** in **k**it	k	καλός	kah**loss**
λ	like **l** in **l**emon	l	λάθος	**lah**thoss
μ	like **m** in **m**an	m	μέσα	**meh**ssah

υ	like n in new	n	νέος	nehoss
ξ	like x in six	ks	έξω	ehkso
π	like p in pot	p	πρός	pross
ρ	like r in red	r	πρίν	preen
σ, ς	1) before β, γ, δ, ζ, μ, ν, ρ, like z in zoo	z	κόσμος	kozmoss
	2) elsewhere, like s in see	s/ss	στό	sto
τ	like t in tea	t	τότε	toteh
φ	like f in five	f	φέρτε	fehrteh
χ	like ch in Scottish loch	kh	άσχημος	ahsskheemoss
ψ	like ps in dropsy	ps	διψώ	dheepso

Groups of letters

αι	like e in get	eh	είναι	eeneh
ει, οι	like ee in see	ee	πείτε	peeteh
ου	like oo in root	oo	μού	moo
αυ	similar to ave in have	ahv	αύτό	ahvto
ευ	like ev in level	ehv	Εύρώπη	ehvropee
γγ	like ng in linger	ngg	'Αγγλία	ahnggleeah
γκ	1) at the beginning of a word like g in go	g	γκαμήλα	gahmeelah
	2) in the middle of a word, like ng in linger	ngg	άγκυρα	ahnggeerah
γξ	like nks in links	ngks	φάλαγξ	fahlahngks
γχ	like ng followed by the ch of Scottish loch	ngkh	μελαγ- χολία	mehlahng- kholeeah
μπ	1) at the beginning of a word like b in beer	b	μπορείτε	boreeteh
	2) in the middle of a word like mb in lumber	mb	'Όλυμπος	oleemboss
ντ	1) at the beginning of a word, like d in dear	d	ντομάτα	domahtah
	2) in the middle of a word, like nd in under	nd	κέντρο	kehndro
τζ	like ds in seeds	dz	τζάκι	dzahkee

Accent marks

These are written in various ways, e.g., ὰ, ά, or ᾶ, but all of them indicate the stressed syllable. The signs for the "breathing" of initial vowels (α, ἁ) can be ignored. A diaeresis (two dots) written over a letter means that the letter is pronounced separately from the previous one, e.g., καιρός is pronounced kehross, but in Κάϊρο, the α and ι are pronounced separately, kaheero.

The alphabet

Here are the characters which comprise the Greek alphabet. The column at left shows the printed capital and small letters, while written letters are shown in the center column. The column at right gives you the name of these letters as pronounced by Greeks.

Printed	Written	Name
A α	ℳ a	**ahl**fah
B β	ℬ β	**vee**tah
Γ γ	Γ γ	**ghah**mah
Δ δ	∂ ∂	**dhehl**tah
E ε	Ɛ ε	**eh**pseelon
Z ζ	Ζ ζ	**zee**tah
H η	Η η	**ee**tah
Θ θ	Θ ∂	**thee**tah
I ι	Ι ι	yee**ot**ah
K κ	Κ u	**kah**pah
Λ λ	Λ λ	**lahm**dhah
M μ	ℳ μ	mee
N ν	N ν	nee
Ξ ξ	Ξ ξ	ksee
O o	Ο o	o**mee**kron
Π π	Π π	pee
P ρ	℘ ρ	ro
Σ σ ς	Σ ς ς	**seegh**mah
T τ	Τ τ	tahf
Υ υ	Υ υ	**ee**pseelon
Φ φ	φ φ	fee
X χ	Χ χ	khee
Ψ ψ	Ψ ψ	psee
Ω ω	ℯ ω	o**mehg**hah

Some basic expressions

Yes.	Ναί.	neh
No.	᾽Οχι.	okhee
Please.	Παρακαλῶ.	pahrahkahlo
Thank you.	Εὐχαριστῶ.	ehvkhahreesto
Thank you very much.	Εὐχαριστῶ πολύ.	ehvkhahreesto polee
That's all right.	Τίποτα.	teepotah

Greetings

Good morning.	Καλημέρα.	kahleemehrah
Good afternoon.	Καλησπέρα.	kahleespehrah
Good evening.	Καλησπέρα.	kahleespehrah
Good night.	Καληνύκτα.	kahleeneektah
Good-bye.	᾽Αντίο.	ahndeeo
See you later.	Εἰς τό ἐπανιδεῖν.	eess to ehpahneedheen
This is Mr....	῾Ο κύριος ...	o keereeoss
This is Mrs....	῾Η κυρία ...	ee keereeah
This is Miss ...	῾Η δεσποινίς ...	ee dhehspeeneess
I'm very pleased to meet you.	Χαίρομαι πού σᾶς γνωρίζω.	khehromeh poo sahss gnoreezo
How are you?	Τί κάνετε;	tee kahnehteh
Very well, thank you.	Πολύ καλά, εὐχαριστῶ.	polee kahlah ehvkhahreesto
And you?	Καί ἐσεῖς;	keh ehsseess
Fine.	Πολύ καλά.	polee kahlah
Excuse me.	Μέ συγχωρεῖτε.	meh seengkhoreeteh

Questions

Where?	Ποῦ;	poo
Where is ... ?	Ποῦ εἶναι...;	poo eeneh
Where are ... ?	Ποῦ εἶναι...;	poo eeneh
When?	Πότε;	poteh
What?	Τί;	tee

How?	Πῶς;	poss
How much?	Πόσο;	posso
How many?	Πόσα;	possah
Who?	Ποιός;	peeoss
Why?	Γιατί;	yeeahtee
Which?	Ποιός/Ποιά/Ποιό;	peeoss/peeah/peeo
What do you call this?	Πῶς λέγεται αὐτό;	poss lehyehteh ahvto
What do you call that?	Πῶς λέγεται ἐκεῖνο;	poss lehyehteh ehkeeno
What does this mean?	Τί σημαίνει αὐτό;	tee seemehnee ahvto
What does that mean?	Τί σημαίνει ἐκεῖνο;	tee seemehnee ehkeeno

Do you speak ... ?

Do you speak English?	Μιλᾶτε ᾽Αγγλικά;	meelahteh ahnggleekah
Do you speak German?	Μιλᾶτε Γερμανικά;	meelahteh yehrmahneekah
Do you speak French?	Μιλᾶτε Γαλλικά;	meelahteh ġahleekah
Do you speak Spanish?	Μιλᾶτε ᾽Ισπανικά;	meelahteh eespahneekah
Do you speak Italian?	Μιλᾶτε ᾽Ιταλικά;	meelahteh eetahleekah
Could you speak more slowly, please?	Μπορεῖτε νά μιλᾶτε πιό ἀργά, παρακαλῶ;	boreeteh nah meelahteh peeo ahrġah pahrahkahlo
Please point to the phrase in the book.	Παρακαλῶ δεῖξτε τή φράση στό βιβλίο.	pahrahkahlo dheeksteh tee frahssee sto veevleeo
Just a minute. I'll see if I can find it in this book.	῞Ενα λεπτό. Θά δῶ ἄν μπορῶ, νά τό βρῶ σ᾽αὐτό τό βιβλίο.	ehnah lehpto. thah dho ahn boro nah to vro s ahvto to veevleeo
I understand.	Καταλαβαίνω.	kahtahlahvehno
I don't understand.	Δέν καταλαβαίνω.	dhehn kahtahlahvehno

Can...?

Can I have...?	Μπορῶ νά ἔχω...;	boro nah **eh**kho
Can we have...?	Μποροῦμε νά ἔχουμε...;	bor**oo**meh nah **eh**-khoomeh
Can you show me...?	Μπορεῖτε νά μοῦ δείξετε...;	bor**ee**teh nah moo **dheek**steh
Can you tell me...?	Μπορεῖτε νά μοῦ πῆτε...;	bor**ee**teh nah moo **pee**teh
Can you help me, please?	Μπορεῖτε νά μέ βοηθήσετε, παρακαλῶ;	bor**ee**teh nah meh voee**thee**sehteh, pahrahkah**lo**

Wanting

I'd like...	Θά ἤθελα...	thah **ee**thehlah
We'd like...	Θά θέλαμε...	thah **theh**lahmeh
Please give me...	Παρακαλῶ δῶστε μου...	pahrahkah**lo dhoss**teh moo
Give it to me, please.	Δῶστε μοῦ το, παρακαλῶ.	**dhoss**teh moo to pahrahkah**lo**
Please bring me...	Παρακαλῶ, φέρτε μου...	pahrahkah**lo fehr**teh moo
Bring it to me, please.	Φέρτε μοῦ το, παρακαλῶ.	**fehr**teh moo to pahrahkah**lo**
I'm hungry.	Πεινῶ.	pee**no**
I'm thirsty.	Διψῶ.	dheep**so**
I'm tired.	Εἶμαι κουρασμένος.	**ee**meh koorah**smeh**noss
I'm lost.	Χάθηκα.	**kah**theekah
It's important.	Εἶναι σοβαρό.	**ee**neh sovah**ro**
It's urgent.	Εἶναι ἐπεῖγον.	**ee**neh eh**pee**ğon
Hurry up!	Γρήγορα!	**ğree**ğorah

It is/There is...

It is/It's...	Εἶναι...	**ee**neh
Is it...?	Εἶναι...;	**ee**neh
It isn't...	Δέν εἶναι...	dhehn **ee**neh
There is/There are...	Ὑπάρχει/ Ὑπάρχουν...	ee**pahr**khee/eep**ahr**khoon

Is there/Are there...?	Ὑπάρχει/ Ὑπάρχουν...;	eepahrkhee/eepahrkhoon
There isn't/There aren't...	Δέν ὑπάρχει/Δέν ὑπάρχουν...	dhehn eepahrkhee/ dhehn eepahrkhoon
There isn't any/ There aren't any.	Δέν ὑπάρχει καθόλου/Δέν ὑπάρχουν καθόλου.	dhehn eepahrkhee kahtholoo/dhehn eepahrkhoon kahtholoo

A few common words

big/small	μεγάλος/μικρός	mehgahloss/meekross
quick/slow	γρήγορος/ἀργός	greegoross/ahrgoss
early/late	νωρίς/ἀργά	noreess/ahrgah
cheap/expensive	φτηνός/ἀκριβός	fteenoss/ahkreevoss
near/far	κοντά/μακρυά	kondah/mahkreeah
hot/cold	ζεστός/κρύος	zehstoss/kreeoss
full/empty	γεμᾶτος/ἄδειος	yehmahtoss/ahdheeoss
easy/difficult	εὔκολος/δύσκολος	ehvkoloss/dheeskoloss
heavy/light	βαρύς/ἐλαφρός	vahreess/ehlahfross
open/shut	ἀνοικτός/κλειστός	ahneektoss/kleestoss
right/wrong	σωστός/λάθος	sostoss/lahthoss
old/new	παληός/καινούργιος	pahleeoss/kehnooryeeoss
old/young	γέρος/νέος	yehross/nehoss
beautiful/ugly	ὡραῖος/ἄσχημος	orehoss/ahsskheemoss
good/bad	καλός/κακός	kahloss/kahkoss
better/worse	καλύτερος/χειρότερος	kahleetehross/kheerotehross

Some prepositions and a few more useful words

at	στό	sto
on	ἐπάνω	ehpahno
in	μέσα	mehssah
to	πρός	pross
from	ἀπό	ahpo
inside	μέσα	mehssah
outside	ἔξω	ehkso
up	ἐπάνω	ehpahno
down	κάτω	kahto
before	πρίν	preen
after	μετά	mehtah
with	μέ	meh
without	χωρίς	khoreess
through	ἀνάμεσα	ahnahmehssah
towards	πρός	pross
until	μέχρι	mehkhree
during	κατά τή διάρκεια	katah tee dheeahrkeeah
and	καί	keh

or	ἤ	ee
not	δέν	dhehn
nothing	τίποτε	teepoteh
none	κανένα	kahnehnah
very	πολύ	polee
also	ἐπίσης	ehpeesseess
soon	σύντομα	seendomah
perhaps	ἴσως	eessoss
here	ἐδῶ	ehdho
there	ἐκεῖ	ehkee
now	τώρα	torah
then	τότε	toteh

Arrival

Your passport, please.	Τό διαβατήριό σας, παρακαλῶ.	to dheeahvahteereeo sahss pahrahkahlo
Here it is.	'Ορίστε.	oreesteh
Have you anything to declare?	Ἔχετε κάτι νά δηλώσετε;	ehkhehteh kahtee nah dheelosehteh
No, nothing at all.	Ὄχι, τίποτε.	okhee teepoteh
Porter!	'Αχθοφόρε!	ahkhthoforeh
Can you help me with my luggage, please?	Μπορεῖτε νά μέ βοηθήσετε μέ τίς ἀποσκευές μου, παρακαλῶ;	boreeteh nah meh vo-eetheessehteh meh teess ahposkehvehss moo pahrahkahlo
That's my suitcase.	Αὐτή εἶναι ἡ βαλίτσα μου.	ahftee eeneh ee vahleetsah moo
Where's the bus to the centre of town, please?	Ποῦ εἶναι τό λεωφορεῖο γιά τό κέντρο τῆς πόλεως, παρακαλῶ;	poo eeneh to lehoforeeo yeeah to kehndro teess polehoss pahrahkahlo
This way, please.	'Από ἐδῶ, παρακαλῶ.	ahpo ehdho pahrahkahlo

Changing money

| Can you change a traveller's cheque, please? | Μπορεῖτε νά ἀλλάξετε ἕνα τράβελερ τσέκ, παρακαλῶ; | boreeteh nah ahlahksehteh ehnah trahvehlehr tsehk pahrahkahlo |
| Where's the nearest bank, please? | Ποῦ εἶναι ἡ πλησιέστερη τράπεζα, παρακαλῶ; | poo eeneh ee pleesseeehstehree trahpehzah pahrahkahlo |

Car rental

I'd like a car.	Θά ἤθελα ἕνα αὐτοκίνητο.	thah eethehlah ehnah ahftokeeneeto
For how long?	Γιά πόσο καιρό;	yeeah posso kehro
A day/Four days/ A week/Two weeks.	Μία ἡμέρα/ Τέσσερεις ἡμέρες/ Μία ἑβδομάδα/ Δύο ἑβδομάδες.	meeah eemehrah/ tehssehreess eemehrehss/ meeah ehvdhomahdhah/ dheeo ehvdhomahdhehss

Taxi

Where can I get a taxi?	Ποῦ μπορῶ νά βρῶ ἕνα ταξί;	poo boro nah vro ehnah tahksee
What's the fare to...?	Ποιά εἶναι ἡ τιμή γιά...;	peeah eeneh ee teemee yeeah
Take me to this address, please.	Πηγαίνετέ με σ'αὐτή τή διεύθυνσι, παρακαλῶ.	peeyehnehteh meh sahftee tee dheeehftheensee pahrahkahlo
I'm in a hurry.	Εἶμαι βιαστικός.	eemeh veeahsteekoss
Could you drive more slowly, please?	Μπορεῖτε νά ὁδηγῆτε πιό ἀργά, παρακαλῶ;	boreeteh nah odheeyeeteh peeo ahrgah pahrahkahlo

Hotel and other accommodation

My name is...	Τό ὄνομά μου εἶναι...	to onomah moo eeneh
Have you a reservation?	Ἔχετε κρατήσει δωμάτιο;	ehkhehteh krahteessee dhomahteeo
Yes, here's the confirmation.	Μάλιστα, ἰδού ἡ διαβεβαίωση.	mahleestah eedhoo ee dheeahvehvehossee
I'd like...	Θά ἤθελα...	thah eethehlah
I'd like a single room/a double room.	Θά ἤθελα ἕνα μονό δωμάτιο/ἕνα διπλό δωμάτιο.	thah eethehlah ehnah mono dhomahteeo/ehnah dheeplo dhomahteeo
a room with a bath/ with a shower	ἕνα δωμάτιο μέ μπάνιο/μέ ντούς	ehnah dhomahteeo meh bahneeo/meh dooss

How much?

What's the price per night/per week/per month?	Ποιά εἶναι ἡ τιμή γιά μία νύχτα/μία ἑβδομάδα/ἕνα μήνα;	peeah eeneh ee teemee yeeah meeah neekhtah/ meeah ehvdhomahdhah/ ehnah meenah
May I see the room?	Μπορῶ νά δῶ τό δωμάτιο;	boro nah dho to dhomahteeo

I'm sorry, I don't like it.	Μέ συγχωρεῖτε, δέν μοῦ ἀρέσει.	meh seenkhoreeteh dhehn moo ahrehssee
Yes, that's fine. I'll take it.	Ναί, εἶναι καλό. Θά τό πάρω.	neh eeneh kahlo. thah to pahro
What's my room number, please?	Ποιός εἶναι ὁ ἀριθμός τοῦ δωματίου μου, παρακαλῶ;	peeoss eeneh o ahreethmoss too dhomahteeoo moo pahrahkahlo
Number 123.	Νούμερο 123.	noomehro 123

Service, please

Who is it?	Ποιός εἶναι;	peeoss eeneh
Just a minute.	Ἕνα λεπτό.	ehnah lehpto
Come in! The door's open.	Ὁρίστε. Ἡ πόρτα εἶναι ἀνοικτή.	oreesteh. ee portah eeneh ahneektee
May we have breakfast in our room?	Μπορούμε νά πάρουμε τό πρόγευμα στό δωμάτιό μας;	boroomeh nah pahroomeh to proyehvmah sto dhomahteeo mahss

Breakfast

I'll have ...	Θά πάρω ...	thah pahro
I'll have some fruit juice.	Θά πάρω ἕνα χυμό φρούτων.	thah pahro ehnah kheemo frooton
a boiled egg	ἕνα βραστό αὐγό	ehnah vrahsto ahvgo
a fried egg	ἕνα τηγανιτό αὐγό	ehnah teeyahneeto ahvgo
some bacon/some ham	χοιρομέρι/ζαμπόν	kheeromehree zahmbon
some toast	μερικά τόστ	mehreekah tost
a pot of tea	τσάϊ	tsahee
a cup of tea	ἕνα φλυτζάνι τσάϊ	ehnah fleentzahnee tsahee
some coffee	καφέ	kahfeh
some chocolate	κακάο	kahkaho
more butter	περισσότερο βούτυρο	pehreessotehro vooteero
some hot water	ζεστό νερό	zehsto nehro

Difficulties

The central heating doesn't work.	Ἡ κεντρική θέρμανση δέν δουλεύει.	ee kehndhreekee thehrmahnsee dhehn dhoolehvee
the light/the socket	τό φῶς/ἡ πρίζα	to foss/ee preezah
the tap/the toilet	τό ρομπινέ/ἡ τουαλέττα	to rombeeneh/ee tooahlehtah

| There's no hot water. | Δέν ἔχει ζεστό νερό. | dhenn **eh**khee zeh**sto** neh**ro** |
| May I see the manager, please? | Μπορῶ νά δῶ τόν διευθυντή, παρακαλῶ; | **bo**ro nah dho ton dheeehftheen**dee** pahrahkah**lo** |

Telephone—Mail

There's a call for you.	Σας ζητοῦν στό τηλέφωνο.	sahss zee**toon** sto tee**leh**fono
Hold the line, please.	Περιμένετε στό ἀκουστικό σας, παρακαλῶ.	pehree**meh**nehteh sto ahkoos**tee**ko sahss pahrahkah**lo**
Operator, I've been cut off.	Δεσποινίς μέ διέκοψαν.	dhehspee**neess** meh dhee**eh**kopsahn
Did anyone telephone me?	Μοῦ τηλεφώνησε κανείς;	moo teelehfo**nee**sseh kah**neess**
Is there any mail for me?	Ὑπάρχουν γράμματα γιά μένα;	ee**pahr**khoon **grah**mahtah yee**ah mehn**nah
Are there any messages for me?	Ὑπάρχουν παραγγελίες γιά μένα;	ee**pahr**khoon pahrzhnggeh**lee**ehss yee**ah mehn**nah

Checking out

May I have my bill, please?	Μπορῶ νά ἔχω τόν λογαριασμό, παρακαλῶ;	**bo**ro nah **eh**kho ton loğahreeah**zmo** pahrahkah**lo**
We're in a great hurry.	Εἴμαστε πολύ βιαστικοί.	**ee**mahsteh po**lee** veeah-stee**kee**
It's been a very enjoyable stay.	Ἡ διαμονή ἦταν πολύ εὐχάριστη.	eedheeahmo**nee ee**tahn po**lee** ehf**khah**reestee

Eating out

Good evening, sir/ Good evening, madam.	Καλησπέρα, κύριε/Καλησπέρα, κυρία.	kahlees**peh**rah **kee**reeeh/kahlees**peh**rah **kee**reeah
Good evening. I'd like a table for two, please.	Καλησπέρα. Θά ἤθελα ἕνα τραπέζι γιά δύο, παρακαλῶ.	kahlees**peh**rah. thah **ee**thehlah **eh**nah trah**peh**zee yee**ah dhee**o pahrahkah**lo**
Do you have a fixed-price menu?	Ἔχετε φαγητό μέ καθωρισμένη τιμή;	**eh**khehteh fahyee**to** meh kahthoreez**meh**nee tee**mee**

124

May I see the à la carte menu?	Μπορῶ νά δῶ τό μενοῦ ἀ-λά-κάρτ;	boro nah dho to mehnoo ahlahkahrt
May we have an ashtray, please?	Μποροῦμε νά ἔχουμε ἕνα στακτοδοχεῖο, παρακαλῶ;	boroomeh nah ehkhoomeh ehnah stahktodhokheeo pahrahkahlo
some bread	ψωμί	psomee
a fork	ἕνα πειρούνι	ehnah peeroonee
a knife	ἕνα μαχαίρι	ehnah mahkhehree
a spoon	ἕνα κουτάλι	ehnan kootahlee
a plate	ἕνα πιάτο	ehnah peeahto
a glass	ἕνα ποτήρι	ehnah poteeree
a napkin	ἕνα τραπεζομάντηλο	ehnah trahpehzomahn-deelo
another chair	μία καρέκλα ἀκόμη	meeah kahrehklah ahkomee
Where's the gentlemen's toilet (men's room)?	Ποῦ εἶναι οἱ τουαλέττες τῶν ἀνδρῶν;	poo eeneh ee tooahlehtehss ton ahndhron
Where's the ladies' toilet (ladies' room)?	Ποῦ εἶναι οἱ τουαλέττες τῶν γυναικῶν;	poo eeneh ee tooahlehtehss ton yeenehkon

Appetizers

I'd like some...	Θά ἤθελα...	thah eethehlah
I'd like some assorted appetizers.	Θά ἤθελα μία ποικιλία ὀρεκτικῶν.	thah eethehlah meeah peekeeleeah orehkteekon
orange juice	ἕνα χυμό πορτοκαλιοῦ	ehnah kheemo portokahleeoo
ham	ζαμπόν	zahmbon
melon	πεπόνι	pehponee
pâté	πατέ	pahteh
smoked salmon	καπνιστό σολωμό	kahpneesto solomo
shrimps (shrimp)	γαρίδες	ğahreedhehss

Soup

Have you any...?	Ἔχετε...;	ehkhehteh
Have you any chicken soup?	Ἔχετε κοτόσουπα;	ehkhehteh kotossoopah
vegetable soup	χορτόσουπα	khortossoopah
onion soup	κρεμμυδόσουπα	krehmeedhossoopah

Fish

I'd like some...	Θά ἤθελα...	thah eethehlah
I'd like some fish.	Θά ἤθελα ψάρι.	thah eethehlah psahree
sole	γλῶσσα	glosah
trout	πέστροφα	pehstrofah
lobster	ἀστακό	ahstahko
crayfish	καραβίδες	kahrahveedhehss
prawns	καβούρια	kahvooreeah
I'd like it...	Θά τό ἤθελα...	thah to eethehlah
I'd like it steamed.	Θά τό ἤθελα στόν ἀτμό.	thah to eethehlah ston ahtmo
grilled	ψητό	pseeto
boiled	βραστό	vrahsto
baked	μαγειρευμένο	mahyeerehvmehno
fried	τηγανιτό	teeģahneeto

Meat—Poultry—Game

I'd like some...	Θά ἤθελα...	thah eethehlah
I'd like some beef.	Θά ἤθελα μοσχάρι.	thah eethehlah mosskhahree
a beef steak	μία μπριζόλα	meeah breezolah
some roast beef	ροζ-μπήφ	rozbeef
a veal cutlet	μία μοσχαρίσια μπριζόλα	meeah mosskhahree-sseeah breezolah
mutton	ἀρνί	ahrnee
lamb	ἀρνάκι γάλακτος	ahrnahkee ģahlahktoss
a pork chop	μία χοιρινή μπριζόλα	meeah kheereenee breezolah
roast pork	ψητό χοιρινό	pseeto kheereeno
hare	λαγό	lahģo
chicken	κοτόπουλο	kotopoolo
roast chicken	κοτόπουλο ψητό	kotopoolo pseeto
duck	πάπια	pahpeeah
How do you like your meat?	Πῶς θέλετε τό κρέας σας;	poss thehlehteh to krehahss sahss
rare	λίγο ψημένο	leeģo pseemehno
medium	μέτριο	mehtreeo
well done	καλοψημένο	kahlopseemehno

Vegetables

What vegetables have you got?	Τί λαχανικά ἔχετε;	tee lahkhahneekah ehkhehteh
I'd like some...	Θά ἤθελα...	thah eethehlah

I'd like some asparagus.	Θά ἤθελα σπαράγγια.	thah **ee**thehlah spah**rahng**geeah
green beans	φασόλια φρέσκα	fah**sso**leeah **freh**skah
mushrooms	μανιτάρια	mahnee**tah**reeah
carrots	καρόττα	kah**ro**tah
onions	κρεμμύδια	kreh**mee**dheeah
red cabbage	κόκκινο λάχανο	**ko**keeno **lahk**hahno
spinach	σπανάκι	spah**nah**kee
rice	ρύζι	**ree**zee
peas	μπιζέλια	bee**zeh**leeah
tomatoes	τομάτες	to**mah**tehss
green salad	πράσινη σαλάτα	**prahs**seenee sah**lah**tah
potatoes	πατάτες	pah**tah**tehss

Desserts

Nothing more, thanks.	Τίποτε ἄλλο, εὐχαριστῶ.	**tee**poteh **ah**lo ehfkhah**ree**sto
Just a small portion, please.	Μία μικρή μερίδα, παρακαλῶ.	**mee**ah mee**kree** meh**ree**dhah pahrah**kah**lo.
Have you any ice-cream?	Ἔχετε παγωτά;	**eh**khehteh pah**ġo**tah
fruit salad	φρουτοσαλάτα	frootossah**lah**tah
fresh fruit	φρέσκα φροῦτα	**freh**skah **froo**tah
cheese	τυρί	tee**ree**

Drink

What would you like to drink?	Τί θά θέλατε νά πιῆτε;	tee thah **theh**lahteh nah **pee**eeteh
I'll have a beer, please.	Θά πάρω μία μπύρα, παρακαλῶ.	thah **pah**ro **mee**ah **bee**rah pahrah**kah**lo
I'll have a whisky, please.	Θά πάρω ἕνα οὐίσκυ, παρακαλῶ.	thah **pah**ro **eh**nah oo**ee**skee pahrah**kah**lo

Wine

I'd like a bottle of wine.	Θά ἤθελα ἕνα μπουκάλι κρασί.	thah **ee**thehlah **eh**nah boo**kah**lee krah**ssee**
red wine	κόκκινο κρασί	**ko**keeno krah**ssee**
rosé wine	ροζέ κρασί	ro**zeh** krah**ssee**
white wine	ἄσπρο κρασί	**ah**spro krah**ssee**
Cheers!	Στήν ὑγειά σας.	steen eeyee**ah** sahss

The bill (check)

May I have the bill (check) please?	Μπορῶ νά ἔχω τό λογαριασμό, παρακαλῶ;	boro nah **eh**kho to lo**ǧ**ahreeahz**mo** pahrahkah**lo**
Is service included?	Τό φιλοδώρημα περιλαμβάνεται;	to feelo**dho**reemah pehreelahm**vah**nehteh
Everything's included.	'Ολα περιλαμβάνονται.	**o**lah pehreelahm**vah**nondheh
Thank you, that was a very good meal.	Εὐχαριστῶ, τό γεῦμα ἦταν πολύ καλό.	ehfkahree**sto** to **yeh**vmah **ee**tahn po**lee** kah**lo**

Travelling

Where's the railway station, please?	Ποῦ εἶναι ὁ σιδηρο-δρομικός σταθμός, παρακαλῶ;	poo **ee**neh o seedheerodhromee**koss** stahth**moss** pahrahkah**lo**
Where's the ticket office, please?	Ποῦ εἶναι τό γραφεῖο ἐκδόσεως εἰσιτηρίων, παρακαλῶ;	poo **ee**neh to **ǧ**rah**fee**o ehk**dho**ssehoss eessee**tee**ree**on** pahrahkah**lo**
I'd like a ticket to...	Θά ἤθελα ενα εἰσιτήριο γιά...	thah **ee**thehlah **eh**nah eessee**tee**ree**o**yeeah
First or second class?	Πρώτη ἤ δευτέρα θέση;	pro**tee** ee dhehf**teh**rah **theh**ssee
First class, please.	Πρώτη θέση, παρακαλῶ.	pro**tee theh**ssee pahrahkah**lo**
Single or return (one way or round-trip)?	'Απλή διαδρομή ἤ μετ'ἐπιστροφῆς;	ah**plee** dheeahdhro**mee** ee mehtehpeestro**feess**
Do I have to change trains?	Πρέπει νά ἀλλάξω τραῖνο;	**preh**pee nah ah**lah**kso **treh**no
What platform does the train leave from?	'Από ποιά ἀποβάθρα φεύγει τό τραῖνο;	ah**po** pee**ah** ahpo**vah**thrah **feh**vyee to **treh**no
Where's the nearest underground (sub-way) station?	Ποῦ εἶναι ὁ πλη-σιέστερος σταθμός τοῦ 'Ηλεκτρικοῦ;	poo **ee**neh o pleessee**eh**-stehross stath**moss** too eelehktree**koo**
Where's the bus station, please?	Ποῦ εἶναι ο σταθμός τῶν λεωφορείων παρακαλῶ;	poo **ee**neh o stath**moss** ton lehofo**ree**on pahrahkah**lo**

When's the first bus to...?	Πότε είναι τό πρῶτο λεωφορεῖο γιά...;	poteh eeneh to proto lehoforeeo yeeah
the last bus	τό τελευταῖο λεωφορεῖο	to tehlehfteho lehoforeeo
the next bus	τό ἐπόμενο λεωφορεῖο	to ehpomehno lehoforeeo
Please let me off at the next stop.	Παρακαλῶ, θέλω νά κατεβῶ στήν ἐπομένη στάση.	pahrahkahlo thehlo nah kahtehvo steen ehpomehnee stahssee

Relaxing

What's on at the cinema (movies)?	Τί παίζουν στόν κινηματογράφο;	tee pehzoon ston keeneemahtografho
What's on at the theatre?	Τί παίζουν στό θέατρο;	tee pehzoon sto thehahtro
What time does the film begin? And the play?	Τί ὥρα ἀρχίζει τό φίλμ; Καί τό ἔργο;	tee orah ahrkheezee to feelm? keh to ehrgo
Are there any tickets for tonight?	Ὑπάρχουν εἰση-τήρια γι'ἀπόψε;	eepahrkhoon eessee-teereeah yeeahpopseh
Where can we go dancing?	Ποῦ μποροῦμε νά πᾶμε νά χορέψουμε;	poo boroomeh nah pahmeh nah khorehpsoomeh
Would you like to dance?	Θά θέλατε νά χορέψετε;	thah thehlahteh nah khorehpsehteh

Introductions

How do you do?	Πῶς εἶσθε;	poss eestheh
How are you?	Τί κάνετε;	tee kahnehteh
Very well, thank you. And you?	Πολύ καλά, εὐχαριστῶ. Καί ἐσεῖς;	polee kahlah ehfkhahreesto. keh ehsseess
May I introduce Miss Philips?	Μπορῶ νά σᾶς συστήσω τή δεσποινίδα Φίλιπς;	boro nah sahss seesteesso tee dhehspeeneedhah Philips
My name is...	Ὀνομάζομαι...	onomahzomeh
I'm very pleased to meet you.	Χαίρω πολύ πού σᾶς γνωρίζω.	khehro polee poo sahss gnoreezo
How long have you been here?	Πόσο καιρό εἶσθε ἐδῶ;	poso kehro eestheh ehdho
It was nice meeting you.	Χάρηκα πού σᾶς γνώρισα.	khahreekah poo sahss gnoreessah

Dating

Would you like a cigarette?	Θά θέλατε ἕνα τσιγάρο;	thah **theh**lahteh **ehnah** tsee**gah**ró
May I get you a drink?	Μπορῶ νά σᾶς φέρω ἕνα ποτό;	boro nah sahss **fehro** **ehnah** poto
Do you have a light, please?	Ἔχετε φωτιά, παρακαλῶ;	**ehkheh**teh foteeah pahrahkahlo
Are you waiting for someone?	Περιμένετε κάποιον;	pehree**mehneh**teh **kah**peeon
Are you free this evening?	Εἶσθε ἐλεύθερη ἀπόψε;	**ees**theh ehlehftthree ah**pop**seh
Where shall we meet?	Ποῦ θά συναντηθοῦμε;	poo thah seenahndee**thoo**meh
What time shall I meet you?	Τί ὥρα θά σᾶς συναντήσω;	tee orah thah sahss seenahn**dees**so
May I take you home?	Μπορῶ νά σᾶς πάω στό σπίτι σας;	boro nah sahss **paho** sto **spee**tee sahss
Thank you, it's been a wonderful evening.	Εὐχαριστῶ, ἦταν μία ὑπέροχη βραδυά.	ehfkahree**esto** eetahn **mee**ah eepehrokhee vrahd**heeah**
What's your telephone number?	Ποιός εἶναι ὁ ἀριθμός τοῦ τηλεφώνου σας;	pee**oss** eeneh o ahreeth**moss** too teelehfonoo sahss
Do you live alone?	Μένετε μόνη σας;	**mehneh**teh **monee** sahss
What time is your last train?	Τί ὥρα εἶναι τό τελευταῖο τραῖνο σας;	tee orah eeneh to tehlehftteho trehno sahss
Good-night...	Καληνύκτα...	kahlee**neek**tah

Banks

Where's the nearest bank, please?	Ποῦ εἶναι ἡ πλησιέστερη τράπεζα, παρακαλῶ;	poo **eeneh** ee pleesseeee**stehree** **trah**pehzah pahrahkahlo
Where can I cash some traveller's cheques?	Ποῦ μπορῶ νά ἐξαργυρώσω μερικά τράβελερς τσέκ;	poo boro nah ehksahryeerosso mehree**kah** trah**veh**lehrs tsehk
What time does the bank open? What time does it close?	Τί ὥρα ἀνοίγει ἡ τράπεζα; Τί ὥρα κλείνει;	tee orah ahneeyee ee **trah**pehzah? tee orah **klee**nee

I'm expecting some money from home. Has it arrived?	Περιμένω χρήματα ἀπό τό σπίτι. Μήπως ἠλθαν;	pehreemehno khreemahtah ahpo to speetee. meeposs eelthahn
Can you give me some small change, please?	Μπορεῖτε νά μοῦ δώσετε μερικά κέρματα, παρακαλῶ;	boreeteh nah moo dhossehteh mehreekah kehrmahtah pahrahkahlo

Shops, stores and services

Where is the nearest chemist's (pharmacy)?	Ποῦ εἶναι τό πλησιέστερο φαρμακεῖο;	poo eeneh to pleesseeehstehro fahrmahkeeo
the nearest hairdresser's	τό πλησιέστερο κουρεῖο	to pleesseeehstehro kooreeo
the photo shop	τό φωτογραφεῖο	to fotograhfeeo
the jeweller's	τό κοσμηματοπωλεῖο	to kozmeemahtopoleeo
the department store	τό ἐμπορικό κατάστημα	to ehmboreeko kahtahsteemah
the police station	τό ἀστυνομικό τμῆμα	to ahsteenomeeko tmeemah
the garage	τό γκαράζ	to gahrahz
How do I get there?	Πῶς νά πάω ἐκεῖ;	poss nah paho ehkee
Is it within walking distance?	Μπορῶ νά πάω μέ τά πόδια;	boro nah paho meh tah podheeah

Service

Can you help me, please?	Μπορεῖτε νά μέ βοηθήσετε, παρακαλῶ;	boreeteh nah meh voeetheessehteh pahrahkahlo
Can you show me this? And that, too.	Μπορεῖτε νά μοῦ δείξετε αὐτό; Καί ἐκεῖνο ἐπίσης.	boreeteh nah moo dheeksehteh ahfto? keh ehkeeno ehpeesseess
It's too expensive/ too big/too small.	Εἶναι πολύ ἀκριβό/ πολύ μεγάλο/ πολύ μικρό.	eeneh poleeahkreevo/polee mehgahlo/ polee meekro
Can you show me some more?	Μπορεῖτε νά μοῦ δείξετε περισσότερα;	boreeteh nah moo dheeksehteh pehreessotehrah
something better	κάτι καλύτερο	kahtee kahleetehro
something cheaper	κάτι φθηνότερο	kahtee ftheenotehro

How much is this? And that?	Πόσο κοστίζει αὐτό; Καί ἐκεῖνο;	**pos**so ko**stee**zee ahf**to**? keh eh**kee**no
It's not quite what I want.	Δέν εἶναι ἀκριβῶς αὐτό πού θέλω.	dhehn **ee**neh ahkree**voss** ahf**to** poo **theh**lo
I like it.	Μοῦ ἀρέσει.	moo ah**reh**see

Chemist's (Pharmacy)

| I'd like something for a cold/for a cough/for travel sickness. | Θά ἤθελα κάτι γιά τό κρύωμα/γιά τό βῆχα/γιά τή ναυτία. | thah **ee**thehlah **kah**tee yeeah to **kree**omah/yeeah to **vee**khah/yeeah tee nahf**tee**ah |
| Can you recommend something for hayfever/for sunburn? | Μπορεῖτε νά μοῦ συστήσετε κάτι γιά τόν ὑψηλό πυρετό/γιά τά ἐγκαύματα τοῦ ἡλίου; | bo**ree**teh nah moo sees**tees**sehteh **kah**tee yeeah ton eep**see**lo peereh**hto**/yeeah tah ehng**gah**vmaht-ah too eeleeoo |

Toiletry

May I have some razor blades?	Μπορῶ νά ἔχω μερικά ξυραφάκια ξυρίσματος;	bo**ro** nah **eh**kho mehree**kah** kseerahfah-keeah kseer**eez**mahtoss
some shaving cream	κρέμα ξυρίσματος	**kreh**mah kseer**eez**-mahtoss
some toothpaste	ὀδοντόπαστα	odhon**do**pahstah
I'd like some soap.	Θά ἤθελαἔνα σαπούνι.	thah **ee**thehlah **eh**nah sah**poo**nee
some suntan oil	λάδι ἡλίου	**lah**dhee eeleeoo

At the barber's

I'd like a haircut, please.	Θά ἤθελα νά μοῦ κόψετε τά μαλλιά παρακαλῶ.	thah **ee**thehlah nah moo **kop**sehteh tah mahleeah pahrahkah**lo**
Short/Leave it long.	Κοντά/'Αφῆστε τα μακρυά.	kon**dah**/ahf**ee**steh tah mahk**ree**ah
A razor cut, please.	Κόψιμο μέ ξυράφι, παρακαλῶ.	**kop**seemo meh kseer**ah**fee pahrahkah**lo**

At the hairdresser's

| I'd like a shampoo and set, please. | Θά ἤθελα λούσιμο καί μίζ-αν-πλί, παρακαλῶ. | thaht **ee**thehlah **loo**seemo keh meezahn**plee** pahrahkah**lo** |

I'd like a bleach.	Θά ήθελα μία ντεκολορασιόν.	thah **ee**thehlah **mee**ah dehkolorahsee**on**
a permanent	μία περμανάντ	**mee**ah pehrmah**nahnd**
a colour rinse	ένα ντεκαπάζ	**eh**nah dehkah**pahz**
a manicure	μανικιούρ	mahneekee**oor**

Photography

| I'd like a film for this camera. | Θά ήθελα ένα φίλμ γι'αύτή τή μηχανή. | thah **ee**thehlah **eh**nah feelm yeeahf**tee** tee meek**hah**nee |
| This camera doesn't work. | Αὐτή ή μηχανή δέν δουλεύει. | ahf**tee** ee meek**hah**nee dehn dhoo**leh**vee |

At the post office

| Where's the nearest post office, please? | Πού είναι τό πλησιέστερο ταχυ-δρομείο, παρακαλώ; | poo **ee**neh to pleessee**eh**stehro tahkhee-dhro**mee**o pahrah**kah**lo |
| I'd like to send this by express (special delivery)/by air mail. | Θά ήθελα νά στείλω αὐτό ἔξπρές/ἀεροπορικῶς. | thah **ee**thehlah nah **stee**lo ahf**to** ehks**prehss**/ ahehroporee**koss** |

Service stations

Where is the nearest service station, please?	Πού είναι τό πλησιέστερο πρατήριο βενζίνης, παρακαλώ;	poo **ee**neh to pleessee**eh**stehro prah**tee**reeo vehn**zee**neess pahrah**kah**lo
Fill her up, please.	Νά τό γεμίσετε, παρακαλώ.	nah to yeh**mee**ssehteh pahrah**kah**lo
Check the oil, please.	Ἐλέγξατε τό λάδι, παρακαλώ.	eh**lehn**ksahteh to **lah**dhee pahrah**kah**lo
Would you check the tyres?	Θά μπορούσατε νά ἐλέγξετε τά λάστιχα;	thah bor**oo**ssahteh nah eh**lehn**ksehteh tah **lah**steekhah

Street directions

| Can you show me on the map where I am? | Μπορείτε νά μού δείξετε στό χάρτη πού είμαι; | bor**ee**teh nah moo **dhee**ksehteh sto **khahr**tee poo **ee**meh |
| You're on the wrong road. | Ἔχετε πάρει λάθος δρόμο. | eh**kheh**teh **pah**ree **lah**thoss **dhro**mo |

133

Go back to . . .	Γυρίστε πίσω στό . . .	yeereesteh peesso sto
Go straight ahead.	Νά πᾶτε εὐθεία.	nah pahteh ehftheeah
It's on the left/on the right.	Εἶναι ἀριστερά/δεξιά.	eeneh ahreestehrah/dhehkseeah

Accidents

May I use your telephone?	Μπορῶ νά χρησιμοποιήσω τό τηλέφωνό σας;	boro nah khreesseemopeeeesso to teelehfono sahss
Call a doctor quickly.	Καλέστε ἕνα γιατρό γρήγορα.	kahlehsteh ehnah yeeahtro greegorah
Call an ambulance.	Καλέστε ἕνα ἀσθενοφόρο.	kahlehsteh ehnah ahsthehnoforo
Please call the police.	Παρακαλῶ καλέστε τήν ἀστυνομία.	pahrahkahlo kahlehsteh teen ahsteenomeeah

Numbers

one	ἕνα	ehnah
two	δύο	dheeo
three	τρία	treeah
four	τέσσερα	tehssehrah
five	πέντε	pehndeh
six	ἕξη	ehksee
seven	ἑπτά	ehptah
eight	ὀκτώ	okto
nine	ἐννέα	ehnehah
ten	δέκα	dhehkah
eleven	ἕντεκα	ehndehkah
twelve	δώδεκα	dhodhehkah
thirteen	δεκατρία	dhehkahtreeah
fourteen	δεκατέσσερα	dhehkahtehssehrah
fifteen	δεκαπέντε	dhehkahpehndeh
sixteen	δεκαέξη	dhehkahehksee
seventeen	δεκαεπτά	dhehkahehptah
eighteen	δεκαοκτώ	dhehkahokto
nineteen	δεκαεννέα	dhehkahehnehah
twenty	εἴκοσι	eekossee
twenty-one	εἴκοσι ἕνα	eekossee ehnah
thirty	τριάντα	treeahndah
forty	σαράντα	sharahndah
fifty	πενήντα	pehneendah
sixty	ἑξήντα	eekseendah
seventy	ἑβδομῆντα	ehvdhomeendah

GREEK

eighty	ὀγδόντα	oǧdhondah
ninety	ἐνενήντα	ehnehneendah
one hundred	ἑκατό	ehkahto
one thousand	χίλια	kheeleeah
ten thousand	δέκα χιλιάδες	dhehkah kheeleeahdhehss

Days

It's Sunday.	Εἶναι Κυριακή.	eeneh keereeahkee
Monday	Δευτέρα	dhehftehrah
Tuesday	Τρίτη	treetee
Wednesday	Τετάρτη	tertahrtee
Thursday	Πέμπτη	pehmptee
Friday	Παρασκευή	pahrahskehvee
Saturday	Σάββατο	shavahto
yesterday	χθές	khthehss
today	σήμερα	seemehrah
tomorrow	αὔριο	ahvreeo
morning/afternoon	πρωί/ἀπόγευμα	proee/ahpoyehvmah
evening/night	βράδυ/νύκτα	vrahdhee/neektah

Months

January	Ἰανουάριος	eeahnooahreeoss
February	Φεβρουάριος	fehvrooahreeoss
March	Μάρτιος	mahrteeoss
April	Ἀπρίλιος	ahpreeleeoss
May	Μάιος	maheeoss
June	Ἰούνιος	eeooneeoss
July	Ἰούλιος	eeooleeoss
August	Αὔγουστος	ahvgoostoss
September	Σεπτέμβριος	sehptehmvreeoss
October	Ὀκτώβριος	oktovreeoss
November	Νοέμβριος	noehmvreeoss
December	Δεκέμβριος	dhehkehmvreeoss
Merry Christmas!	Καλά Χριστούγεννα.	kahlah khreestooyehnah
Happy New Year!	Εὐτυχισμένος ὁ καινούργιος χρόνος.	ehfteekheezmehnoss o kehnooryeeoss khronoss

ITALIAN

Guide to Pronunciation

Letter	Approximate pronunciation	Symbol	Example	
Consonants				
b, d, f, k, l, m, n, p, q, t, v	are pronounced as in English			
c	1) before **e** and **i**, like **ch** in **ch**ip	ch	**cerco**	**chayr**koa
	2) elsewhere, like **c** in **c**at	k	**conto**	**koan**toa
ch	like **c** in **c**at	k	**che**	kay
g	1) before **e** and **i**, like **j** in **j**et	j	**leggero**	layd**jai**roa
	2) elsewhere, like **g** in **g**o	g	**grande**	**grahn**day
gh	like **g** in **g**o	g	**ghiaccio**	gee**aht**cheeoa
gl	like **lli** in million	ly	**gli**	lyee
gn	like **ni** in onion	ñ	**bagno**	**bar**ñoa
h	always silent		**ha**	ah

r	trilled like a Scottish r	r	caro	karroa
s	1) generally like s in sit	s/ss	casa	karssah
			questo	kooaystoa
	2) sometimes like z in zoo	z	viso	veezoa
sc	1) before e, i, like sh in shut	sh	uscita	oosheetah
	2) elsewhere, like sk in skin	sk	scarpa	skahrpah
z or zz	1) generally like ts in hits	ts	grazie	grahtseeay
	2) sometimes like ds in roads	dz	romanzo	roamahndzoa

Vowels

a	1) short, like a in car, but shorter	ah	gatto	gahttoa
	2) long, like a in car	ar	casa	karssah
e	1) can always be pronounced like ay in gay	ay	sera	sayrah
	2) in correct speech, it is sometimes pronounced like e in get or, when long, more like ai in hair	eh	bello	behlloa
		ai	bene	bainay
i	like the ee in meet	ee	vini	veenee
o	1) can always be pronounced like oa in goat	oa	sole	soalay
	2) in correct speech, it is sometimes pronounced like o in got, or when long, more like aw in law	o	notte	nottay
		aw	rosa	rawzah
u	like the oo in foot	oo	fumo	foomoa

Two or more vowels

In groups of vowels, a, e, and o are strong vowels, and i and u are weak vowels. When two strong vowels are next to each other, they are pronounced as two separate syllables, e.g., *beato* = bayahtoa. When a strong and weak vowel are next to each other, the weak one is pronounced more quickly and with less stress (less loudly) than the strong one, e.g., *piede* = peeayday; such sounds are diphthongs and constitute only one syllable. If the weak vowel is stressed, then it is pronounced as a separate syllable, e.g., *due* = **doo**ay. Two weak vowels together are pronounced as a diphthong, and it is generally the second one that is more strongly stressed, e.g., *guida* = gooeedah.

Stressing of words

Generally, the vowel of the next to the last syllable is stressed. When a final vowel is stressed, it has an accent written over it (´ or `). Normally an accent is used only when the stress falls on a final vowel, and not when it falls on syllables before the next to the last one.

ITALIAN

Some basic expressions

Yes.	**Si.**	see
No.	**No.**	no
Please.	**Per favore.**	pair fah**voa**ray
Thank you.	**Grazie.**	**grah**tseeay
Thank you very much.	**Mille grazie.**	**meel**lay **grah**tseeay
That's all right.	**Prego.**	**pray**goa

Greetings

Good morning.	**Bongiorno.**	boan**joar**noa
Good afternoon.	**Bongiorno.**	boan**joar**noa
Good evening.	**Buona sera.**	boo**aw**nah **say**rah
Good night.	**Buona notte.**	boo**aw**nah **not**tay
Good-bye.	**Arrivederci.**	ahreevay**dair**chee
See you later.	**A più tardi.**	a pyoo **tahr**dee
This is Mr. . . .	**Questo è il signor . . .**	koo**ayss**toa ay eel see**ñor**
This is Mrs. . . .	**Questa è la signora . . .**	koo**ayss**tah ay lah see**ñoa**rah
This is Miss . . .	**Questa è la signorina . . .**	koo**ayss**tah ay lah see**ñoa**reenah
I'm very pleased to meet you.	**Piacere.**	peeah**chay**ray
How are you?	**Come sta?**	**koa**may stah
Very well, thank you.	**Molto bene. Grazie.**	**moal**toa **bai**nay. **grah**tseeay
And you?	**E lei?**	ay **laiee**
Fine.	**Bene.**	**bai**nay
Excuse me.	**Mi scusi.**	mee **skoo**zee

Questions

Where?	**Dove?**	**doa**vay
Where is . . . ?	**Dov'è . . . ?**	doa**vai**
Where are . . . ?	**Dove sono . . . ?**	**doa**vay **soa**noa

ITALIAN

When?	Quando?	kwahndoa
What?	Cosa?	kawssah
How?	Come?	koamay
How much?	Quanto?	kwahntoa
How many?	Quanti?	kwahntee
Who?	Chi?	kee
Why?	Perchè?	pehrkay
Which?	Quale?	kwarlay
What do you call this?	Come si chiama questo?	koamay see keearmah kooaysstoa
What do you call that?	Come si chiama quello?	koamay see keearmah kooaylloa
What does this mean?	Cosa significa questo?	kawssah seeñeefeekah kooaystoa
What does that mean?	Cosa significa quello?	kawssah seeñeefeekah kooaylloa

ITALIAN

Do you speak ... ?

Do you speak English?	Parla inglese?	pahrlah eengglayssay
Do you speak German?	Parla tedesco?	pahrlah taydayskoa
Do you speak French?	Parla francese?	pahrlah frahnchayzay
Do you speak Spanish?	Parla spagnolo?	pahrlah spahñoaloa
Do you speak Italian?	Parla italiano?	pahrlah eetahlyarnoa
Could you speak more slowly, please?	Può parlare più adagio, per piacere?	pwo pahrlarray peeoo ahdarjoa pair peeahchayray
Please point to the phrase in the book.	Per favore, mi indichi la frase nel libro.	pair fahvoaray mee eendeekee lah frarzay nehl leebroa
Just a minute. I'll see if I can find it in this book.	Un momento. Vedo se posso trovarla nel libro.	oon moamayntoa. vaydoa say posssoa troavarrlah nayl leebroa
I understand.	Capisco.	kahpeesskoa
I don't understand.	Non capisco.	noan kahpeesskao

Can...?

Can I have...?	**Posso avere...?**	**poss**soa ah**vay**ray
Can we have...?	**Possiamo avere...?**	possseear**moa** ah**vay**ray
Can you show me...?	**Può indicarmi...?**	pwo eendee**karr**mee
Can you tell me...?	**Può dirmi...?**	pwo **deer**mee
Can you help me, please?	**Può aiutarmi, per piacere?**	pwo igh**oo**tarrmee pair peeah**chay**ray

Wanting

I'd like...	**Vorrei...**	vor**rai**ee
We'd like...	**Vorremmo...**	vor**rehm**moa
Please give me...	**Per favore, mi dia...**	pair fah**voa**ray mee **dee**ah
Give it to me, please.	**Me lo dia, per favore.**	may loa **dee**ah pair fah**voa**ray
Please bring me...	**Per favore, mi porti...**	pair fah**voa**ray mee **por**tee
Bring it to me, please.	**Me lo porti, per favore.**	may loa **por**tee pair fah**voa**ray
I'm hungry.	**Ho fame.**	oa **far**may
I'm thirsty.	**Ho sete.**	oa **say**tay
I'm tired.	**Sono stanco.**	**soa**noa **stahng**koa
I'm lost.	**Mi sono perso.**	mee **soa**noa **pehr**soa
It's important.	**È importante.**	ay eempor**tahn**tay
It's urgent.	**È urgente.**	ay oor**jehn**tay
Hurry up!	**Si affretti!**	see ahf**fray**ttee

It is/There is...

It is/It's...	**È...**	ai
Is it...?	**È...?**	ai
It isn't...	**Non è...**	noan ai
There is/There are...	**C'è/Ci sono...**	chai/chee **soa**noa
Is there/Are there...?	**C'è/Ci sono...?**	chai/chee **soa**noa

ITALIAN

| There isn't/There aren't... | **Non c'è/Non ci sono...** | noan chai/noan chee soanoa |
| There isn't any/There aren't any. | **Non ce n'è/Non ce ne sono.** | noan chay nai/noan chay nay soanoa |

A few common words

big/small	**grande/piccolo**	grahnday/peekkoaloa
quick/slow	**rapido/lento**	rarpeedoa/lehntoa
early/late	**presto/tardi**	prehsstoa/tahrdee
cheap/expensive	**economico/costoso**	aykoanomeekoa/kosstoasoa
near/far	**vicino/lontano**	veecheenoa/lontarnoa
hot/cold	**caldo/freddo**	kahldoa/frayddoa
full/empty	**pieno/vuoto**	peeaynoa/vooawtoa
easy/difficult	**facile/difficile**	farcheelay/deefeecheelay
heavy/light	**pesante/leggero**	paysahntay/laydjairoa
open/shut	**aperto/chiuso**	ahpehrtoa/keeoossoa
right/wrong	**giusto/sbagliato**	joosstoa/zbahlyartoa
old/new	**vecchio/nuovo**	vehkkeeoa/nooawvoa
old/young	**vecchio/giovane**	vehkkeeoa/joavahnay
beautiful/ugly	**bello/brutto**	behlloa/broottoa
good/bad	**buono/cattivo**	booawnoa/kahtteevoa
better/worse	**migliore/peggiore**	meelyoaray/paydjoaray

Some prepositions and a few more useful words

at	**a**	ah
on	**sopra**	soaprah
in	**in**	een
to	**a**	ah
from	**da**	dah
inside	**dentro**	dayntroa
outside	**fuori**	fooawree
up	**sù**	soo
down	**giù**	joo
before	**prima di**	preemah dee
after	**dopo di**	dawpoa dee
with	**con**	kon
without	**senza**	sayntsah
through	**attraverso**	ahttrahvehrsoa
towards	**verso**	vehrsoa
until	**fino a**	feenoa
during	**durante**	doorahntay
and	**e**	ay
or	**o**	oa
not	**non**	noan
nothing	**niente**	neeehntay
none	**nessuno**	naysssoonoa

very	molto	**moal**toa
also	anche	**ahng**kay
soon	presto	**prehss**toa
perhaps	forse	**for**say
here	qui	koo**ee**
there	là	lah
now	ora	**oa**rah
then	poi	poy

Arrival

Your passport, please.	Il passaporto, per favore.	eel pahsssah**por**toa pair fah**voa**ray
Here it is.	Eccolo.	**ehk**koaloa
Have you anything to declare?	Ha qualcosa da dichiarare?	ah kwahl**kaw**ssah dah deekeeah**rar**ray
No, nothing at all.	No. Non ho nulla.	noa noan oa **nool**lah
Porter!	Facchino!	fahk**kee**noa
Can you help me with my luggage, please?	Può prendere le mie valige, per favore?	pwo **prehn**dayray lay **mee**ay vahlee**jay** pair fah**voa**ray
That's my suitcase.	Quella è la mia valigia.	koo**ayl**lah ai lah **mee**ah vahlee**jah**
Where's the bus to the centre of town, please?	Dov'è l'autobus per il centro della città, per favore?	doa**vai** lowtoa**booss** pair eel **chehn**troa **dayl**lah cheet**tah** pair fah**voa**ray
This way, please.	Da questa parte, per piacere.	dah koo**ayss**tah **pahr**tay pair peeah**chay**ray

Changing money

| Can you change a traveller's cheque, please? | Può cambiarmi un traveller's cheque, per favore? | pwo kahmbee**arr**mee oon ''traveller's cheque'' pair fah**voa**ray |
| Where's the nearest bank, please? | Dov'è la banca più vicina, per favore? | doa**vai** lah **bahng**kah pee**oo** vee**chee**nah pair fah**voa**ray |

Car rental

I'd like a car.	Vorrei un'automobile.	vor**raie** oon owtoa**maw**beelay
For how long?	Per quanto tempo?	pair koo**ahn**toa **tehm**poa
A day/Four days/ A week/Two weeks.	Un giorno/Quattro giorni/Una settimana/Due settimane.	oon **joar**noa/koo**ahtt**roa **joar**nee/**oo**nah saytee**mar**nah/**doo**ay saytee**mar**nay

ITALIAN

ITALIAN

Taxi

Where can I get a taxi?	**Dove posso trovare un tassi?**	doavay **poss**soa troa**var**-ray oon tahss**see**
What's the fare to . . . ?	**Quanto costa la corsa per . . . ?**	**kwahn**toa **koss**tah lah **kor**sah pair
Take me to this address, please.	**Mi porti a questo indirizzo, per favore.**	mee **por**tee ah kooa**yss**toa eendee**reett**soa pair fah**voa**ray
I'm in a hurry.	**Ho fretta.**	oa **fray**ttah
Could you drive more slowly, please?	**Può guidare più adagio, per favore?**	pwo gooee**dar**ray pee**oo** ah**dar**joa pair fah**voa**ray

Hotel and other accommodation

My name is . . .	**Mi chiamo . . .**	mee kee**ear**moa
Have you a reservation?	**Ha fatto la prenotazione?**	ah **faht**toa lah praynoatahtsee**oa**nay
Yes, here's the confirmation.	**Sì; ecco la conferma.**	see **ehk**koa lah kon**fehr**mah
I'd like . . .	**Vorrei . . .**	vor**raiee**
I'd like a single room/a double room.	**Vorrei una camera singola/per due persone.**	vor**raiee** **oo**nah **kar**mayrah **seeng**goalah/pair **doo**ay payr**soa**nay
a room with a bath/with a shower	**una camera con bagno/con doccia**	**oo**nah **kar**mayrah kon **bar**ñoa/kon **dot**chah

How much?

What's the price per night/per week/per month?	**Qual è il prezzo per una notte/per una settimana/per un mese?**	kwah**lai** eel **preht**tsoa pàir **oo**nah **not**tay/pair **oo**nah saytteemar**nah**/pair oon **may**ssay
May I see the room?	**Posso vedere la camera?**	**poss**soa vay**day**ray lah **kar**mayrah
I'm sorry, I don't like it.	**Mi dispiace: non è di mio gradimento.**	mee despee**ar**chay noan ai dee **mee**oa grahdee**mayn**toa
Yes, that's fine. I'll take it.	**Sì, va bene. La prendo.**	see vah **bai**nay lah **prayn**doa
What's my room number, please?	**Qual è il numero della mia camera?**	kwah**lai** eel **noo**mayroa **dayl**lah **mee**ah **kar**mayrah
Number 123.	**Numero 123.**	**noo**mayroa 123

Service, please

Who is it?	**Chi è?**	kee ai
Just a minute.	**Un momento, per favore.**	oon moa**mayn**toa pair fah**voa**ray
Come in! The door's open.	**Avanti! La porta è aperta.**	ah**vahn**tee lah **por**tah ai ah**pehr**tah
May we have breakfast in our room?	**Possiamo fare la prima colazione in camera?**	posss**eear**moa **far**ray lah **pree**mah koalahtsee**oo**anay een **kar**mayran

Breakfast

I'll have...	**Vorrei...**	vor**rai**ee
I'll have some fruit juice.	**Vorrei un succo di frutta.**	vor**rai**ee oon **sook**koa dee **froot**tah
a boiled egg	**un uovo alla "coque"**	oon oo**aw**voa **ahl**lah kok
a fried egg	**un uovo al tegame**	oon oo**aw**voa ahl tay**gar**may
some bacon/some ham	**della pancetta affumicata/del prosciutto**	**dayl**lah pahn**cheht**tah ahffoomee**kar**tah/dayl proa**shoot**toa
some toast	**del pane tostato**	dayl **par**nay toass**tar**toa
a pot of tea	**del té**	dayl tay
a cup of tea	**una tazza di té**	**oo**nah **taht**tsah dee tay
some coffee	**del caffé**	dayl kahff**fay**
some chocolate	**della cioccolata**	**dayl**lah choakkoa**lar**tah
more butter	**un altro po'di burro**	oon **ahl**troa po dee **boor**roa
some hot water	**dell'acqua calda**	dayl**ahk**kooah **kahl**dah

Difficulties

The central heating doesn't work.	**Il riscaldamento centrale non funziona.**	eel reesskahldah**mayn**toa chayn**trar**lay noan foon-tsee**oa**nah
the light/the socket	**la luce/la presa**	lah **loo**chay/lah **pray**sah
the tap/the toilet	**il rubinetto/il gabinetto**	eel roobee**nayt**toa/eel gahbee**nayt**toa
There's no hot water.	**Non c'è acqua calda.**	noan chai **ahk**kooah **kahl**dah
May I see the manager, please?	**Posso vedere il direttore, per piacere?**	**poss**soa vay**day**ray eel deerayt**toa**ray pair peeah**chay**ray

ITALIAN

Telephone—Mail

There's a call for you.	C'è una telefonata per lei.	chai oonah taylayfoanartah pair laiee
Hold the line, please.	Resti in linea, per piacere.	rehsstee een leenayah pair peeahchayray
Operator, I've been cut off.	Signorina, mi hanno interrotto.	seeñoareenah mee ahnnoa eentehrrottoa
Did anyone telephone me?	Mi ha telefonato qualcuno?	mee ah taylayfoanartoa kwahlkoonoa
Is there any mail for me?	C'è posta per me?	chai posstah pair may
Are there any messages for me?	Ci sono comunicazioni per me?	chee soanoa komoonee-kahtseeoanee pair may

Checking out

May I have my bill, please?	Posso avere il mio conto, per favore?	posssoa ahvayray eel meeoa koantoa pair fahvoaray
We're in a great hurry.	Abbiamo molta fretta.	ahbbeearmoa moaltah frayttah
It's been a very enjoyable stay.	È stato un soggiorno molto piacevole.	ai startoa oon soadjoarnoa moaltoa peeahchayvoalay

Eating out

Good evening, sir/ Good evening, madam.	Buona sera, signore/Buona sera, signora.	booawnah sayrah seeñoaray/booawnah sayrah seeñoarrah
Good evening. I'd like a table for two, please.	Buona sera. Vorrei una tavola per due, per favore.	booawnah sayrah. vorraiee oonah tarvoalah pair dooay pair fahvoaray
Do you have a fixed-price menu?	Avete un menu a prezzo fisso?	ahvaytay oon maynoo ah prehttsoa feesssoa
May I see the à la carte menu?	Posso vedere il menu a scelta?	posssoa vaydayray eel maynoo ah shayltah
May we have an ashtray, please?	Posso avere un portacenere, per favore?	posssoa ahvayray oon portahchaynayray pair fahvoaray
some bread	un po' di pane	oon po dee parnay
a fork	una forchetta	oonah forkehttah
a knife	un coltello	oon koaltehlloa

a spoon	un cucchiaio	oon kookkeeighoa
a plate	un piatto	oon peeahttoa
a glass	un bicchiere	oon beekkeeairay
a napkin	un tovagliolo	oon toavahlyawloa
another chair	un'altra sedia	oonahltrah saideeah
Where's the gentle-men's toilet (men's room)?	Dove sono i gabinetti per uomini?	doavay soanoa ee gahbeenayttee pair ooomeenee
Where's the ladies' toilet (ladies' room)?	Dove sono i gabinetti per signore?	doavay soanoa ee gahbeenayttee pair seeñoaray

Appetizers

I'd like some . . .	Vorrei . . .	vorraiee
I'd like some assorted appetizers.	Vorrei degli antipasti assortiti.	vorraiee daylyee ahntee-pahsstee ahssorteetee
orange juice	un succo d'arancia	oon sookkoa dahrahnchah
ham	del prosciutto	day proashoottoa
melon	del melone	dayl mayloanay
pâté	del pâté	dayl pahtay
smoked salmon	del salmone affu-micato	dayl sahlmoanay ahffoomeekartoa
shrimps (shrimp)	dei gamberetti	daiee gahmbayrayttee

Soup

Have you any . . . ?	Ha . . . ?	ah
Have you any chicken soup?	Ha un brodo di pollo?	ah oon brawdoa dee poalloa
vegetable soup	una minestra di verdure	oonah meenehsstrah dee vehrdooray
onion soup	una minestra di cipolle	oonah meenehsstrah dee cheepoallay

Fish

I'd like some . . .	Vorrei . . .	vorraiee
I'd like some fish.	Vorrei del pesce.	vorraiee dayl payshay
sole	della sogliola	dayllah sawlyoalah
trout	delle trote	dayllay trawtay
lobster	un'aragosta	oon ahrahgoasstah
crayfish	dei gamberi d'acqua dolce	daiee gahmbayree dahkkooah dolchay
prawns	dei gamberi	daiee gahmbayree

ITALIAN

I'd like it ...	**Li vorrei ...**	lee vorraiee
I'd like it steamed.	**Li vorrei al vapore.**	lee vorraiee ahl vahpoaray
grilled	**alla griglia**	ahllah greelyah
boiled	**bolliti**	bolleetee
baked	**al forno**	ahl fornoa
fried	**fritti**	freettee

Meat—Poultry—Game

I'd like some ...	**Vorrei ...**	vorraiee
I'd like some beef.	**Vorrei del manzo.**	vorraiee dayl **mahn**dzoa
a beef steak	**una bistecca di manzo**	oonah bees**tayk**kah dee **mahn**dzoa
some roast beef	**un arrosto di manzo**	oon ahr**roass**toa dee **mahn**dzoa
a veal cutlet	**una cotoletta di vitello**	oonah koatoa**layt**tah dee vee**tehl**loa
mutton	**del montone**	dayl moan**toa**nay
lamb	**dell'agnello**	dayl ah**ñehl**loa
a pork chop	**una braciola di maiale**	oonah brah**choa**lah dee mi**ghar**lay
roast pork	**un arrosto di maiale**	oon ahr**ross**toa dee mi**ghar**lay
hare	**della lepre**	**dayl**lah **lai**pray
chicken	**del pollo**	dayl **poal**loa
roast chicken	**del pollo arrosto**	dayl **poal**loa ahr**roass**toa
duck	**dell'anatra**	dayl **ar**nahtrah
How do you like your meat?	**Come vuole la carne?**	**koa**may voo**aw**lay lah **kahr**nay
rare	**al sangue**	ahl **sahn**gooay
medium	**non troppo cotta**	noan **trop**poa **kot**tah
well done	**ben cotta**	bain **kot**tah

Vegetables

What vegetables have you got?	**Quali legumi ha?**	**koo**arlee lay**goo**mee ah
I'd like some ...	**Vorrei ...**	vorraiee
I'd like some asparagus.	**Vorrei degli asparagi.**	vorraiee **day**lyee ah**spar**rahjee
green beans	**dei fagiolini**	daiee fahjoa**lee**nee
mushrooms	**dei funghi**	daiee **foong**gee
carrots	**delle carote**	**dayl**lay kah**raw**tay
onions	**delle cipolle**	**dayl**lay chee**poal**lay
red cabbage	**dei cavoli rossi**	daiee **kah**voalee **ross**see

spinach	**degli spinaci**	**day**lyee spee**nar**chee
rice	**del riso**	dayl **ree**soa
peas	**dei piselli**	**dai**ee pee**seh**llee
tomatoes	**dei pomodori**	**dai**ee poamoa**daw**ree
green salad	**dell'insalata**	dayl eensah**lar**tah
potatoes	**delle patate**	**day**llay pah**tar**tay

Desserts

Nothing more, thanks.	**Nient'altro. Grazie.**	neeehntahltroa **grah**tseeay
Just a small portion, please.	**Solo una piccola porzione, per favore.**	**soa**loa **oo**nah **peek**koalah portsee**oa**nay pair fah**voa**ray
Have you any ice-cream?	**Ha un gelato?**	ah oon jay**lar**toa
fruit salad	**una macedonia**	**oo**nah mahchay**daw**neeah
fresh fruit	**della frutta fresca**	**day**llah **froot**tah **frayss**kah
cheese	**del formaggio**	dayl for**mahd**joa

Drink

What would you like to drink?	**Cosa desidera da bere?**	**kaw**ssah day**zee**dayrah dah **bay**ray
I'll have a beer, please.	**Mi dia una birra, per piacere.**	mee **dee**ah **oo**nah **beer**rah pair peeah**chay**ray
I'll have a whisky, please.	**Mi dia un whisky, per favore.**	mee **dee**ah oon whisky (**wiss**kee) pair fah**voa**ray

Wine

I'd like a bottle of wine.	**Vorrei una bottiglia di vino.**	vor**rai**ee **oo**nah bot**tee**lyah dee **vee**noa
red wine	**di vino rosso**	dee **vee**noa **roass**soa
rosé wine	**di rosé**	dee roa**zay**
white wine	**di vino bianco**	dee**vee**noa beeahngkoa
Cheers!	**Salute!**	sah**loo**tay

The bill (check)

May I have the bill (check) please?	**Posso avere il mio conto, per piacere?**	**poss**soa ah**vay**ray eel **mee**oa **koan**toa pair peeah**chay**ray
Is service included?	**È compreso il servizio?**	ai koam**pray**zoa eel sayr**veet**seeoa

ITALIAN

| Everything's included. | Tutto compreso. | toottoa koamprayzoa |
| Thank you, that was a very good meal. | Grazie. Abbiamo mangiato molto bene. | grahtseeay ahbbeearmoa mahnjartoa moaltoa bainay |

Travelling

Where's the railway station, please?	Dove si trova la stazione, per favore?	doavay see trawvah lah stahtseeoanay pair fahvoaray
Where's the ticket office, please?	Dove si trova lo sportello dei biglietti, per favore?	doavay see trawvah loa sportehlloa daiee beelyayttee pair fahvoaray
I'd like a ticket to ...	Vorrei un biglietto per ...	vorraiee oon beelyayttoa pair
First or second class?	Di prima o di seconda classe?	dee preemah oa dee saykoandah klahsssay
First class, please.	Di prima classe, per piacere.	dee preemah klahsssay pair peeahchayray
Single or return (one way or round-trip)?	Andata o andata e ritorno?	ahndartah oa ahndartah ay reetornoa
Do I have to change trains?	Devo cambiare treno?	dayvoa kahmbeearray traynoa
What platform does the train leave from?	Da che binario parte il treno?	dah kay beenarreeoa pahrtay eel traynoa
Where's the nearest underground (subway) station?	Dov'è la più vicina stazione della metropolitana?	doavai lah peeoo vee-cheenah stahtseeoanay dayllah may-troapoaleetarnah
Where's the bus station, please?	Dov'è la stazione degli autobus, per piacere?	doavai lah stahtseeoanay daylyee owtoabooss pair peeahchayray
When's the first bus to ...?	Quando passa il primo autobus per ...?	kwahndoa pahsssah eel preemoa owtoabooss pair
the last bus/the next bus	l'ultimo autobus/il prossimo autobus	loolteemoa owtoabooss/ eel prossseemoa owtoabooss
Please let me off at the next stop.	Mi faccia scendere alla prossima fermata, per piacere.	mee fahtchah shayndayray ahllah prossseemah fehrmartah pair peeahchayray

Relaxing

What's on at the cinema (movies)?	**Cosa danno al cinema?**	**kaw**ssah **dahn**noa ahl **chee**naymah
What's on at the theatre?	**Cosa danno al teatro?**	**kaw**ssah **dahn**noa ahl tay**ar**troa
What time does the film begin? And the play?	**A che ora incomincia il film? E la rappresentazione?**	ah kay **oa**rah eengkoa-**meen**cheeah eel feelm? ay lah rahppraysssayntah-**tsee**oanay
Are there any tickets for tonight?	**Ci sono ancora posti liberi per questa sera?**	chee **soa**noa ahng**koa**rah **poa**stee **lee**bayree pair **koo**aysstah **say**rah
Where can we go dancing?	**Dove possiamo andare a ballare?**	**doa**vay posss**eear**moa ahn**dar**ray ah bahll**ar**ray
Would you like to dance?	**Vuole ballare?**	vooa**way** bahll**ar**ray

Introductions

How do you do?	**Bongiorno.**	boan**joar**noa
How are you?	**Come sta?**	**koa**may stah
Very well, thank you. And you?	**Molto bene, grazie. E lei?**	**moal**toa **bai**nay **grah**tseeay. ay **laie**e
May I introduce Miss Philips?	**Posso presentarle la signorina Philips?**	**posss**soa prayzayn**tarr**lay lah seeñoa**ree**nah Philips
My name is...	**Mi chiamo...**	mee kee**ar**moa
I'm very pleased to meet you.	**Sono molto lieto di fare la sua conoscenza.**	**soa**noa **moal**toa lee**ay**toa dee **far**ray lah **soo**ah koanoa**shehn**tsah
How long have you been here?	**Da quanto tempo è qui?**	dah **kwahn**toa **tehm**poa ai koo**ee**
It was nice meeting you.	**Sono lieto di aver fatto la sua conoscenza.**	**soa**noa lee**ay**toa dee ah**vayr faht**toa lah **soo**ah koanoa**shehn**tsah

Dating

Would you like a cigarette?	**Accetta una sigaretta?**	aht**chayt**tah **oo**nah seegah**rayt**tah
May I get you a drink?	**Posso offrirle da bere?**	**posss**soa offf**ree**rlay dah **bay**ray

Do you have a light, please?	**Mi fa accendere, per piacere?**	mee fah aht**chehn**dayray pair peeah**chay**ray
Are you waiting for someone?	**Attende qualcuno?**	aht**tehn**dayray kooahl-**koo**noa
Are you free this evening?	**È libera, stasera?**	ai **lee**bayrah stah**say**rah
Where shall we meet?	**Dove possiamo incontrarci?**	**doa**vay posssee**ar**moa eengkon**trar**rchee
What time shall I meet you?	**A che ora la vedrò?**	ah kay **oar**ah lah vay**droa**
May I take you home?	**Posso accompagnarla a casa?**	**poss**soa ahkkoampah-ñar**rl**ah ah **kar**ssah
Thank you, it's been a wonderful evening.	**Grazie! È stata una magnifica serata.**	**graht**seeay! ai **star**tah **oo**nah man**ñee**feekah say-**rar**tah
What's your telephone number?	**Qual'è il suo numero di telefono?**	kwahl**ai** eel **soo**oa **noo**mayroa dee tay**lai**foanoa
Do you live alone?	**Vive sola?**	**vee**vay **soa**lah
What time is your last train?	**A che ora parte il suo ultimo treno?**	ah kay **oar**ah **pahr**tay eel **soo**oa **ool**teemoa **tray**noa
Good-night...	**Buona notte...**	**bwo**nah **not**tay

Banks

Where's the nearest bank, please?	**Dov'è la banca più vicina, per favore?**	**doa**vai lah **bahng**kah pee**oo** vee**chee**nah pair fah**voa**ray
Where can I cash some traveller's cheques?	**Dove posso cambiare un traveller's cheque?**	**doa**vay **poss**soa kahm-bee**ar**ray oon "traveller's cheque"
What time does the bank open/What time does it close?	**A che ora apre la banca/A che ora chiude?**	ah kay **oar**ah **ah**pray la **bahng**kah/ah kay **oar**ah kee**oo**day
I'm expecting some money from home. Has it arrived?	**Aspetto del denaro da casa. È arrivato?**	ah**spayt**toa dayl day**nar**roa dah **kar**ssah. ai ahr-ree**var**toa
Can you give me some small change, please?	**Potrebbe darmi della moneta spicciola, per favore?**	poa**trayb**bay **darr**mee **dayl**-lah moa**nay**tah speet**choa**-lah pair fah**voa**ray

ITALIAN

Shops, stores and services

Where is the nearest chemist's (pharmacy)?	Dov'è la più vicina farmacia?	doavai lah peeoo vee-cheenah fahrmahcheeah
the nearest hair-dresser's	il parrucchiere più vicino	eel pahrrookkeeairay peeoo veecheenoa
the photo shop	il fotografo	eel foatawgrahfoa
the jeweller's	la gioielleria	lah joyayllayreeah
the department store	il grande magazzino	eel grahnday mahgahddzeenoa
the police station	la questura (il posto di polizia)	lah kooaysstoorah (eel poasstoa dee poalee-tseeah)
the garage	l'autorimessa	lowtoareemaysssah
How do I get there?	Come ci si può arrivare?	koamay chee see pwo ahrreevarray
Is it within walking distance?	Ci si può andare anche a piedi?	chee see pwo ahndarray ahngkay ah peeaydee

Service

Can you help me, please?	Può aiutarmi, per piacere?	pwo ighootarrmee pair peeahchayray
Can you show me this? And that, too.	Può mostrarmi questo? E anche quello.	pwo moasstrarrmee kooaysstoa? ay ahngkay kooaylloa
It's too expensive/ too big/too small.	È troppo caro/ troppo grande/ troppo piccolo.	ay troppoa karroa/troppoa grahnday/troppoa peek-koaloa
Can you show me some more?	Mi può mostrare una scelta più ampia?	mee pwo moasstrarray oonah shaylltah peeoo ahmpeeah
something better something cheaper	qualcosa migliore qualcosa di più economico	kwahlkawssah meelyoaray kwahlkawssah dee peeoo aykoanawmeekoa
How much is this? And that?	Quanto costa questo? E quello?	kwahntoa kosstah kooaysstoa? ay kooaylloa
It's not quite what I want.	Non è proprio quello che volevo.	noan ay prawpreeoa kooaylloah kay voalayvoa
I like it.	Questo mi piace.	kooaysstoa mee peearchay

ITALIAN

152

Chemist's (Pharmacy)

I'd like something for a cold/for a cough/for travel sickness.	Vorrei qualcosa per il raffreddore/per la tosse/per il mal di moto.	vorraiee kwahl**kaw**ssah pair eel rahffrayd**doa**ray/ pair lah **toass**say/pair eel mahl dee **maw**toa
Can you recommend something for hay-fever/for sunburn?	Può consigliarmi qualcosa per la febbre del fieno/per una scottatura di sole?	pwo koanseel**yarr**mee kwahl**kaw**ssah pair lah **fayb**bray dayl fee**al**noa/ pair oonah skottah**too**rah dee **soa**lay

Toiletry

May I have some razor blades?	Potrei avere delle lamette da barba?	poatraiee ahvayray dayllay lah**mayt**tay dah **bahr**bah
some shaving cream	una crema da barba	oonah **krai**mah dah **bahr**bah
some toothpaste	un dentifricio	oon daynteefree**choa**
I'd like some soap.	Vorrei una saponetta.	vorraiee oonah sahpoa**nayt**tah
some suntan oil	dell'olio per la tintarella	dayl **aw**lyoa pair lah teen-tah**rehl**lah

At the barber's

I'd like a haircut, please.	Vorrei farmi tagliare i capelli, per favore.	vorraiee **farr**mee tah**lyar**ray ee kah**payl**lee pair fah**voa**ray
Short/Leave it long.	Corti/Li lasci lunghi.	**koar**tee/lee **lah**shee **loong**gee
A razor cut, please.	Un taglio col rasoio, per piacere.	oon **tar**lyoa koal rah**saw**eeoa pair peeah**chay**ray

At the hairdresser's

I'd like a shampoo and set, please.	Vorrei uno shampoo e una messa in piega, per piacere.	vorraiee oonoa "shampoo" ay oonah **mayss**sah een peeaigah pair peeah**chay**ray
I'd like a bleach.	Vorrei una decolorazione.	vorraiee oona day-koaloarahtsee**oa**nay
a permanent	una permanente	oonah payr mahnehntay
a colour rinse	un "cachet"	oon kah**shay**
a manicure	una manicure	oonah mahnee**koo**ray

Photography

I'd like a film for this camera.	**Vorrei un rullino per questa macchina fotografica.**	vorra**ee** oon roo**lee**noa pair koo**ayss**tah **mahk**-keenah foatoa**grar**feekah
This camera doesn't work.	**Questa macchina fotografica non funziona.**	koo**ayss**tah **mahk**keenah foatoa**grar**feekah noan foontsee**oa**nah

At the post office

Where's the nearest post office, please?	**Dove si trova l'ufficio postale più vicino, per favore?**	**doa**vay see **traw**vah loo**ffee**choa poa**sstar**lay pee**oo** vee**chee**noa pair fah**voa**ray
I'd like to send this by express (special delivery)/by air mail.	**Vorrei spedire questo per espresso/per via aerea.**	vorra**ee** spay**dee**ray koo**ayss**toa pair ayss**prehss**soa/pair vee**ah** ahairayah

Service stations

Where is the nearest service station, please?	**Dove si trova la più vicina stazione di rifornimento, per favore?**	**doa**vay see **traw**vah lah pee**oo** vee**chee**nah stah-tseeoanay dee reefornee-**mayn**toa pair fah**voa**ray
Fill her up, please.	**Faccia il pieno, per favore.**	**faht**chah eel pee**ai**noa pair fah**voa**ray
Check the oil, please.	**Controlli l'olio, per favore.**	koan**troal**lee **law**lyoa pair fah**voa**ray
Would you check the tyres?	**Vorrebbe controllare le gomme?**	vor**rayb**bay koantroal-**lar**ray lay **gom**may

Street directions

Can you show me on the map where I am?	**Può indicarmi sulla carta dove mi trovo?**	pwo eendee**karr**mee sool-lah **kahr**tah **doa**vay mee **traw**voa
You're on the wrong road.	**È sulla strada sba-gliata.**	ay **soo**lah **strar**dah zbahl**yar**tah
Go back to . . .	**Ritorni a . . .**	ree**toar**nee ah
Go straight ahead.	**Continui diritto.**	koan**tee**noooee dee**reet**toa
It's on the left/on the right.	**È a sinistra/a destra.**	ai ah seenee**ss**trah/ah **dehs**trah

Accidents

May I use your telephone?	**Potrei usare il suo telefono?**	poatraiee oozarray eel soooa taylaifoanoa
Call a doctor quickly.	**Chiami subito un medico.**	keearmee soobeetoa oon maideekoa
Call an ambulance.	**Chiami un'auto-ambulanza.**	keearmee oon owtoaahm-boolahntsah
Please call the police.	**Per piacere, chiami la polizia.**	pair peeahchayray keearmee lah poaleetseeah

Numbers

one	**uno**	oonoa
two	**due**	dooay
three	**tre**	tray
four	**quattro**	kooahttroa
five	**cinque**	cheengkooay
six	**sei**	sehee
seven	**sette**	sehttay
eight	**otto**	ottoa
nine	**nove**	nawvay
ten	**dieci**	deealchee
eleven	**undici**	oondeechee
twelve	**dodici**	doadeechee
thirteen	**tredici**	traydeechee
fourteen	**quattordici**	kooahttordeechee
fifteen	**quindici**	kooeendeechee
sixteen	**sedici**	saydeechee
seventeen	**diciassette**	deechahsssehttay
eighteen	**diciotto**	deechottoa
nineteen	**diciannove**	deechahnawvay
twenty	**venti**	vayntee
twenty-one	**ventuno**	vayntoonoa
thirty	**trenta**	trayntah
forty	**quaranta**	kooahrahntah
fifty	**cinquanta**	cheengkooahntah
sixty	**sessanta**	sayssssahntah
seventy	**settanta**	sayttahntah
eighty	**ottanta**	oattahntah
ninety	**novanta**	noavahntah
one hundred	**cento**	chehntoa
one thousand	**mille**	meellay
ten thousand	**diecimila**	deeehcheemeelah

Days

It's Sunday.	È domenica.	ai doamayneekah
Monday	lunedì	loonaydee
Tuesday	martedì	mahrtaydee
Wednesday	mercoledì	mehrkoalaydee
Thursday	giovedì	joavaydee
Friday	venerdì	vaynayrdee
Saturday	sabato	sarbahtoa
yesterday	ieri	eeairee
today	oggi	odjee
tomorrow	domani	doamarnee
morning/afternoon	mattino/pomeriggio	mahtteenoa/poamay-reedjoa
evening/night	sera/notte	sayrah/nottay

Months

January	gennaio	jaynighoa
February	febbraio	fehbbrighoa
March	marzo	mahrtsoa
April	aprile	ahpreelay
May	maggio	mahdjoa
June	giugno	jooñoa
July	luglio	loolyoa
August	agosto	ahgoasstoa
September	settembre	sayttehmbray
October	ottobre	oattoabray
November	novembre	noavehmbray
December	dicembre	deechehmbray
Merry Christmas!	Buon Natale!	bwon nahtarlay!
Happy New Year!	Buon Anno!	bwon ahnnoa

ITALIAN

NORWEGIAN

Guide to Pronunciation

Letter	Approximate pronunciation	Symbol	Example	

Consonants

b, d, f, h, m, n, p, t, v	as in English			
g	1) before **i**, **y** or **ei**, like **y** in yet	y	**gi**	yee
	2) otherwise, like **g** in **g**o	g	**gate**	**g**arter
j, gj, hj, lj	like **y** in yet	y	**ja**	yar
			hjem	yehm
k	1) before **i**, **y** or **j**, like **ch** in German **ich**, or something like **ch** in Scottish lo**ch**; it is similar to the first sound of **huge**	kh	**kirke**	**kh**eerker
			kyst	**kh**ewst
	2) otherwise like **k** in kit	k	**kaffe**	**k**ahffer
l	always as in lee, never as in bell	l	**tale**	tarler

| r | in southwestern Norway, it is pronounced in the back of the mouth (as in French), elsewhere it is slightly rolled in the front of the mouth | r | rask | rahsk |

N.B. In the groups **rd**, **rl**, **rn** and **rt**, the **r** tends not to be pronounced but influences the pronunciation of the following consonant, which is then pronounced with the tongue behind the upper teeth ridge (turned upwards at the front). We don't use a special symbol for this retroflex pronunciation of **d**, **l**, **n** or **t**.

rs	is generally pronounced like **sh** in **sh**ut in eastern Norway	sh	norsk	noshk
s	always as in **s**o	s/ss	rose	roosser
sj, skj, sk	when followed by **i**, **y** or **øy**, like **sh** in **sh**ut	sh	sjø	shur
			ski	shee

N.B. The letters **c**, **q**, **w**, **z** are only found in foreign words, and tend to be pronounced as in the language of origin.

Vowels

In Norwegian, vowels in stressed syllables are long when followed by, at most, one pronounced consonant. They are generally short when followed by two or more consonants.

a	1) when long, like **a** in c**a**r	ar	dag	darg
	2) when short, fairly like **u** in c**u**t or **o** in American c**o**llege	ah	vaske	vahsker
e	1) when long, like **ay**, in s**ay**, but a pure sound, *not* a diphthong	ay	se	say
	2) when short, like **e** in g**e**t	eh	penn	pehn
	3) when followed by **r**, like **a** in b**a**d; long or short	ææ æ	her sterk	hæær stærk
	4) when unstressed, like **er** in oth**er**	er	nese	naysser
i	1) when long, like **ee** in s**ee**, but with the tongue more raised, and the lips more drawn back at the sides	ee	ti	tee
	2) when short, like **ee** in m**ee**t	i	drikke	drikker
o	1) when long, like **oo** in s**oo**n, but with the lips more rounded (when followed by **-rt**, **-st**, **-m** and **-nd**, it can be short	oo	god	goo
			ost	oost
	2) when short, generally like **o** in h**o**t	o	tolv	tol

u	a difficult sound; something like the **ew** in f**ew**, or Scottish **oo** in g**oo**d; you will find it very hard to distinguish from Norwegian **y**, so we use the same symbol for both	ew	**mur**	mewr
y	put your tongue in the position for the **ee** in b**ee**, and then round your lips as for the **oo** in p**oo**l: the vowel you pronounce like this should be more or less correct	ew	**by** **tynn**	bew tewn
æ	1) before **r** like **a** in b**a**d; usually long but sometimes short	ææ	**lære**	læærer
		æ	**lærd**	læd
	2) otherwise, like **ay** in s**ay**	ay	**hæl**	hayl
å	1) when long, like **aw** in s**aw**	aw	**på**	paw
	2) when short (rare), more like **o** in h**o**t	o	**gått**	got
ø	like **u** in f**u**r; either long or short	ur	**dør** **søtt**	durr surt

Diphthongs

au	this sounds like **ow** in n**ow**, but, in fact, the first part is a Norwegian ø-sound	ow	**sau**	sow
ei	like **ay** in s**ay** but often reminiscent of **igh** in s**igh**	ay	**vei**	vay
øy	fairly like **oy** in b**oy**	oy	**høy**	hoy

Silent letters

1) The letter **g** is generally silent in the endings **-lig** and **-ig**.
2) The letter **d** is generally silent after **l** or **n** or after **r** at the end of a word (with lengthening of the vowel) or often after a long vowel, e.g. ho**l**de, lan**d**, gå**r**d.
3) The letter **v** is silent in a few words, e.g., sel**v**, tol**v**, hal**v**, søl**v**.

NORWEGIAN

Some basic expressions

Yes.	**Ja.**	yar
No.	**Nei.**	nay
Please.	**Vennligst.**	**vehn**ligst
Thank you.	**Takk.**	tahk
Thank you very much.	**Mange takk.**	**mahng**er tahk
That's all right.	**Ingen årsak.**	**ing**ern **aw**shahk

Greetings

Good morning.	**God morgen.**	goo **maw**ern
Good afternoon.	**God dag.**	goo darg
Good evening.	**God kveld.**	goo kvehl
Good night.	**God natt.**	goo naht
Good-bye.	**Adjø.**	ah**dyur**
See you later.	**På gjensyn.**	paw **yehn**sewn
This is Mr.	**Dette er herr ...**	**deht**ter ær haer
This is Mrs.	**Dette er fru ...**	**deht**ter ær frew
This is Miss ...	**Dette er frøken ...**	**deht**ter ær **frur**kern
I'm very pleased to meet you.	**Det gleder meg å treffe Dem.**	day **glay**derr may aw **trehf**fer dehm
How are you?	**Hvordan går det?**	**voor**dahn gawr day
Very well, thank you. And you?	**Bare bra, takk. Og med Dem?**	**bar**rer brar tahk. awg may(d) dehm
Fine.	**Fint.**	fint
Excuse me.	**Unnskyld.**	**oon**shewl

Questions

Where?	**Hvor?**	voor
Where is ...?	**Hvor er ...?**	voor ær
Where are ...?	**Hvor er ...?**	voor ær
When?	**Når?**	nawr

What?	**Hva?**	var
How?	**Hvordan?**	**voor**dahn
How much?	**Hvor mye?**	**voor** mewer
How many?	**Hvor mange?**	**voor** mahnger
Who?	**Hvem?**	vehm
Why?	**Hvorfor?**	**voor**for
Which?	**Hvilken?**	**vil**kern
What do you call this?	**Hva heter dette?**	var **hay**terr **deht**ter
What do you call that?	**Hva heter det?**	var **hay**terr day
What does this mean?	**Hva betyr dette?**	var ber**tewr deht**ter
What does that mean?	**Hva betyr det?**	var ber**tewr** day

NORWEGIAN

Do you speak ... ?

Do you speak English?	**Snakker De engelsk?**	**snahk**kerr dee **ehng**erlsk
Do you speak German?	**Snakker De tysk?**	**snahk**kerr dee tewsk
Do you speak French?	**Snakker De fransk?**	**snahk**kerr dee frahnsk
Do you speak Spanish?	**Snakker De spansk?**	**snahk**kerr dee spahnsk
Do you speak Italian?	**Snakker De italiensk?**	**snahk**kerr de itahlee**ehnsk**
Could you speak more slowly, please?	**Kunne De snakke litt saktere?**	**kewn**ner dee **snahk**ker lit **sahk**terrer
Please point to the phrase in the book.	**Kunne De peke på setningen i boken.**	**kewn**ner dee **pay**ker paw **seht**ningern ee **book**ern
Just a minute. I'll see if I can find it in this book.	**Et øyeblikk. Jeg skal se om jeg kan finne det i denne boken.**	eht **oy**erblik yay skal say om yay karn **fin**ner day ee **dehn**ner **book**ern
I understand.	**Jeg forstår.**	yay for**shtawr**
I don't understand.	**Jeg forstår ikke.**	yay for**shtawr ik**ker

Can...?

Can I have...?	Kan jeg få...?	kahn yay faw
Can we have...?	Kan vi få...?	kahn vee faw
Can you show me...?	Kan De vise meg...?	kahn dee **vee**sser may
Can you tell me...?	Kan De si meg...?	kahn dee see may
Can you help me, please?	Kan De være så vennlig å hjelpe meg?	kahn dee **væær**er saw **vehn**lee aw **yehl**per may

Wanting

I'd like...	Jeg vil gjerne ha...	yay vil **yæær**ner har
We'd like...	Vi ville gjerne ha...	vee **vil**er **yæær**ner har
Please give me...	Vennligst, gi meg...	**vehn**ligst yee may
Give it to me, please.	Vennligst, gi det til meg.	**vehn**ligst yee day til may
Please bring me...	Vennligst, hent...til meg.	**vehn**ligst hehnt...til may
Bring it to me, please.	Vennligst, hent det til meg.	**vehn**ligst hehnt day til may
I'm hungry.	Jeg er sulten.	yay ær **sewl**tern
I'm thirsty.	Jeg er tørst.	yay ær tursht
I'm tired.	Jeg er trett.	yay ær treht
I'm lost.	Jeg har gått meg vill.	yay har got may vil
It's important.	Det er viktig.	day ær **vik**tee
It's urgent.	Det haster.	day **hahss**terr
Hurry up!	Skynd Dem!	shewn dehm

It is/There is...

It is/It's...	Det er...	day ær
Is it...?	Er det...?	ær day
It isn't...	Det er ikke...	day ær **ik**ker
There is/There are...	Det finnes...	day **finn**erss
Is there/Are there...?	Finnes det...?	**finn**erss day

NORWEGIAN

| There isn't/There aren't ... | **Det finnes ikke ...** | day finnerss ikker |
| There isn't any/ There aren't any. | **Det finnes ingen.** | day finnerss ingern |

A few common words

big/small	**stor/liten**	stoor/**lee**tern
quick/slow	**hurtig/langsom**	**hew**tee/**lahng**som
early/late	**tidlig/sen**	**teed**lee/sayn
cheap/expensive	**billig/dyr**	**bil**lee/dewr
near/far	**nær/langt borte**	næær/lahngt **boo**ter
hot/cold	**varm/kald**	vahrm/kahl
full/empty	**full/tom**	fewl/tom
easy/difficult	**lett/vanskelig**	leht/**vahn**skerlee
heavy/light	**tung/lett**	tewng/leht
open/shut	**åpen/lukket**	**aw**pern/**lewk**kert
right/wrong	**riktig/gal**	**rik**tee/garl
old/new	**gammel/ny**	**gahm**merl/new
old/young	**gammel/ung**	**gahm**merl/ewng
beautiful/ugly	**pen/stygg**	payn/stewg
good/bad	**god/dårlig**	goo/**dawr**lee
better/worse	**bedre/verre**	**bay**drer/**vær**rer

Some prepositions and a few more useful words

at	**ved**	vay(d)
on	**på**	paw
in	**i**	ee
to	**til**	til
from	**fra**	frar
inside	**innenfor**	**in**nernfor
outside	**utenfor**	**ew**ternfor
up	**opp**	op
down	**ned**	nay(d)
before	**før**	furr
after	**etter**	**eht**terr
with	**med**	may(d)
without	**uten**	**ew**tern
through	**gjennom**	**yehn**nom
towards	**mot**	moot
until	**til**	til
during	**i løpet av**	ee **lur**pert ahv
and	**og**	awg
or	**eller**	**ehl**lerr
not	**ikke**	**ik**ker
nothing	**ingenting**	**ing**ernting

none	**ingen**	**ing**ern
very	**veldig**	**vehl**dee
also	**også**	**awg**saw
soon	**snart**	snahrt
perhaps	**kanskje**	**kahn**sher
here	**her**	hæær
there	**der**	dæær
now	**nå**	naw
then	**da**	dar

Arrival

Your passport, please.	**Passet Deres, takk.**	**pahss**sert **day**rerss tahk
Here it is.	**Vær så god.**	væær shaw goo
Have you anything to declare?	**Har De noe å for-tolle?**	harr dee **noo**er aw for-**toll**er
No, nothing at all.	**Nei, ingen ting.**	nay **ing**ernting
Porter!	**Bærer!**	**bææ**rerr
Can you help me with my luggage, please?	**Kan De hjelpe meg med bagasjen?**	kahn dee **yehl**per may may(d) bah**gars**hern
That's my suitcase.	**Det er min kuffert.**	day ær meen **kewf**ferrt
Where's the bus to the centre of town, please?	**Hvor tar man bus-sen inn til centrum?**	voor tarr mahn **bewss**sern in til **sehn**trewm
This way, please.	**Denne vei.**	**dehn**ner vay

Changing money

| Can you change a traveller's cheque, please? | **Kan De innløse en reisesjekk?** | kahn dee **in**lursser ayn **righ**ssershehk |
| Where's the nearest bank, please? | **Hvor ligger nærmeste bank?** | voor **lig**gerr **nææ**rmerster bahnk |

Car rental

I'd like a car.	**Jeg vil gjerne leie en bil.**	yay vil **yææ**ner **lay**er ayn beel
For how long?	**Hvor lenge?**	voor **lehng**er
A day/Four days/ A week/Two weeks.	**En dag/Fire dager/ En uke/To uker.**	ayn darg/**fee**rer **darg**err/ ayn **ewk**er/too **ewk**err

NORWEGIAN

Taxi

Where can I get a taxi?	Hvor kan jeg få tak i en drosje?	voor kahn yay faw tark ee ayn drosher
What's the fare to ...?	Hva koster det til ...?	var kossterr day til
Take me to this address, please.	Vennligst, kjør meg til denne adressen.	vehnligst khurr may til dehnner ahdrehsssern
I'm in a hurry.	Jeg har det travelt.	yay harr day trarverlt
Could you drive more slowly, please?	Kunne De kjøre litt saktere?	kewnner dee khurrer lit sahkterrer

Hotel and other accommodation

My name is ...	Mitt navn er ...	mit nahvn ær
Have you a reservation?	Har De reservert?	harr dee raysehrvayrt
Yes, here's the confirmation.	Ja, her er bekreftelsen.	yar hææær ær berkrehfterlssern
I'd like ...	Jeg vil gjerne ha ...	yay vil yææner har
I'd like a single room/a double room.	Jeg vil gjerne ha et enkelt rom/et dobbelt rom.	yay vil yææner har eht ehngkerlt room/eht dobberlt room
a room with a bath/ with a shower	et rom med bad/ med dusj	eht room may(d) bard/ may(d) dewsh

How much?

What's the price per night/per week/per month?	Hva koster det for en natt/for en uke/for en måned?	var kossterr day for ayn naht/for ayn ewker/for ayn mawnerd
May I see the room?	Kan jeg få se rommet?	kahn yay faw say roommert
I'm sorry, I don't like it.	Jeg beklager, men jeg liker det ikke.	yay berklagerr mayn yay leekerr day ikker
Yes, that's fine. I'll take it.	Ja, det er bra. Jeg tar det.	yar day ær brar yay tarr day
What's my room number, please?	Hvilket værelse-nummer har jeg?	vilkert væærerlssernewm-merr harr yay
Number 123.	Nummer 123.	newmmerr 123

| Where's the gentle-men's toilet (men's room)? | **Hvor er herre-toalettet?** | voor ær **hæ**rerr-twahlehtter(t) |
| Where's the ladies' toilet (ladies' room)? | **Hvor er dametoalettet?** | voor ær **d**armer-twahlehtter(t) |

Appetizers

I'd like some ...	**Jeg vil gjerne ha ...**	yay vil **yææ**ner har
I'd like some assorted appetizers.	**Jeg vil gjerne ha noen assorterte hors-d'œuvres.**	yay vil **yææ**ner har nooern ahssor**t**airter or**d**urvr
orange juice	**appelsinsaft**	ah**p**perlsseenssahft
ham	**skinke**	**shing**ker
melon	**melon**	may**loon**
pâté	**postei**	pooss**t**ay
smoked salmon	**røkelaks**	**r**urkerlahks
shrimps (shrimp)	**reker**	**r**aykerr

Soup

Have you any ... ?	**Har de ... ?**	harr dee
Have you any chicken soup?	**Har De hønse-suppe?**	harr dee **h**urnsserssewpper
vegetable soup	**grønnsaksuppe**	**gr**urnssahksewpper
onion soup	**løksuppe**	**l**urksewpper

Fish

I'd like some ...	**Jeg vil gjerne ha ...**	yay vil **yææ**ner har
I'd like some fish.	**Jeg vil gjerne ha fisk.**	yay vil **yææ**ner har fisk
sole	**sjøtunge**	**sh**urtewnger
trout	**ørret**	**u**rrrert
lobster	**hummer**	**h**ewmmerr
crayfish	**kreps**	krehps
prawns	**store reker**	**st**oorer **r**aykerr
I'd like it ...	**Jeg vil gjerne ha det ...**	yay vil **yææ**ner har day
I'd like it steamed.	**Jeg vil gjerne ha det dampet.**	yay vil **yææ**ner har day **d**ahmpert
grilled	**griljert**	gri**ly**airt
boiled	**kokt**	kookt
baked	**ovnstekt**	**oovn**staykt
fried	**stekt**	staykt

Service, please

Who is it?	**Hvem er det?**	vehm ær day
Just a minute.	**Et øyeblikk.**	eht **oy**erblik
Come in! The door's open.	**Kom inn! Døren er åpen.**	kom in **durr**ern ær **aw**pern
May we have breakfast in our room?	**Kan vi få frokost på rommet?**	kahn vee faw **froo**koost paw **room**mert

Breakfast

I'll have ...	**Jeg vil ha ...**	yay vil har
I'll have some fruit juice.	**Jeg vil ha litt fruktsaft.**	yay vil har lit **frewkt**sahft
a boiled egg	**et kokt egg**	eht kookt ehg
a fried egg	**et speilegg**	eht **spay**lehg
some bacon/some ham	**litt bacon/litt skinke**	lit **bay**kern/lit **shing**ker
some toast	**litt ristet loff**	litt **riss**tert loof
a pot of tea	**en kanne te**	ayn **kahn**ner tay
a cup of tea	**en kopp te**	ayn kop tay
some coffee	**litt kaffe**	lit **kahf**fer
some chocolate	**litt sjokolade**	lit shookoo**lar**der
more butter	**mer smør**	mair smurr
some hot water	**litt varmt vann**	lit vahrmt vahn

Difficulties

The central heating doesn't work.	**Sentralvarmen virker ikke.**	sehn**trarl**vahrmern **veer**ker **ikk**er
the light/the socket	**lyset/støpslet**	**lew**sser(t)/**sturp**sler(t)
the tap/the toilet	**vannkranen/ toalettet**	**vahn**krarnern/twah**leht**ter(t)
There's no hot water.	**Det er ikke noe varmt vann.**	day ær **ikk**er **noo**er vahrmt vahn
May I see the manager, please?	**Kan jeg få snakke med direktøren?**	kahn yay faw **snahk**ker may(d) deerehk**tur**rern

Telephone—Mail

There's a call for you.	**Det er telefon til Dem.**	day ær tayler**foon** til dehm
Hold the line, please.	**Ikke legg på røret.**	**ikk**er lehg paw **rur**rer(t)

NORWEGIAN

Operator, I've been cut off.	**Frøken, jeg er blitt avbrutt.**	**frur**kern yay ær blit **ahv**brewt
Did anyone telephone me?	**Har noen ringt til meg?**	harr **noo**ern ringt til may
Is there any mail for me?	**Er det noe post til meg?**	ær day **noo**er post til may
Are there any messages for me?	**Er det noen beskjed til meg?**	ær day **noo**ern ber**shay(d)** til may

Checking out

May I have my bill, please?	**Kan jeg få regningen, takk.**	kahn yay faw **ray**ningern tahk
We're in a great hurry.	**Vi har det svært travelt.**	vee harr day svæt **trar**verlt
It's been a very enjoyable stay.	**Det har vært et meget hyggelig opphold.**	day harr væt eht **may**ert **hewg**gerlee **op**hol

Eating out

Good evening, sir/ Good evening, madam.	**God aften.**	goo **ahf**tern
Good evening. I'd like a table for two, please.	**God aften. Jeg vil gjerne ha et bord for to, takk.**	goo **ahf**tern. yay vil **yææ**ner har eht boor for too tahk
Do you have a fixed-price menu?	**Har De en fastsatt meny?**	harr dee ayn **fahst**saht may**new**
May I see the à la carte menu?	**Kan jeg få se menyen?**	kahn yay faw say may**new**ern
May we have an ashtray, please?	**Kan vi få et askebeger.**	kahn vee faw eht **ahs**ker**bay**gerr
some bread	**litt brød**	lit brurd
a fork	**en gaffel**	ayn **gahf**ferl
a knife	**en kniv**	ayn kneev
a spoon	**en skje**	ayn shay
a plate	**en tallerken**	ayn **tahl**lerrkern
a glass	**et glass**	eht glahss
a napkin	**en serviett**	ayn sær**vieht**
another chair	**en stol til**	ayn stool til

NORWEGIAN

Meat—Poultry—Game

| I'd like some ... | **Jeg vil gjerne ha ...** | yay vil **yææ**ner har |
| I'd like some beef. | **Jeg vil gjerne ha oksekjøtt.** | yay vil **yææ**ner har **ook**serkhurt |

a beef steak	**en biff**	ayn bif
some roast beef	**roastbeef**	**roast**beef
a veal cutlet	**en kalve-kotelett**	ayn **kahl**verkotterleht
mutton	**fårekjøtt**	**fawr**erkhurt
lamb	**lammekjøtt**	**lahm**merkhurt
a pork chop	**en svinekotelett**	ayn **svee**nerkotterleht
roast pork	**svinestek**	**svee**nerstayk
hare	**hare**	**harr**er
chicken	**kylling**	**khew**lling
roast chicken	**stekt kylling**	staykt **kewl**ling
duck	**and**	ahnd

| How do you like your meat? | **Hvordan vil De ha kjøttet tilberedt?** | **voor**dahn vil dee har **khurt**tert tilber**reht** |

rare	**blodig**	**bloo**dee
medium	**medium**	**may**diewm
well done	**godt stekt**	got staykt

NORWEGIAN

Vegetables

What vegetables have you got?	**Hvilke grønnsaker har De?**	**vil**ker **grurn**ssakerr harr dee
I'd like some ...	**Jeg vil gjerne ha ...**	yay vil **yææ**ner har
I'd like some asparagus.	**Jeg vil gjerne ha asparges.**	yay vil **yææ**ner har ah**spar**gerss

green beans	**grønne bønner**	**grurn**ner **burn**nerr
mushrooms	**sopp**	sop
carrots	**gulrøtter**	**gewl**rurtterr
onions	**løk**	lurk
red cabbage	**rødkål**	**rurd**kawl
spinach	**spinat**	spin**art**
rice	**ris**	rees
peas	**erter**	**æ**terr
tomatoes	**tomater**	too**mart**err
green salad	**grønn salat**	grurn sah**lart**
potatoes	**poteter**	poo**tayt**err

Desserts

| Nothing more, thanks. | **Takk, jeg er forsynt.** | tahk yay ær fo**shewnt** |

Just a small portion, please.	**Bare en liten porsjon.**	barrer ayn **lee**tern por**shoon**
Have you any ice-cream?	**Har De iskrem?**	harr dee **ees**krehm
fruit salad	**frukt-salat**	**frewkt**sahlart
fresh fruit	**frisk frukt**	frisk frewkt
cheese	**ost**	oost

Drink

What would you like to drink?	**Hva vil de ha å drikke?**	var vil dee har aw **drik**ker
I'll have a beer, please.	**Jeg vil gjerne ha en øl.**	yay vil **yææ**ner har ayn url
I'll have a whisky, please.	**Jeg vil gjerne ha en whisky.**	yay vil **yææ**ner har ayn **wiss**kee

Wine

I'd like a bottle of wine.	**Jeg vil gjerne ha en flaske vin.**	yay vil **yææ**ner har ayn **flah**sker veen
red wine	**rødvin**	**rur(d)**vin
rosé wine	**rosévin**	roa**say**vin
white wine	**hvitvin**	**veet**vin
Cheers!	**Skål!**	skawl

The bill (check)

May I have the bill (check) please?	**Kan jeg få regningen, takk!**	karn yay faw **ray**ningern tahk
Is service included?	**Er service inkludert?**	ær sær**vee**sser ing-klew**dai(r)t**
Everything's included.	**Alt er inkludert.**	ahlt ær ingklew**dai(r)t**
Thank you, that was a very good meal.	**Takk, det var et utmerket måltid.**	tahk day varr eht **ewt**mærkert **mawl**tid

Travelling

Where's the railway station, please?	**Hvor ligger jernbanestasjonen?**	voor **ligg**err **yææn**barner-stahs**hoo**nern
Where's the ticket office, please?	**Hvor er billettkontoret?**	voor ær bill**eht**kontoorert
I'd like a ticket to ...	**Jeg vil gjerne ha en billett til ...**	yay vil **yææ**ner har ayn bill**eht** til

First or second class?	Første eller annen klasse?	furshter ehllerr ahnnern klahssser
First class, please.	Første, takk.	furshter tahk
Single or return (one way or round-trip)?	Enveis eller tur-retur?	aynvayss ehller tewr-rertewr
Do I have to change trains?	Må jeg bytte tog?	maw yay bewtter tawg
What platform does the train leave from?	Fra hvilken platform går toget?	frar vilkern plahtform gawr tawgert
Where's the nearest underground (subway) station?	Hvor ligger nærmeste under-grunnstasjon?	voor liggerr nærmersster ewnnergrewnstahshoon
Where's the bus station, please?	Hvor er buss-stasjonen?	voor ær bewss-stahshoonern
When's the first bus to...?	Når går den første bussen til...?	nawr gawr dayn furshter bewsssern til
the last bus the next bus	den siste bussen den neste bussen	dayn sisster bewsssern dayn nehssster bewsssern
Please let me off at the next stop.	Vil De slippe meg av på neste stop-pested?	vil dee slipper may ahv paw nehssster stopper-stehd

Relaxing

What's on at the cinema (movies)?	Hva går på kino?	var gawr paw kheenoo
What's on at the theatre?	Hva går på teatret?	var gawr paw tayartrer(t)
What time does the film begin? And the play?	Når begynner filmen? Og stykket?	nawr beryewnnerr filmern? awg stewkkert
Are there any tickets for tonight?	Er det noen billetter igjen til i kveld?	ær day nooern billehtterr eeyern til ee kvehl
Where can we go dancing?	Hvor kan vi gå for å danse?	voor kahn vee gaw for aw dahnser
Would you like to dance?	Vil De danse?	vil dee dahnser

Introductions

| How do you do? | God dag. | goo darg |
| How are you? | Hvordan står det til? | voordahn stawr day til |

Very well, thank you. And you?	**Bare bra, takk. Og med Dem?**	**bar**rer brar tahk. awg may(d) dehm
May I introduce Miss Philips?	**Kan jeg få presentere frøken Philips?**	kahn yay faw praysahng-**tay**rert frurkern Philips
My name is ...	**Mitt navn er ...**	mit nahvn ær
I'm very pleased to meet you.	**Det gleder meg å treffe Dem.**	day **glay**derr may aw **treh**ffert dehm
How long have you been here?	**Hvor lenge har De vært her?**	voor **lehng**er harr dee væt hær
It was nice meeting you.	**Det var hyggelig å treffe Dem.**	day varr **hewg**gerlee aw **treh**ffer dehm

Dating

Would you like a cigarette?	**Vil De ha en sigarett?**	vil dee har ayn sigah**reht**
May I get you a drink?	**Kan jeg by Dem på en drink?**	kahn yay bew dehm paw ayn drink
Do you have a light, please?	**Unnskyld, har De en fyrstikk?**	**ewn**shewl harr dee ayn **few**shtik
Are you waiting for someone?	**Venter De på noen?**	**vehn**terr dee paw **noo**ern
Are you free this evening?	**Er De ledig i kveld?**	ær dee **lay**dee ee kvehl
Where shall we meet?	**Hvor skal vi møtes?**	voor skahl ve **mur**terss
What time shall I meet you?	**Når skal jeg møte Dem?**	nawr skahl ,yay **mur**ter dehm
May I take you home?	**Kan jeg få følge Dem hjem?**	kahn yay faw **fur**ler dehm yehm
Thank you, it's been a wonderful evening.	**Mange takk, det har vært en hyggelig kveld.**	**mahng**er tahk day harr væt ayn **hewg**gerlee kvehl
What's your telephone number?	**Hva er telefonnummeret Deres?**	var ær tayler**foon**-newmmerrer(t) **day**rerss
Do you live alone?	**Bor De alene?**	boor dee ah**lay**ner
What time is your last train?	**Når går det siste toget Deres?**	nawr gawr day **siss**ter **taw**ger(t) **day**rerss
Good-night ...	**God natt ...**	goo naht

Banks

Where's the nearest bank, please?	Unnskyld, hvor ligger nærmeste bank?	ewnshewl voor liggerr nærmerster bahnk
Where can I cash some traveller's cheques?	Hvor kan jeg innløse noen reisesjekker?	voor kahn yay inlursser nooern righssershehkkerr
What time does the bank open/What time does it close?	Når åpner banken/ Når stenger den?	nawr awpnerr bahngkern/nawr stehngerr dehn
I'm expecting some money from home. Has it arrived?	Jeg venter penger hjemmefra. Har de kommet?	yay vehnterr pehngerr yehmmerfrar. harr dee kommert
Can you give me some small change, please?	Kan De gi meg litt vekslepenger?	kahn dee yee may lit vehkslerpehngerr

Shops, stores and services

Where is the nearest chemist's (pharmacy)?	Hvor er nærmeste apotek?	voor ær nærmerster ahpotayk
the nearest hairdresser's	den nærmeste frisør	dehn nærmerster frissurr
the photo shop	fotoforretningen	footooforrehtningern
the jeweller's	gullsmeden	gewlssmaydern
the department store	varemagasinet	varrermahgahsseener(t)
the police station	politistasjonen	pooliteestahshoonern
the garage	parkeringshuset	pahrkayringsshewsser(t)
How do I get there?	Hvordan kommer jeg dit?	voordahn kommerr yay deet
Is it within walking distance?	Er det for langt å gå dit?	ær day for lahngt aw gaw deet

Service

Can you help me, please?	Kan De være så vennlig å hjelpe meg?	kahn dee væærer saw vehnlee aw yehlper may
Can you show me this? And that, too.	Kan De vise meg den? Og den også.	kahn dee veeser may dehn awg dehn awgsaw
It's too expensive/ too big/too small.	Det er for dyrt/for stort/for lite.	day ær for dewrt/for stoot/for leeter

Can you show me some more?	Kan De vise meg flere?	kahn dee **vee**sser may **flay**rer
something better	noe bedre	**noo**er **bay**drer
something cheaper	noe billigere	**noo**er **bil**ligerrer
How much is this? And that?	Hvor mye koster dette? Og det?	voor **mew**er **koss**terr **deh**tter? awg day
It's not quite what I want.	Det er ikke akkurat hva jeg vil ha.	day ær **ikk**er ahk**hew**rart var yay vil har
I like it.	Jeg liker det.	yay **lee**kerr day

Chemist's (Pharmacy)

| I'd like something for a cold/for a cough/for travel sickness. | Jeg vil gjerne ha noe for en forkjølelse/mot hoste/mot reisesyke. | yay vil **yææ**ner har **noo**er for ayn for**khur**lerlser/moot **hooss**ter/moot **righ**sserssewker |
| Can you recommend something for hayfever/for sunburn? | Kan De anbefale noe mot høysnue/mot sol brenthet? | kahn dee ahnber**far**ler **noo**er moot **hoys**snewer/moot **sool**brehnthayt |

Toiletry

May I have some razor blades?	Kan jeg få noen barberblader?	kahn yay faw **noo**ern bahr**bayr**blarderr
some shaving cream	en barberkrem	ayn bahr**bayr**krehm
some toothpaste	en tannpasta	ayn **tahn**pahsstah
I'd like some soap.	Jeg vil gjerne ha en såpe.	yay vil **yææ**ner har ayn **saw**per
some suntan oil	en solbadolje	ayn **sool**bardolyer

At the barber's

I'd like a haircut, please.	Jeg vil gjerne ha håret klippet.	yay vil **yææ**ner har **haw**rer(t) **klip**pert
Short/Leave it long.	Kort/La det være langt.	kot/lar day **vææ**rer lahngt
A razor cut, please.	Skåret med barber kniv.	**skaw**rert may(d) bahr**bayr**kneev

At the hairdresser's

| I'd like a shampoo and set, please. | Jeg vil gjerne ha vask og legg. | yay vil **yææ**ner har vahsk awg lehg |

I'd like a bleach.	**Jeg vil gjerne ha det bleket.**	yay vil **yææ**ner har day **blay**kert
a permanent	**en permanent**	ayn pehrmah**nehnt**
a colour rinse	**en farge-skylling**	ayn **fahr**yer shewlling
a manicure	**en manikyr**	ayn mahnee**kewr**

Photography

| I'd like a film for this camera. | **Jeg ville gjerne ha en film til dette apparatet.** | yay vil **yææ**ner har ayn film til **deht**ter ahppah**rar**ter(t) |
| This camera doesn't work. | **Dette apparatet virker ikke.** | **deht**ter ahppah**rar**tert **veer**ker **ik**ker |

At the post office

| Where s the nearest post office, please? | **Hvor ligger det nærmeste post-kontoret?** | voor **lig**gerr day **nær**merster **post**kontoorert |
| I'd like to send this by express (special delivery)/by air mail. | **Jeg vil gjerne sende dette som ilpost/med luftpost.** | yay vil **yææ**ner **sehn**ner **deht**ter som **eel**post/may(d) **lewft**post |

Service stations

Where is the nearest service station, please?	**Kan De si meg hvor den nærmeste ben-sinstasjonen ligger?**	kahn dee see may voor dehn **nær**merster behn-**seen**stahshoonern **lig**gerr
Fill her up, please.	**Full tank, takk.**	fewl tahnk tahk
Check the oil, please.	**Vil de kontrollere oljen!**	vil dee kontroll**ay**rer **ol**yern
Would you check the tyres?	**Vil De kontrollere dekkene!**	vil dee kontroll**ay**rer **dehk**kerner

Street directions

Can you show me on the map where I am?	**Kan De vise meg hvor jeg er på dette kartet?**	kahn dee **vee**sser may voor yay ær paw **deht**ter **kah**ter(t)
You're on the wrong road.	**De er på feil vei.**	dee ær paw fayl vay
Go back to ...	**Kjør tilbake til ...**	khurr til**bar**ker til
Go straight ahead.	**Kjør rett frem.**	khurr reht frehm
It's on the left/on the right.	**Det er på venstre/på høyre side.**	day ær paw **vehn**strer/paw **hoy**rer **see**der

NORWEGIAN

Accidents

May I use your telephone?	**Kan jeg få låne telefonen Deres?**	kahn yay faw lawner tayler**foo**nern **day**rerss
Call a doctor quickly.	**Tilkall en lege øyeblikkelig.**	**til**kahl ayn **lay**ger oyerblikkerlee
Call an ambulance.	**Ring etter en sykebil.**	ring **eht**terr ayn **sew**kerbeel
Please call the police.	**Vennligst ring til politiet.**	**vehn**ligst ring til pooli**tee**er(t)

Numbers

one	**en**	ayn
two	**to**	too
three	**tre**	tray
four	**fire**	feerer
five	**fem**	fehm
six	**seks**	sehks
seven	**sju**	shew
eight	**åtte**	otter
nine	**ni**	nee
ten	**ti**	tee
eleven	**elleve**	ehlver
twelve	**tolv**	tol
thirteen	**tretten**	**treht**tern
fourteen	**fjorten**	**fyoo**tern
fifteen	**femten**	**fehm**tern
sixteen	**seksten**	**sigh**stern
seventeen	**sytten**	**sewt**tern
eighteen	**atten**	**aht**tern
nineteen	**nitten**	**nit**tern
twenty	**tjue**	**tyew**er
twenty-one	**tjueen**	**tyew**erayn
thirty	**tretti**	**treht**tee
forty	**førti**	**fur**tee
fifty	**femti**	**fehm**tee
sixty	**seksti**	**sehks**tee
seventy	**sytti**	**sewt**tee
eighty	**åtti**	**ot**tee
ninety	**nitti**	**nit**tee
one hundred	**hundre**	**hewn**rer
one thousand	**tusen**	**tew**ssern
ten thousand	**titusen**	**tee**tewssern

NORWEGIAN

Days

It's Sunday.	Det er søndag.	day ær **surn**darg
Monday	**mandag**	**mahn**darg
Tuesday	**tirsdag**	**teerss**darg
Wednesday	**onsdag**	**onss**darg
Thursday	**torsdag**	**torsh**darg
Friday	**fredag**	**fray**darg
Saturday	**lørdag**	**lur**darg
yesterday	**i går**	ee gawr
today	**i dag**	ee darg
tomorrow	**i morgen**	ee **maw**ern
morning/afternoon	**morgen/ettermiddag**	**maw**ern/**eht**terrmiddarg
evening/night	**aften/natt**	**ahf**tern/naht

Months

January	**januar**	yahne**warr**
February	**februar**	faybre**warr**
March	**mars**	mahsh
April	**april**	ah**preel**
May	**mai**	**migh**
June	**juni**	**yew**nee
July	**juli**	**yew**lee
August	**august**	**ow**gewst
September	**september**	seh**ptehm**berr
October	**oktober**	ok**taw**berr
November	**november**	no**vehm**berr
December	**desember**	days**sehm**berr
Merry Christmas!	**God Jul! Godt**	goo yewl! got newttawr
Happy New Year!	**Nyttår!**	

NORWEGIAN

POLISH

Guide to Pronunciation

Note that Polish has some diacritical letters—letters with accent marks—which we do not know in English.

Letter	Approximate pronunciation	Symbol	Example	
Consonants				
b, f, k, l, m, p, z	are pronounced as in English			
cz	like **ch** in **ch**urch	ch	**cz**y	**ch**i
dż	like **j** in **J**am	j	**dż**em	**j**ehm
g	as in **g**irl	g	**g**uma	**g**umah
j	like **y** in **y**et	y	**j**ak	**y**ahk
ł	like **w** in **w**in	w	**ł**adny	**wah**dni
n	as in English but put your tongue against the front teeth and not the teeth ridge	n	**n**a	nah
s	as in **s**it	s/ss	**s**am	**s**ahm
sz	like **sh** in **sh**ine	sh	**sz**al	**sh**ahl
t, d	as in English but put your tongue against the front teeth and not against the teeth ridge	t d	**t**ak **d**om	tahk dom
w	like **v** in **v**an	v	**w**oda	**v**odah
ż or rz	like **s** in plea**s**ure	zh	**ż**lazo **rz**eka	**zheh**lahzo **zheh**kah

Sounds distinctly different

An often recurring phenomenon in the Slavic languages is "softening", or the "softened" pronunciation of consonants. Examples of this in Polish are **ć**, **dź**, **ń**, **ś** and **ź**. A similar effect can be produced by pronouncing **y** as in yet— but very, very short—after the consonant.

c	like the English sequence **ts** in **ts**e**ts**e pronounced quickly	ts	**co**	tso
ć	pronounced like the Polish **c** but softer	tsh	**ciało**	**tshah**wo
dz	like the English sequence **ds** in be**ds** pronounced quickly	dz	**dzwonek**	**dz**vonehk
dź or dzi	pronounced like the Polish **dz** but softer	dzh	**dziať**	**dz**hahw
h or ch	similar to English **h** but with much more friction	h	**herbata** **chudy**	heh**rbah**tah **hoo**di
ń or ni	pronounced like the English **n** but softer	ñ	**nie**	ñeh
r	like the Scottish **r** (vibration of the tip of the tongue); note that it is also pronounced at the end of words	r	**rak**	rahk
ś or si	pronounced like the English **s** but softer	s'	**się** **ktoś**	s'eh ktos'
ź or zi	pronounced like the English **z** but softer	z'	**zielony**	z'eh**lo**ni

Notice that voiced sounds become completely devoiced at the end of a word or in the context of other voiceless sounds, i.e., they are pronounced like their voiceless counterparts (e.g., **b** of chleb is pronounced like **p**; **w** of rów is pronounced like **f**; **rz** and **z** in przez like **sz** and **s**, etc.).

Vowels

a	like English **u** in c**u**lt or American **o** in c**o**llege	ah	**tak**	tahk
e	like **e** in t**e**n	eh	**lek**	lehk
i	like **ee** in f**ee**t	ee	**ile**	eeleh
y	like **i** in f**i**t	i	**ty**	ti
o	like **o** in c**o**t	o	**kot**	kot
u or ó	a sound between the English **u** in p**u**t and **oo** in b**oo**ts	oo	**drut**	droot
ą	is pronounced **on** before a consonant; when it's the final letter, it is pronounced like French **an** in fiancé	on / awng	**prąd** / **są**	pront / sawng
ę	is pronounced **en** before a consonant or like **e** in b**e**d when it is the final letter	ehn / eh	**pęd** / **tę**	pehnt / teh

Some diphthongs

ej	like **a** in t**a**ke	ay	**dobrej**	**dob**ray
aj	like **i** in l**i**ke	igh	**daj**	digh

The stress falls in Polish on the next to the last syllable, e.g. **głodny** (**gwod**ni), **drogeria** (dro**geh**ryah).

Some basic expressions

Yes.	**Tak.**	tahk
No.	**Nie.**	ñeh
Please.	**Proszę.**	**pro**sheh
Thank you.	**Dziękuję.**	dzhehn**koo**yeh
Thank you very much.	**Dziękuję bardzo.**	dzhehn**koo**yeh **bah**rdzo
That's all right.	**Proszę bardzo.**	**pro**sheh **bah**rdzo

Greetings

Good morning.	**Dzień dobry.**	dzhehñ **do**bri
Good afternoon.	**Dzień dobry.**	dzhehñ **do**bri
Good evening.	**Dobry wieczór.**	**do**bri **vyeh**choor
Good night.	**Dobranoc.**	do**brah**nots
Good-bye.	**Do widzenia.**	do veed**zeh**ñah
See you later.	**Do zobaczenia.**	do zobah**cheh**ñah
This is Mr....	**To jest pan ...**	to yehst pahn
This is Mrs....	**To jest pani ...**	to yehst **pah**ñee
This is Miss ...	**To jest pani ...**	to yehst **pah**ñee
I'm very pleased to meet you.	**Miło mi pana/panią poznać.**	**mee**wo mee **pah**na/**pah**ñawng **po**znahtsh
How are you?	**Jak się pan/pani miewa?**	yahk s'eh pahn/**pah**ñee **myeh**vah
Very well, thank you.	**Bardzo dobrze, dziękuję.**	**bah**rdzo **do**bzheh dzhehn**koo**yeh
And you?	**A pan/pani?**	ah pahn/**pah**ñee
Fine.	**Dobrze.**	**do**bzheh
Excuse me.	**Przepraszam.**	psheh**prah**shahm

Questions

Where?	**Gdzie?**	gdzheh
Where is ... ?	**Gdzie jest ... ?**	gdzheh yehst
Where are ... ?	**Gdzie są ... ?**	gdzheh sawng
When?	**Kiedy?**	**kyeh**di

What?	**Co?**	tso
How?	**Jak?**	yahk
How much?	**Ile?**	eeleh
How many?	**Ile?**	eeleh
Who?	**Kto?**	kto
Why?	**Dlaczego?**	dlahchehgo
Which?	**Który?**	ktoori
What do you call this?	**Jak się to nazywa?**	yahk s'eh to nahzivah
What do you call that?	**Jak się tamto nazywa?**	yahk s'eh tahmto nahzivah
What does this mean?	**Co to znaczy?**	tso to **znah**chi
What does that mean?	**Co tamto znaczy?**	tso **tahm**to znahchi

Do you speak . . . ?

Do you speak English?	**Czy pan/pani mówi po angielsku?**	chi pahn/**pah**ñee **moo**vee po ahn**gyehl**skoo
Do you speak German?	**Czy pan/pani mówi po niemiecku?**	chi pahn/**pah**ñee **moo**vee po nyeh**myeht**skoo
Do you speak French?	**Czy pan/pani mówi po francusku?**	chi pahn/**pah**ñee **moo**vee po frahn**tsoo**skoo
Do you speak Spanish?	**Czy pan/pani mówi po hiszpańsku?**	chi pahn/**pah**ñee **moo**vee po heesh**pahñ**skoo
Do you speak Italian?	**Czy pan/pani mówi po włosku?**	chi pahn/**pah**ñee **moo**vee po **vwos**koo
Could you speak more slowly, please?	**Proszę mówić trochę wolniej.**	**pro**sheh **moo**veetsh **tro**heh vol**ñay**
Please point to the phrase in the book.	**Proszę wskazać odpowiednie zdanie w moich rozmówkach.**	**pro**sheh **fskah**zahtsh odpo**vyehd**ñeh **zdah**ñeh fmoeeh roz**moof**kahh
Just a minute. I'll see if I can find it in this book.	**Chwileczkę. Zobaczę czy to jest w moich rozmówkach.**	hfee**leh**chkeh. zo**bah**cheh chi to yehst fmoeeh roz**moof**kahh
I understand.	**Rozumiem.**	ro**zoo**myehm
I don't understand.	**Nie rozumiem.**	ñeh ro**zoo**myehm

Can...?

Can I have...?	**Czy mogę dostać...?**	chi **mo**geh **doss**tahtsh
Can we have...?	**Czy możemy dostać...?**	chi mo**zheh**my **doss**tahtsh
Can you show me...?	**Czy może mi pan/pani pokazać...?**	chi **mo**zheh mee pahn/**pah**ñee po**kah**zahtsh
Can you tell me...?	**Czy może mi pan/pani powiedzieć...?**	chi **mo**zheh mee pahn/**pah**ñee po**vyeh**dzhehtsh
Can you help me, please?	**Czy może mi pan/pani pomóc?**	chi **mo**zheh mee pahn/**pah**ñee po**moots**

Wanting

I'd like...	**Chciałbym...**	**htshahw**bim
We'd like...	**Chcielibyśmy...**	**htsheh**leebis'mi
Please give me...	**Proszę mi dać...**	**pro**sheh mee dahsh
Give it to me, please.	**Proszę mi to dać.**	**pro**sheh mee to dahtsh
Please bring me...	**Proszę przynieść mi...**	**pro**sheh **pshiñ**ehs'tsh mee
Bring it to me, please.	**Proszę mi to przynieść.**	**pro**sheh mee to **pshiñ**ehs'tsh
I'm hungry.	**Jestem głodny.**	**yehss**tehm **gwod**ni
I'm thirsty.	**Chce mi się pić.**	htseh mee s'eh peetsh
I'm tired.	**Jestem zmęczony.**	**yehss**tehm zmehn**cho**ni
I'm lost.	**Zgubiłem się.**	zgoo**bee**wehm s'eh
It's important.	**To ważne.**	to **vahzh**neh
It's urgent.	**To pilne.**	to **peel**neh
Hurry up!	**Niech się pan/pani pospieszy!**	ñehh s'eh pahn/**pah**ñee pos**pyeh**shi

It is/There is...

It is/It's...	**To jest...**	to yehst
Is it...?	**Czy to jest...?**	chi to yehst
It isn't...	**To nie jest...**	to ñeh yehst

There is/There are . . .	**Jest/Są . . .**	yehst/sawng
Is there/Are there . . . ?	**Czy jest/Czy są . . . ?**	chi yehst/chi sawng
There isn't/There aren't . . .	**Nie ma . . .**	ñeh mah
There isn't any/ There aren't any.	**Nie ma.**	ñeh mah

A few common words

big/small	**duży/mały**	doozhi/mahwi
quick/slow	**szybki/wolny**	shipkee/volni
early/late	**wczesny/późny**	fchehssni/pooz'ni
cheap/expensive	**tani/drogi**	tahñee/drogee
near/far	**bliski/daleki**	bleesskee/dahlehkee
hot/cold	**gorący/zimny**	gorontsi/z'eemni
full/empty	**pełny/pusty**	pehwni/poossti
easy/difficult	**łatwy/trudny**	wahtfi/troodni
heavy/light	**ciężki/lekki**	tshehnshkee/lehkkee
open/shut	**otwarty/zamknięty**	otfahrti/zahmkñehnti
right/wrong	**słuszny/niesłuszny**	swooshni/ñehswooshni
old/new	**stary/nowy**	stahri/novi
old/young	**stary/młody**	stahri/mwodi
beautiful/ugly	**piękny/brzydki**	pyehnkni/bzhitkee
good/bad	**dobry/zły**	dobri/zwi
better/worse	**lepiej/gorzej**	lehpyay/gozhay

A few prepositions and some more useful words

at	**w**	v
on	**na**	nah
in	**w**	v
to	**do**	do
from	**z**	z
inside	**wewnątrz**	vehvnontsh
outside	**na zewnątrz**	nah zehvnontsh
up	**do góry**	do goori
down	**na dół**	nah doow
before	**przed**	psheht
after	**po**	po
with	**z**	z
without	**bez**	behss
through	**przez**	pshehss
towards	**w kierunku**	fkyehroonkoo
until	**aż do**	ahzh do

during	**podczas**	**pot**chahss
and	**i**	ee
or	**lub**	loop
not	**nie**	ñeh
nothing	**nic**	ñeets
none	**żaden**	**zhah**dehn
very	**bardzo**	**bahr**dzo
also	**także**	**tahg**zheh
soon	**wkrótce**	f**kroott**seh
perhaps	**może**	**mo**zheh
here	**tutaj**	**too**tigh
there	**tam**	tahm
now	**teraz**	**teh**rahss
then	**potem**	**po**tehm

Arrival

Your passport, please.	**Paszport proszę.**	**pahsh**port **pro**sheh
Here it is.	**Proszę.**	**pro**sheh
Have you anything to declare?	**Czy ma pan/pani coś do zadeklarowania?**	chi mah pahn/**pah**ñee tsos' do zahdehklahro**vah**ñah
No, nothing at all.	**Nie, nic nie mam.**	ñeh ñeets ñeh mahm
Porter!	**Bagażowy!**	bahgah**zho**vi
Can you help me with my luggage, please?	**Proszę pomóc mi nieść te walizki.**	**pro**sheh **po**moots mee ñehs'tsh teh vah**lee**skee
That's my suitcase.	**To moja walizka.**	to **mo**yah vah**lee**skah
Where's the bus for the centre of town, please?	**Gdzie jest autobus do centrum?**	gdzheh yehst ahw**to**booss do **tsehn**troom
This way, please.	**Proszę tędy.**	**pro**sheh **tehn**di

Changing money

Can you change a traveller's cheque, please?	**Czy może pan/pani wymienić mi czek podróżny?**	chi **mo**zheh pahn/**pah**ñee vimye**ñee**tsh mee chehk pod**roozh**ni
Where's the nearest bank, please?	**Gdzie jest najbliższy bank?**	gdzheh yehst nigh**blee**shshi bahnk

Car rental

I'd like a car.	**Chcę wynająć samochód.**	htseh vi**nam**yontsh sah**mo**hoot
For how long?	**Na jak długo?**	nah yahk **dwoo**go
A day/Four days/ A week/Two weeks.	**Jeden dzień/Cztery dni/Tydzień/Dwa tygodnie.**	**yeh**dehn dzhehñ/**chtehri** dñee/**ti**dzhehñ/dvah ti**god**ñeh

Taxi

Where can I get a taxi?	**Gdzie są taksówki?**	gdzheh sawng tahk**soof**kee
What's the fare to...?	**Ile kosztuje przejazd do...?**	**ee**leh kosh**too**yeh **psheh**yahst do
Take me to this address, please.	**Proszę mnie zawieźć na ten adres.**	**prosh'eh** mñeh **zah**vyehs'tsh nah tehn **ah**drehss
I'm in a hurry.	**Spieszy mi się.**	**spyeh**shi mee s'eh
Could you drive more slowly, please?	**Proszę jechać wolniej.**	**prosheh vehhahtsh vol**ñay

Hotel and other accommodation

My name is...	**Nazywam się...**	nah**zi**vahm s'eh
Have you a reservation?	**Czy ma pan/pani rezerwację?**	chi mah pahn/**pah**ñee rehzehr**vaht**syeh
Yes, here's the confirmation.	**Tak, oto kwit.**	tahk **o**to kfeet
I'd like...	**Proszę...**	**prosheh**
I'd like a single room/a double room.	**Proszę pojedyńczy pokój/podwójny pokój.**	**prosheh** poyeh**diñ**chi **po**kooy/pod**voo**yni **po**kooy
a room with a bath/ with a shower	**pokól z łazienką/ z prysznicem**	**po**kooy zwah**z'ehn**kawng/ sprish**ñeet**sehm

How much?

What's the price per night/per week/per month?	**Ile kostuje za noc/za tydzień/za miesiąc?**	**ee**leh kosh**too**yeh zah nots/zah **ti**dzhehñ/zah **myehs'**onts
May I see the room?	**Czy mogę zobaczyć pokój?**	chi **mo**gem zo**bah**chitsh **po**kooy

I'm sorry, I don't like it.	**Niestety nie podoba mi się.**	ñehsstehti ñeh podobah mee s'eh
Yes, that's fine. I'll take it.	**Dobrze. Biorę go.**	dobzheh. byoreh go
What's my room number, please?	**Jaki jest numer mojego pokoju?**	yahkee yehst noomehr moyehgo pokoyoo
Number 123.	**Numer 123.**	noomehr 123

Service, please

Who is it?	**Kto tam?**	kto tahm
Just a minute.	**Chwileczkę.**	hfeelehchkeh
Come in! The door's open.	**Proszę! Drzwi otwarte.**	prosheh!, jvee otfahrteh
May we have breakfast in our room?	**Czy możemy zjeść śniadanie w pokoju?**	chi mozhehmi zyehs'tsh s'ñahdahñeh fpokoyoo

Breakfast

I'll have...	**Proszę...**	prosheh
I'll have some fruit juice.	**Proszę sok.**	prosheh sok
a boiled egg	**jajko gotowane**	yighko gotovahneh
a fried egg	**jajko smażone**	yighko smahzhoneh
some bacon/some ham	**bekon/szynkę**	behkon/shinkeh
some toast	**grzanki**	gzhahnkee
a pot of tea	**dzbanek herbaty**	dzbahnehk hehrbahti
a cup of tea	**filiżankę herbaty**	feeleezhahnkeh hehrbahti
some coffee	**kawę**	kahveh
some chocolate	**gorącą czekoladę**	gorontsawng chehkolahdeh
more butter	**trochę więcej masła**	troheh vyehntsay mahsswah
some hot water	**trochę gorącej wody**	troheh gorontsay vodi

Difficulties

The central heating doesn't work.	**Centralne ogrze-wanie nie działa.**	tsehntrahlneh ogzheh-vahñeh ñeh dzhahwah
the light/the socket	**światło/gniazdko**	s'fyahtwo/gñahsstko
the tap/the toilet	**kurek/ubikacja**	koorehk/oobeekahtsyah

| There's no hot water. | Nie ma ciepłej wody. | ñeh mah **tsheh**pway vo**d**i |
| May I see the manager, please? | Chciałbym porozmawiać z kierownikiem. | **htshahw**bim porozmahvyahtsh skehrovneekehm |

Telephone—Mail

There's a call for you.	Telefon do pana/pani.	teh**leh**fon do pahnah/pahñee
Hold the line, please.	Proszę się nie rozłanczać.	prosheh s'eh ñeh rozwonchahtsh
Operator, I've been cut off.	Proszę pana, przerwano mi.	prosheh **pah**nah pshehrvahno mee
Did anyone telephone me?	Czy ktoś do mnie dzwonił?	chi ktos' do mñeh **dzvo**ñeew
Is there any mail for me?	Czy jest dla mnie poczta?	chi yehst dlah mñeh **poch**tah
Are there any messages for me?	Czy jest jakaś wiadomość dla mnie?	chi yehst **yah**kahs' vyah**do**mos'tsh dlah mñeh

Checking out

May I have my bill, please?	Proszę rachunek.	prosheh rah**hoo**nehk
We're in a great hurry.	Bardzo się spieszymy.	**bahr**dzo s'eh spyeh**shi**mi
It's been a very enjoyable stay.	Bardzo miło spędziliśmy tutaj czas.	**bahr**dzo **mee**wo spehndzhee**lees**'mi **too**tigh chahss

Eating out

Good evening, sir/ Good evening, madam.	Dobry wieczór panu/Dobry wieczór pani.	**dobr**i vyeh**choor pah**noo/**dobr**i vyeh**choor pah**ñee
Good evening. I'd like a table for two, please.	Dobry wieczór. Proszę o stolik dla dwóch osób.	**dobr**i vyeh**choor**. prosheh o **sto**leek dlah dyooh **o**soop
Do you have a fixed-price menu?	Czy są obiady firmowe?	chi sawng o**byah**di feer**mo**veh
May I see the à la carte menu?	Proszę kartę.	prosheh **kahr**teh

190

May we have an ashtray, please?	**Proszę popielniczkę.**	prosheh popyehlñeechkeh
some bread	**pieczywo**	pyehchivo
a fork	**widelec**	veedehlehts
a knife	**nóż**	noosh
a spoon	**łyżkę**	wishkeh
a plate	**talerz**	tahlehsh
a glass	**szklankę**	shklahnkeh
a napkin	**serwetkę**	sehrvehtkeh
another chair	**jeszcze jedno krzesło**	yehshcheh yehdno kshehsswo

| Where's the gentlemen's toilet (men's room)? | **Gdzie jest toaleta dla panów?** | gdzheh yehst twahlehtah dlah pahnoof |
| Where's the ladies' toilet (ladies' room)? | **Gdzie jest toaleta dla pań?** | gdzheh yehst twahlehtah dlah pahñ |

Appetizers

I'd like some . . .	**Proszę . . .**	prosheh
I'd like some assorted appetizers.	**Proszę zestaw zakąsek.**	prosheh zehsstahf zahkonsehk
orange juice	**sok pomarańczowy**	sok pomahrahñchovi
ham	**szynkę**	shinkeh
melon	**melona**	mehlonah
pâté	**pasztet**	pahshteht
smoked salmon	**wędzonego łososia**	vehndzonehgo wossos'ah
shrimps (shrimp)	**krewetki**	krehvehtkee

Soup

Have you any . . . ?	**Czy jest . . . ?**	chi yehst
Have you any chicken soup?	**Czy jest rosół?**	chi yehst rossoow
vegetable soup	**zupa jarzynowa**	zoopah yahzhinovah
onion soup	**zupa cebulowa**	zoopah tsehboolovah

Fish

I'd like some . . .	**Proszę . . .**	prosheh
I'd like some fish.	**Proszę rybę.**	prosheh ribeh
sole	**solę**	soleh
trout	**pstrąga**	pstrongah
lobster	**homara**	homahrah
crayfish	**langustę**	lahngoossteh
prawns	**krewetki**	krehvehtkee

I'd like it . . .	**Proszę rybę . . .**	**pro**sheh **ri**beh
I'd like it steamed.	**Proszę rybę duszoną.**	**pro**sheh **ri**beh doo**sho**nawng
grilled	**z rusztu**	**zroosh**too
boiled	**gotowaną**	goto**vah**nawng
baked	**zapiekaną**	zahpyeh**kah**nawng
fried	**smażoną**	smah**zho**nawng

Meat—Poultry—Game

I'd like some . . .	**Proszę . . .**	**pro**sheh
I'd like some beef.	**Proszę wołowinę.**	**pro**sheh vowo**vee**neh
a beef steak	**befsztyk**	**behf**shtik
some roast beef	**pieczeń wołową**	**pyeh**chehñ vowo**vawng**
a veal cutlet	**sznycel cielęcy**	**shnit**sehl tsheh**leh**ntsi
mutton	**baraninę**	bahrah**ñee**neh
lamb	**młodą baraninę**	**mwo**dawng bahrah**ñee**neh
a pork chop	**kotlet schabowy**	**kot**leht shah**bo**vi
roast pork	**pieczeń wieprzową**	**pyeh**chehñ vyehp**sho**vawng
hare	**zająca**	zah**yon**tsah
chicken	**kurczę**	**koor**cheh
roast chicken	**kurczę pieczone**	**koor**cheh pyeh**cho**neh
duck	**kaczkę**	**kah**chkeh
How do you like your meat?	**Jak ma być podane?**	yahk mah bitsh po**dah**neh
rare	**po angielsku**	po ahn**gehl**skoo
medium	**średnio wysmażone**	**s'rehd**ño vissmah**zho**neh
well done	**mocno wysmażone**	**mots**no vissmah**zho**neh

Vegetables

What vegetables have you got?	**Jakie są jarzyny?**	**yah**keh sawng yamh**zhi**ni
I'd like some . . .	**Proszę . . .**	**pro**sheh
I'd like some asparagus.	**Proszę szparagi.**	**pro**sheh shpah**rah**gee
green beans	**zieloną fasolkę**	z'ehlo**nawng** fah**ssol**keh
mushrooms	**pieczarki**	pyeh**char**kee
carrots	**marchewkę**	mahr**hehf**keh
onions	**cebulę**	tseh**boo**leh
red cabbage	**czerwoną kapustę**	chehr**vo**nawng kah**pooss**teh
spinach	**szpinak**	**shpee**nahk
rice	**ryż**	rish

peas	**groszek**	groshehk
tomatoes	**pomidory**	pomeedori
green salad	**sałatkę**	sahwahtkeh
potatoes	**ziemniaki**	z'ehmñahkee

Desserts

Nothing more, thanks.	**To wszystko, dziękuję.**	to fshisstko dzhehnkooyeh
Just a small portion, please.	**Małą porcję proszę.**	mahwawng portsyeh prosheh
Have you any ice-cream?	**Czy są lody?**	chi sawng lodi
fruit salad	**kompot**	kompot
fresh fruit	**świeże owoce**	s'fyehzheh ovotseh
cheese	**ser**	sehr

Drink

What would you like to drink?	**Czego pan/pani się napije?**	chehgo pahn/pahñee s'eh nahpeeyeh
I'll have a beer, please.	**Proszę piwo.**	prosheh peevo
I'll have a whisky, please.	**Proszę whisky.**	prosheh wisskee

Wine

I'd like a bottle of wine.	**Proszę butelkę wina.**	prosheh bootehlkeh veenah
red wine	**czerwonego wina**	chehrvonehgo veenah
rosé wine	**słodkiego wina**	swotkehgo veenah
white wine	**białego wina**	byahwehgo veenah
Cheers!	**Na zdrowie!**	nah zdrovyeh

The bill (check)

May I have the bill (check) please?	**Proszę o rachunek.**	prosheh o rahhoonehk
Is service included?	**Włącznie z obsługą?**	vwonchñeh zopswoogawng
Everything's included.	**Rachunek obejmuje wszystko.**	rahhoonehk obaymooyeh fshisstko
Thank you, that was a very good meal.	**Dziękuję, jedzenie było bardzo dobre.**	dzhehnkooyeh yehdzehñeh biwo bahrdzo dobreh

Travelling

Where's the railway station, please?	**Przepraszam, gdzie jest stacja kolejowa?**	psheh**prah**shahm gdzeh yehst **stah**tsyah koleh**yo**vah
Where's the ticket office, please?	**Przepraszam, gdzie jest kasa biletowa?**	psheh**prah**shahm gdzeh yehst **kah**ssah beeleh**to**vah
I'd like a ticket to . . .	**Proszę bilet do . . .**	pro**sheh** **beeleht** do
First or second class?	**Pierwszej czy drugiej klasy?**	**pyehr**shay chi **droogay** **klah**ssi
First class, please.	**Proszę pierwszą klasę.**	pro**sheh** **pyehr**shawng **klah**sseh
Single or return (one way or round-trip)?	**Zwykły bilet czy powrotny?**	**zvik**wi **beeleht** chi po**vrot**ni
Do I have to change trains?	**Czy muszę się przesiadać?**	chi **moo**sheh s'eh pshehs'**ay**dahtsh
What platform does the train leave from?	**Z którego peronu odchodzi pociąg?**	sk**too**rehgo peh**ro**noo oth**odz**hee **pot**shonk
Where's the nearest underground station?	**Gdzie jest najbliższa stacja metro?**	**gdzeh** yehst **nigh**bleeshshah **stah**tsyah **meh**tro
Where's the bus station, please?	**Gdzie jest dworzec autobusowy?**	**gdzeh** yehst **dvo**zhehts ahwto**boo**ssovi
When's the first bus to . . . ?	**Kiedy odchodzi pierwszy autobus do . . . ?**	**keh**di oth**odz**hee **pyehr**shi ahwto**booss** do
the last bus the next bus	**ostatni autobus następny autobus**	oss**tah**tñee ahwto**booss** nahss**tehm**pni ahwto**booss**
Please let me off at the next stop.	**Proszę mnie wypuścić na następnym przystanku.**	pro**sheh** mñeh vi**poos**'tsheetsh nah nahss**tehm**pnim pshiss**tahn**koo

Relaxing

What's on at the cinema (movies)?	**Co grają w kinie?**	tso **grah**yawng f**kee**ñeh
What's on at the theatre?	**Co grają w teatrze?**	tso **grah**yawng f**teh**ah**chsheh**
What time does the film begin? And the play?	**O której zaczyna się film? A sztuka?**	o k**too**ray zah**chi**nah s'eh feelm? ah **shtoo**kah
Are there any tickets for tonight?	**Czy są bilety na dzisiaj wieczór?**	chi sawng bee**leh**ti nah **dzhee**ss'igh **vyeh**choor

194

| Where can we go dancing? | Gdzie można pójść potańczyć? | gdzeh mozhnah pooys'tsh potahñchitsh |
| Would you like to dance? | Czy mogę prosić? | chi mogeh pross'eetsh |

Introductions

How do you do?	Dzień dobry.	dzhehñ dobri
How are you?	Jak się pan/pani ma?	yahk s'eh pahn/pahñee mah
Very well, thank you. And you?	Dobrze, dziękuję. A pan/pani?	dobzheh dzhehnkooyeh. ah pahn/pahñee
May I introduce Miss Philips?	To jest pani Philips.	to yehst pahñee Philips
My name is...	Nazywam się...	nahzivahm s'eh
I'm very pleased to meet you.	Miło mi pana/panią poznać.	meewo mee pahnah/pahñawng poznahtsh
How long have you been here?	Od jak dawna pan/pani jest tutaj?	od yahk dahvnah pahn/pahñee yehst tootigh
It was nice meeting you.	Miło mi było pana/panią poznać.	meewo mee biwo pahnah/pahñawng poznahtsh

Dating

Would you like a cigarette?	Czy zapali pani?	chi zahpahlee pahñee
May I get you a drink?	Czy nie zechciałaby pani napić się czegoś?	chi ñeh zehhtshahwahbi pahñee nahpeetsh s'eh chehgos'
Do you have a light, please?	Czy mogę prosić o ogień?	chi mogeh pross'eetsh o ogehñ
Are you waiting for someone?	Czy pan/pani na kogoś czeka?	chi pahn/pahñee nah kogos' chehkah
Are you free this evening?	Czy pan/pani ma dzisiaj wolny wieczór?	chi pahn/pahñee mah dzheess'igh volni vyehchoor
Where shall we meet?	Gdzie się spotkamy?	gdzeh s'eh spotkahmi
What time shall I meet you?	O której się spotkamy?	o ktooray s'eh spotkahmi
May I take you home?	Czy mogę panią odwieźć do domu?	chi mogeh pahñawng odvyehs'tsh do domoo

Thank you, it's been a wonderful evening.	**Dziękuję za cudowny wieczór.**	dzhehn**koo**yeh zah tsoo**dov**ni **vyeh**choor
What's your telephone number?	**Jaki jest pana/pani numer telefonu?**	**yah**kee yehst pahnah/**pah**ñee noomehr tehleh**fo**noo
Do you live alone?	**Czy pani mieszka sama?**	chi **pah**ñee **myehsh**kah **sah**mah
What time is your last train?	**O której ma pan/pani ostatni pociąg?**	o **kto**tray mah pahn/**pah**ñee ostahtnee **pot**shonk
Good-night . . .	**Dobranoc . . .**	do**brah**nots

Banks

Where's the nearest bank, please?	**Przepraszam, gdzie jest najbliższy bank?**	psheh**prah**shahm gdzheh yehst nigh**bleesh**shi bahnk
Where can I cash some traveller's cheques?	**Gdzie mogę wymienić czeki po-dróżne?**	gdzheh mogeh vimyeh**ñee**tsh **chehk**kee podroozhneh
What time does the bank open? What time does it close?	**O której otwiera się bank? O której się zamyka?**	o **ktoo**ray otfyehrah s'eh bahnk o **ktoo**ray s'eh zah**mi**kah
I'm expecting some money from home. Has it arrived?	**Oczekuję na przekaz pieniężny z domu. Czy już nad-szedł?**	oche**koo**yeh nah psheh**kahss** pyeh**ñehnzh**ni **zdo**moo. chi yoosh **naht**sheht
Can you give me some small change, please?	**Proszę mi dać drobne.**	**pro**sheh mee dahtsh **drob**neh

Shops, stores and services

Where is the nearest chemist's (pharmacy)?	**Gdzie jest najbliższa apteka?**	gdzheh yehst nigh**bleesh**shah ahp**teh**kah
the nearest hair-dresser's	**zakład fryzjerski**	**zah**kwaht friz **yehr**skee
the photo shop	**fotooptyka**	foto**op**tikah
the jeweller's	**jubiler**	yoo**bee**lehr
the department store	**dom towarowy**	dom tovah**ro**vi
the police station	**posterunek milicji**	posteh**roo**nehk mee**lee**etsyee
the garage	**warsztat samochodowy**	**vahr**shtaht sahmoho**do**ví

| How do I get there? | Jak tam się mogę, dostać? | yahk tahm s'eh mogeh dosstahtsh |
| Is it within walking distance? | Czy dojdę tam pieszo? | chi doydeh tahm pyehsho |

Service

Can you help me, please?	Proszę pana/panią!	prosheh pahnah/pahñawng
Can you show me this? And that, too.	Proszę mi to pokazać! A także tamto!	prosheh mee to pokahzahtsh! ah tahgzheh tahmto
It's too expensive/ too big/too small.	Jest za drogi/za duży/za mały.	yehst zah drogee/zah doozhi/zah mahwi
Can you show me some more?	Czy może mi pan/pani pokazać trochę więcej?	chi mozheh mee pahn/pahñee pokahzahtsh troheh vyehntsay
something better something cheaper	coś lepszego coś tańszego	tsos'lehpshehgo tsos' tahñshehgo
How much is this? And that?	Ile to kosztuje? A tamto?	eeleh to koshtooyeh? ah tahmto
It's not quite what I want.	Nie to chciałem.	ñeh to htshahwehm
I like it.	Podoba mi się to.	podobah mee s'eh to

Chemist's (Pharmacy)

| I'd like something for a cold/for a cough/for travel sickness. | Proszę coś na przeziębienie/na kaszel/na mdłości. | prosheh tsos' nah pshehz'ehmbyehñeh/nah kahshehl/nah mdwos'tshee |
| Can you recommend something for hay-fever/for sunburn? | Czy może mi pan/pani polecić coś na katar sienny/na oparzenie słoneczne? | chi mozheh mee pahn/pahñee polehtsheetsh tsos' nah kahtahr s'ehnni/nah opahzhehñeh swonehchneh |

Toiletry

May I have some razor blades?	Poproszę żyletki.	poprosheh zhilehtkee
some shaving cream some toothpaste	krem do golenia pastę do zębów	krehm do golehñah pahssteh do zehmboof
I'd like some soap.	Proszę mydło.	prosheh midwo
some suntan oil	olejek do opalania	olehyehk do opahlahñah

At the barber's

I'd like a haircut, please.	Proszę mnie ostrzyc.	prosheh mñeh osstshits
Short/Leave it long.	Krótko/Długo.	krootko/dwoogo
A razor cut, please.	Strzyżenie brzytwą, proszę.	stshizhehñeh bzhitfawng prosheh

At the hairdresser's

I'd like a shampoo and set, please.	Proszę mycie i trwałe ufarbowanie.	prosheh mitsheh ee trfahweh oofahrbovahñeh
I'd like a bleach.	Proszę rozjaśnić.	prosheh rozyahs'ñeetsh
a permanent	trwała	trfahwawng
a colour rinse	płukankę koloryzującą	pwookahnkeh kolorizooyontsawng
a manicure	manicure	mahñeekyoor

Photography

| I'd like a film for this camera. | Proszę film do tego aparatu. | prosheh feelm do tehgo ahpahrahtoo |
| This camera doesn't work. | Popsuł mi się aparat. | popsoow mee s'eh ahpahraht |

At the post office

| Where's the nearest post office, please? | Przepraszam, gdzie jest najbliższa poczta? | pshehprahshahm gdzheh yehst nighbleeshshah pochtah |
| I'd like to send this by express (special delivery)/by air mail. | Chcę to nadać ekspresem/pocztą lotniczą. | htseh to nahdahtsh ehksprehssehm/pochtawng lotñeechawng |

Service stations

Where is the nearest service station, please?	Przepraszam, gdzie jest najbliższa stacja benzynowa?	pshehprahshahm gdzheh yehst nighbleeshshah stahtsyah behnzinovah
Fill her up, please.	Proszę napełnić zbiornik.	prosheh nahpehwñeetsh zbyorñeek
Check the oil, please.	Proszę sprawdzić olej.	prosheh sprahvdzheetsh olay
Would you check the tyres?	Proszę sprawdzić opony.	prosheh sprahvdzheetsh oponi

Street directions

Can you show me on the map where I am?	Czy może pan/pani pokazać mi na mapie gdzie teraz jestem?	chi mozheh pahn/pahñee pokahzahtsh mee nah mahpyeh gdzheh tehrahss yehsstehm
You're on the wrong road.	Pan/pani jedzie nie tą szosą.	pahn/pahñee yehdzheh ñeh tawng shossawng
Go back to...	Proszę zawrócić do...	prosheh zahvrootsheetsh do
Go straight ahead.	Proszę jechać prosto.	prosheh yehhahtsh prossto
It's on the left/on the right.	To jest na lewo/na prawo.	to yehst nah lehvo/nah prahvo

Accidents

May I use your telephone?	Czy mogę skorzystać z telefonu?	chi mogeh skozhisstahtsh stehlehfonoo
Call a doctor quickly.	Proszę wezwać lekarza, szybko.	prosheh vehzvahtsh lehkahzhah shipko
Call an ambulance.	Proszę wezwać pogotowie.	prosheh vehzvahtsh pogotovyeh
Please call the police.	Proszę wezwać milicję.	prosheh vehzvahtsh meeleetsyeh

Numbers

one	jeden	yehdehn
two	dwa	dvah
three	trzy	chshi
four	cztery	chtehri
five	pięć	pyehñtsh
six	sześć	shehs'tsh
seven	siedem	s'ehdehm
eight	osiem	os'ehm
nine	dziewięć	dzhehvyehñtsh
ten	dziesięć	dzhehs'ehñtsh
eleven	jedenaście	yehdehnahs'tsheh
twelve	dwanaście	dvahnahs'tsheh
thirteen	trzynaście	chshinahs'tsheh
fourteen	czternaście	chtehrnahs'tsheh
fifteen	piętnaście	pyehtnahs'tsheh
sixteen	szesnaście	shehssnahs'tsheh
seventeen	siedemnaście	s'ehdehmnahs'tsheh
eighteen	osiemnaście	os'ehmnahs'tsheh
nineteen	dziewiętnaście	dzhehvyehtnahs'tsheh

194

199

twenty	dwadzieścia	dvah**dzhehs**'tshah
twenty-one	dwadzieścia jeden	dvah**dzhehs**'tshah **yeh**dehn
thirty	trzydzieści	chshi**dzhehs**'tshee
forty	czterdzieści	chtehr**dzhehs**'tshee
fifty	pięćdziesiąt	pyehñ**dzhehs**'ont
sixty	sześćdziesiąt	shehs'**dzhehs**'ont
seventy	siedemdziesiąt	s'ehdehm**dzhehs**'ont
eighty	osiemdziesiąt	os'ehm**dzhehs**'ont
ninety	dziewięćdziesiąt	dzhehvyehñ**dzhehs**'ont
one hundred	sto	sto
one thousand	tysiąc	tis'onts
ten thousand	dziesięć tysięcy	**dzhehs**'ehñtsh tis'**ehn**tsi

Days

It's Sunday.	Jest niedziela.	yehst ñeh**dzhehl**ah
Monday	poniedziałek	poñeh**dzhah**wehk
Tuesday	wtorek	ftorehk
Wednesday	środa	s'rodah
Thursday	czwartek	chfahrtehk
Friday	piątek	pyontehk
Saturday	sobota	sobotah
yesterday	wczoraj	fchorigh
today	dzisiaj	dzhees'igh
tomorrow	jutro	yootro
morning/afternoon	rano/popołudnie	rahno/popowoodñeh
evening/night	wieczór/noc	vyehchoor/nots

Months

January	styczeń	stichehñ
February	luty	looti
March	marzec	mahzhehts
April	kwiecień	kfyehtshehñ
May	maj	migh
June	czerwiec	chehrvyehts
July	lipiec	leepyehts
August	sierpień	s'ehrpyehñ
September	wrzesień	vzhehss'ehñ
October	październik	pahz'**dzhehr**ñeek
November	listopad	leesstopaht
December	grudzień	groodzhehñ
Merry Christmas!	Wesołych Świąt!	vehsowih s'fyont!
Happy New Year!	Szczęśliwego Nowego Roku!	schehehns'leevehgo novehgo rokoo

PORTUGUESE

Guide to Pronunciation

Letter	Approximate pronunciation	Symbol	Example	

Consonants

f, k, l, p, t, v	as in English			
b	as in English, but often less decisive (more like **v**)	b	boca	**bo**aker
		bh	abrir	erb**reer**
c	1) before **e** and **i**, like **s** in s**i**t	s	cedo	**say**dhoo
	2) elsewhere, like **k** in **k**ill	k	casa	**kah**zer
ç	like **s** in s**i**t	s	comecar	koomer**sahr**
ch	like **sh** in **sh**ut	sh	chamar	sher**mahr**
d	as in English, but often less decisive (more like **th** in **th**is)	d	dia	**dee**er
		dh	nada	**nah**dher
g	1) before **a**, **o** and **u** or a consonant, or after **l**, **n** and **r**, like **g** in **g**o	g	garfo	**gahr**foo
	2) between vowels, like a soft version of the **ch** in Scottish lo**ch**	ǧ	rogar	roo**ǧahr**
	3) before **e** and **i**, like **s** in pleasure	zh	gelo	**zhay**loo

h	always silent		**homem**	omahng^y
j	like **s** in plea**s**ure	zh	**já**	zhah
lh	like **lli** in mi**lli**on	ly	**olho**	olyoo
m	1) between a vowel and a consonant, or at the end of a word ("finally"), it indicates that the vowel is nasalized (see "Nasal vowels")		**embalar** **bom**	ahng^ybah**lah** bawng
	2) elsewhere like **m** in **m**et	m	**mais**	mighsh
n	1) when initial or between vowels, like **n** in **n**o	n	**novo**	no**a**voo
	2) in a consonant group and in plural endings it nasalizes the preceding vowel, but is generally silent		**branco**	**brah**ngkoo
			homens	omahng^ysh
nh	like **ni** in o**ni**on	ny	**vinho**	vee**ny**oo
q	like **k** in **k**ill	k	**quadro**	kwah**dh**roo
r	strongly trilled as in Scottish speech	r	**rua**	roo**e**r
s	1) when initial, after a consonant or written **ss**, like **s** in **s**it	s	**saber**	ser**bhayr**
	2) between vowels (not necessarily in the same word), like **z** in ra**z**or	z	**casa** **as aves**	kah**z**er erz ah**v**ersh
	3) when final, or before **c, f, p, q, t**, like **sh** in **sh**ut	sh	**país**	peree**sh**
	4) elsewhere, like **s** in plea**s**ure	zh	**cisne**	see**zh**ner
x	1) generally like **sh** in **sh**ut	sh	**baixo**	bigh**shoo**
	2) in **ex-** before a vowel, like **z** in ra**z**or	z	**exacto**	i**z**ahtoo
z	1) when initial or between vowels like **z** in ra**z**or	z	**zero**	**z**ehroo
	2) when final or before **c, f, p, q, s** or **t**, like **sh** in **sh**ut	sh	**feliz**	ferlee**sh**
	3) elsewhere like **s** in plea**s**ure	zh	**luz da**	loo**zh** der

Vowels

a				
	1) when stressed (see under "Stressing") it is like a mixture of the **u** in c**u**t and the **a** in p**a**rty	ah	**nado**	**nah**dhoo
	2) when unstressed or before **m**, **n** or **nh** but not in the same syllable like **a** in **a**bout	er	**porta**	**port**er
e				
	1) when stressed generally like **e** in g**e**t	eh	**pertu**	**pehr**too
	2) when stressed sometimes like **a** in l**a**te	ay	**cabelo**	ker**bhay**loo
	3) when unstressed, like **er** in oth**er**	er	**pesado**	per**zah**dhoo
	4) at the beginning of a word, and in certain other cases, like **i** in h**i**t	i	**antes** **exacto**	**ern**tish i**zah**too
é	like **e** in g**e**t	eh	**café**	ker**feh**
ê	like **a** in l**a**te	ay	**mès**	maysh
i				
	1) when stressed like **ee** in s**ee**d	ee	**riso**	**ree**zoo
	2) when unstressed, like **i** in com**i**ng	i	**final**	fi**nahl**
o				
	1) when stressed, like **o** in r**o**d	o	**fora**	**for**er
	2) when unstressed, usually like **oo** in f**oo**t	oo	**caso**	**kah**zoo
	3) sometimes when stressed or unstressed, like **o** in n**o**te (most common o-sound)	oa	**voltar** **Lisboa**	voal**tahr** lizh**voa**er
ô, ou	like **o** in n**o**te	oa	**pôs**	poash
u				
	1) generally like **oo** in s**oo**n	oo	**número**	**noo**merroo
	2) silent in **gu** and **qu** before **e** or **i**		**querer**	ker**rayr**

Diphthongs

A diphthong is two vowels pronounced as a single vowel sound, e.g., in English **boy** there is a diphthong consisting of **o** plus a weak **i** sound. In Portuguese diphthongs, **a**, **e** and **o** are strong vowels and **i** and **u** are weak vowels. In diphthongs the strong vowels are pronounced with more stress (louder) than the weak ones, e.g., **ai** is pronounced like **igh** in s**igh**, and **au** like **ow** in h**ow**. Sometimes the weak vowels can combine to make a diphthong. Apart from these generalizations the exact pronunciation of Portuguese diphthongs is not easy to predict.

Nasal vowels

These are pronounced through the mouth and through the nose at the same time, just as in the French nasal vowels (e.g., in the French **bon**) and quite similar to the nasal twang heard in some areas of America and Britain.

ã, am, an	something like **ung** in l**ung**, or like **an** in French d**ans**	ahng **maçã**	mer**sahng**
em, en	something like **ing** in s**ing**, but recalling also the **a** in l**a**te	ayng **cento**	**sayng**too
im, in	a nasalized version of the **ea** in l**ea**rn	eeng **cinco**	**seeng**koo
õ, om, on	like **orn** in c**orn**cob or like **on** in French b**on**	awng **bom**	bawng
um, un	something like a North of England pronunciation of **ung** in l**ung** (a nasalized version of **u** in p**u**t)	oong **um**	oong

Semi-nasalized diphthongs

In these, the first element is nasalized and combined with a weak **i** (pronounced like **y** in y**et**) or **u** pronounced like **w** in w**as**).

ãe, ãi, êm, final en, usually final em	pronounced as **ã** followed by **y** in y**et**	ahng^y **mãe**	mahng^y
		sêm	sahng^y
ão, final unstressed am	pronounced as **ã** followed by **w** in w**as**	ahng^w **mão**	mahng^w
õe, oi	pronounced as **õ** followed by **y** in y**et**	awng^y **põe**	pawng^y
ui	like nasal vowel **u** followed by **y** in y**et**	oong^y **muito**	**moong**^ytoo

Stressing

1) If a word ends with **a**, **e** or **o**, the stress falls on the next to the last syllable, e.g., **rosa** (pronounced **roa**zer). Plural endings **m** and **s** are generally disregarded.
2) All other words are stressed on the last syllable, e.g., **animal** (pronounced ernee**mahl**).

Words not stressed in accordance with these rules have an accent (´ or `) over the vowel of the stressed syllable.

Some basic expressions

Yes.	**Sim.**	seeng
No.	**Não.**	nahng^w
Please.	**Por favor.**	poor fervoar
Thank you.	**Obrigado.**	obreegahdhoo
Thank you very much.	**Muito obrigado.**	moong^ytoo obreegahdhoo
That's all right.	**Não tem de quê.**	nahng^w tayng der kay

Greetings

Good morning.	**Bom dia.**	bawng deeer
Good afternoon.	**Boa tarde.**	boaer tahrder
Good evening.	**Boa noite.**	boaer noyter
Good night.	**Boa noite.**	boaer noyter
Good-bye.	**Adeus.**	erdhehoosh
See you later.	**Até logo.**	ertay loagoo
This is Mr....	**Apresento-lhe o Senhor...**	erprerzayntoolyer oo sayñoar
This is Mrs....	**Apresento-lhe a Senhora...**	erprerzayntoolyer er sayñoarer
This is Miss...	**Apresento-lhe a Menina...**	erprerzayntoolyer er merneener
I'm very pleased to meet you.	**Muito prazer em conhecê-lo.**	moong^ytoo prerthehr ayng kooñerthayloo
How are you?	**Como está?**	koamoo ishtah
Very well, thank you.	**Muito bem, obrigado.**	moong^ytoo bayng obreegahdhoo
And you?	**E você?**	ee vosay
Fine.	**Bem.**	bayng
Excuse me.	**Desculpe.**	dehshkoolper

Questions

Where?	**Onde?**	onder
Where is...?	**Onde está...?**	onder ishtah
Where are...?	**Onde estão...?**	onder ishtahng^w

When?	Quando?	kwahndoo
What?	O quê?	oo kay
How?	Como?	koamoo
How much?	Quanto?	kwahntoo
How many?	Quantos?	kwahntoosh
Who?	Quem?	kayng
Why?	Porquê?	poorkay
Which?	Qual?	kwahl
What do you call this?	Como se chama isto?	koamoo ser shermer eeshtoo
What do you call that?	Como se chama aquilo?	koamoo ser shermer erkeeloo
What does this mean?	Que significa isto?	kay seegneefeeker eeshtoo
What does that mean?	Que significa aquilo?	kay seegneefeeker erkeeloo

PORTUGUESE

Do you speak ... ?

Do you speak English?	Fala inglês?	fahler eengglaysh
Do you speak German?	Fala alemão?	fahler erlermahng^w
Do you speak French?	Fala francês?	fahler frahngsaysh
Do you speak Spanish?	Fala espanhol?	fahler ishperñol
Do you speak Italian?	Fala italiano?	fahler eeterlyahnoo
Could you speak more slowly, please?	Pode falar mais devagar, por favor?	poahdher ferlahr mighsh dervergahr poor fervoar
Please point to the phrase in the book.	Por favor, indique-me a frase no livro.	poor fervoar eendeekermer er frahzer noo leevroo
Just a minute. I'll see if I can find it in this book.	Um momento por favor, vou ver se posso encontrá-la neste livro.	oong moomayngtoo poor fervoar voa vayr ser posssoo ingkontrahrler nehster leevroo
I understand.	Compreendo.	kawngpriayngdoo
I don't understand.	Não compreendo.	nahng^w kawngpriayngdoo

Can ... ?

Can I have ... ?	**Pode dar-me?**	poa**dher** dahr**mer**
Can we have ... ?	**Pode dar-nos ... ?**	poa**dher** dahr**noosh**
Can you show me ... ?	**Pode mostrar-me ... ?**	poa**dher** moosh**trahr**mer
Can you tell me ... ?	**Pode dizer-me ... ?**	poa**dher** dee**zehr**mer
Can you help me, please?	**Pode ajudar-me, por favor?**	poa**dher** erzhood**dahr**mer poor fer**voar**

Wanting

I'd like ...	**Queria ...**	kerr**eeer**
We'd like ...	**Queríamos ...**	kerr**eeer**moosh
Please give me ...	**Por favor, dê-me ...**	poor fer**voar day**mer
Give it to me, please.	**Dê-mo, por favor.**	**day**moo poor fer**voar**
Please bring me ...	**Por favor, traga-me ...**	poor fer**voar** trah**g̃er**mer
Bring it to me, please.	**Traga-mo, por favor.**	trah**g̃er** moo poor fer**voar**
I'm hungry.	**Tenho fome.**	**teh**ñoo fomer
I'm thirsty.	**Tenho sede.**	**teh**ñoo **sehd**her
I'm tired.	**Estou cansado.**	ish**toa** kern**sah**dhoo
I'm lost.	**Estou perdido.**	ish**toa** perr**dheed**hoo
It's important.	**É importante.**	eh impoor**tahn**ter
It's urgent.	**É urgente.**	eh oor**zhehn**ter
Hurry up!	**Depressa!**	der**prehs**er

It is/There is ...

It is/It's ...	**É ...**	eh
Is it ... ?	**É ... ?**	eh
It isn't ...	**Não é ...**	nahng^w eh
There is/There are ...	**Há ...**	ah
Is there/Are there ... ?	**Há ... ?**	ah

PORTUGUESE

There isn't/There aren't ...	**Não há ...**	nawng^w ah

| There isn't any/
There aren't any. | **Não há nenhum/
Não há nenhuns
(Não há nenhuma/
Não há nenhumas).** | nawng^w ah niñoong/
nawng^w ah niñoongsh
(nawng^w ah niñoongmer/
nawng^w ah niñoong-
mersh) |

A few common words

big/small	**grande/pequeno**	grahnder/perkehnoo
quick/slow	**rápido/lento**	rahpeedhoo/lehntoo
early/late	**cedo/tarde**	sehdhoo/tahrder
cheap/expensive	**barato/caro**	berrahtoo/kahroo
near/far	**perto/longe**	pehrtoo/lawngzher
hot/cold	**quente/frio**	kehnter/freeoo
full/empty	**cheio/vazio**	shayoo/verzeeoo
easy/difficult	**fácil/difícil**	fahseel/derfeeseel
heavy/light	**pesado/leve**	perzahdhoo/lehver
open/shut	**aberto/fechado**	erbehrtoo/fershahdhoo
right/wrong	**certo/errado**	sehrtoo/ehrrahdhoo
old/new	**velho/novo**	vehlyoo/noavoo
old/young	**idoso/jovem**	eedhoazoo/zhovayng
beautiful/ugly	**belo/feio**	behloo/fayoo
good/bad	**bom/mau**	bawng/mow
better/worse	**melhor/pior**	milyor/peeor

Some prepositions and a few more useful words

at	**a**	ah
on	**sobre**	soabrer
in	**em**	ayng
to	**para**	perrer
from	**de**	der
inside	**dentro**	dehntroo
outside	**fora**	forer
up	**em cima**	ayng seemer
down	**em baixo**	ayng bighshoo
before	**antes**	erntish
after	**depois**	derpoysh
with	**com**	kawng
without	**sem**	sayng
through	**através**	ertrervehsh
towards	**para**	perrer
until	**até**	erteh
during	**durante**	doorahnter

and	**e**	ee
or	**ou**	oa
not	**não**	nawng^w
nothing	**nada**	**nah**dher
none	**nenhum**	ning**ñoong**
very	**muito**	**moong**^y too
also	**também**	tahng**bayng**
soon	**em breve**	ayng **brehv**er
perhaps	**talvez**	tahl**vaysh**
here	**aqui**	er**kee**
there	**ali**	er**lee**
now	**agora**	er**gor**er
then	**depois**	der**poysh**

Arrival

Your passport, please.	**O passaporte, por favor.**	oo pahser**por**ter poor fer**voar**
Here it is.	**Aqui está.**	er**kee** ish**tah**
Have you anything to declare?	**Tem alguma coisa declarar?**	tayng ahl**goo**mer **koy**zer er dherkler**rahr**
No, nothing at all.	**Não, nada.**	nawng^w **nah**dher
Porter!	**Bagageiro!**	ber**g**er**zhay**roo
Can you help me with my luggage, please?	**Pode levar-me a bagagem, por favor?**	**poa**dher ler**vahr**mer er ber**gah**zhayng poor fer**voar**
That's my suitcase.	**Esta é a minha mala.**	**ehsh**ter eh er **mee**ñer **mah**ler
Where's the bus to the centre of town, please?	**Onde posso apanhar o autocarro para o centro da cidade, por favor?**	**on**der **poss**oo erper**ñahr** oo owtoo**kahr**roo **per**rer oo **sehn**troo der seedhah-dher poor fer**voar**
This way, please.	**Por aqui, por favor.**	poor er**kee** poor fer**voar**

Changing money

Can you change a traveller's cheque, please?	**Pode cambiar-me um cheque de viagem, por favor?**	**poa**dher kerm**byahr**mer oong shehk der vyah-**zhayng** poor fer**voar**
Where's the nearest bank, please?	**Onde fica o banco mais próximo, por favor?**	**on**der **fee**ker oo **bahng**-koo mighsh **pros**eemoo poor fer**voar**

PORTUGUESE

Car rental

I'd like a car.	Queria alugar um carro.	kerreeer erlooğahr oong kahrroo
For how long?	Por quanto tempo?	poor kwahntoo tayngpoo
A day/Four days/ A week/Two weeks	Um dia/Quatro dias/Uma semana/ Duas semanas.	oong deeer/kwahtroo deeersh/oomer sermahner/dooersh sermahnersh

Taxi

Where can I get a taxi?	Onde posso encontrar um táxi?	onder posssoo ingkontrahr oong tahksee
What's the fare to ...?	Qual é o preço do percurso para ...?	kwahl ay oo prehsoo doo perrkoorsoo perrer
Take me to this address, please.	Leve-me a esta morada, por favor.	lehvermer er ehshter moorahdher poor fervoar
I'm in a hurry.	Estou com pressa.	ishtoa kawng prehser
Could you drive more slowly, please?	Pode ir mais devagar, por favor?	poadher eer mighsh dervergahr poor fervoar

Hotel and other accommodation

My name is...	O meu nome é ...	oo mehoo noamer eh
Have you a reservation?	Reservou?	rerzerrvoa
Yes, here's the confirmation.	Sim, aqui está a confirmação.	seeng erkee ishtah er kawngfeermersahng[w]
I'd like...	Quero...	kehròo
I'd like a single room/a double room.	Quero um quarto de uma cama/um quarto de casal.	kehroo oong kwahrtoo der oomer kermer/oong kwahrtoo der kerzahl
a room with a bath/with a shower	um quarto com banho/com chuveiro	oong kwahrtoo kawng bahñoo/kawng shoovayroo

How much?

What's the price per night/per week/per month?	Qual é o preço por noite/por semana/ por mês?	kwahl eh oo prehsoo poor noyter/poor sermahner/poor maysh
May I see the room?	Posso ver o quarto?	posssoo vehr oo kwahrtoo

I'm sorry, I don't like it.	**Lamento, mas não gosto.**	lermehntoo mersh nahng^wgoshtoo
Yes, that's fine. I'll take it.	**Sim, está bem. Fico com ele.**	seeng ishtah bayng. feekoo kawng ehler
What's my room number, please?	**Qual é o número do meu quarto, por favor?**	kwahl eh oo noomerroo doo mehoo kwahrtoo poor fervoar
Number 123.	**Número 123.**	noomerroo 123.

Service, please

Who is it?	**Quem é?**	kayng eh
Just a minute.	**Um momento.**	oong moomehntoo
Come in! The door's open.	**Entre! A porta está aberta.**	ehntrer er porter ishtah erbehrter
May we have breakfast in our room?	**Podemos ter o pequeno almoço no quarto?**	poodhehmoosh tehr oo perkehnoo ahlmosoo nookwahrtoo

Breakfast

I'll have ...	**Tomo ...**	tomoo
I'll have some fruit juice.	**Tomo sumo de fruta.**	tomoo soomoo der frooter
a boiled egg	**um ovo kozido**	oong ovoo koozeedhoo
a fried egg	**um ovo estrelado**	oong ovoo ishtrerlahdhoo
some bacon/some ham	**toucinho/presunto**	toaseeñoo/prerzoontoo
some toast	**torradas**	toorrahdhersh
a pot of tea	**um bule de chá**	oong booler der shah
a cup of tea	**uma chávena de chá**	oomer shahverner der shah
some coffee	**café**	kerfeh
some chocolate	**chocolate**	shookoolahter
more butter	**mais manteiga**	mighsh merntayǧer
some hot water	**água quente**	ahgwer kaynter

Difficulties

The central heating doesn't work.	**O aquecimento central não funciona.**	oo erkehseemehntoo sehntrahl nahng^w foonsyoaner
the light/the socket	**a luz/a tomada**	er loosh/er toomahdher
the tap/the toilet	**a torneira/a casa de banho**	er toornayrer/er kahzer der bahñoo

| There's no hot water. | **Não há água quente.** | nahng^w ah ah\u0302gwer kaynter |
| May I see the manager, please? | **Posso falar com o director, por favor?** | **posss**oo fer**lahr** kawng oo deere**h**toar poor fer**voar** |

Telephone—Mail

There's a call for you.	**Há uma chamada para si.**	ah **oo**mer sher**mah**dher **perrer see
Hold the line, please.	**Aguarde um momento, por favor.**	er**gwahr**der oong moo**mehn**too poor fer**voar**
Operator, I've been cut off.	**Telefonista, cortaram-me a ligação.**	terler**foo**neesh**ter koor**tah**remmer er leeger-**sahng**^w
Did anyone telephone me?	**Alguém me chamou?**	ahl**gayng** mer sher**moa**
Is there any mail for me?	**Há correio para mim?**	ah koor**ray**oo perrer meeng
Are there any messages for me?	**Há alguma mensagem para mim.**	ah ahl**goo**mer mayng**sah**zhayng **perrer meeng

Checking out

May I have my bill, please?	**Pode dar-me a conta, por favor?**	**poad**her **dahr**mer er **kon**ter poor fer**voar**
We're in a great hurry.	**Temos muita pressa.**	**tay**moosh **moong**^yter **preh**ser
It's been a very enjoyable stay.	**Tivemos uma óptima estadia.**	tee**veh**moosh **oo**mer **ot**eemer ishter**dhee**er

Eating out

Good evening, sir/ Good evening, madam.	**Boa noite, Senhor/Boa noite, Senhora.**	**boa**er **noy**ter say**ñoar/boa**er **noy**ter say**ñoa**rer
Good evening. I'd like a table for two, please.	**Boa noite. Desejo uma mesa para dois, por favor.**	**boa**er **noy**ter. der**zeh**zhoo **oo**mer **may**zer **perrer doysh poor fer**voar**
Do you have a fixed-price menu?	**Tem um menu de preço fixo?**	tayng oong meh**noo** der **preh**soo **feek**soo
May I see the à la carte menu?	**Pode dar-me o menu?**	**poad**her **dahr**mer oo meh**noo**

May we have an ashtray, please?	**Pode-nos dar um cinzeiro, por favor?**	**poa**dhernoosh dahr oong seenzayroo poor fer**voar**
some bread	**pão**	pahng^w
a fork	**um garfo**	oong **gahr**foo
a knife	**uma faca**	oomer **fah**ker
a spoon	**uma colher**	oomer kool**yehr**
a plate	**um prato**	oong **prah**too
a glass	**um copo**	oong **ko**poo
a napkin	**um guardanapo**	oong gwerr**der**nahpoo
another chair	**outra cadeira**	oatrer ker**dhay**rer
Where's the gentlemen's toilet (men's room)?	**Onde é a casa de banho dos cavalheiros?**	onder eh er **kah**zer der **bah**ñoo doosh kerver**lyay**roosh
Where's the ladies' toilet (ladies' room)?	**Onde é a casa de banho das senhoras?**	onder eh er **kah**zer der **bah**ñoo dersh say**ñoa**rersh

Appetizers

I'd like some . . .	**Queria . . .**	ker**ree**er
I'd like some assorted appetizers.	**Queria uns acepipes variados.**	ker**ree**er oongsh erser**pee**persh verr**yah**doosh
orange juice	**um sumo de laranja**	oong **soo**moo der ler**rahng**zher
ham	**fiambre**	**fyahng**brer
melon	**melão**	mer**lahng**^{w}
pâté	**pâté**	pah**tay**
smoked salmon	**salmão fumado**	sahl**mahng**^{w} foomahdhoo
shrimps (shrimp)	**camarões**	kermer**rawng**^{y}sh

Soup

Have you any . . . ?	**Tem . . . ?**	tayng
Have you any chicken soup?	**Tem caldo de galinha?**	tayng **kahl**doo der gerlee-ñer
vegetable soup	**sopa de legumes**	**soa**per der ler**goo**mersh
onion soup	**sopa de cebola**	**soa**per der cer**boa**ler

Fish

I'd like some . . .	**Queria . . .**	ker**ree**er
I'd like some fish.	**Queria peixe.**	ker**ree**er **pay**sher
sole	**linguado**	ling**gwah**dhoo
trout	**truta**	**troo**ter
lobster	**lagosta**	ler**ġoash**ter
crayfish	**caranguejo**	kerrerng**gay**zhoo
prawns	**lagostins**	lergoosh**teeng**sh

PORTUGUESE

I'd like it . . .	**Quero-o . . .**	keh**roo**oo
I'd like it steamed.	**Quero-o cozido a vapor.**	keh**roo**oo koo**zee**dhoo er ver**poar**
grilled	**grelhado**	gri**lyah**dhoo
boiled	**cozido**	koo**zee**dhoo
baked	**no forno**	noo **foar**noo
fried	**frito**	**free**too

Meat—Poultry—Game

I'd like some . . .	**Queria . . .**	ker**reeer**
I'd like some beef.	**Queria carne de vaca.**	ker**reeer kahr**ner der **vah**ker
a beef steak	**um bife**	oong **bee**fer
some roast beef	**rósbife**	roz**bee**fer
a veal cutlet	**uma costeleta de vitela**	**oo**mer koosht**er**layter der vee**teh**ler
mutton	**carneiro**	kerr**nay**roo
lamb	**borrego**	boo**ray**goo
a pork chop	**uma costeleta de porco**	**oo**mer koosht**er**layter der **poar**koo
roast pork	**porco assado**	**poar**koo er**sah**dhoo
hare	**lebre**	**leh**brer
chicken	**frango**	**frahng**goo
roast chicken	**frango assado**	**frahng**goo er**sah**dhoo
duck	**pato**	**pah**too
How do you like your meat?	**Como deseja a carne?**	**koa**moo der**zay**zher er **kahr**ner
rare	**mal passada**	mahl per**sah**dher
medium	**médio**	**meh**dyoo
well done	**bem passada**	bayng per**sah**dher

Vegetables

What vegetables have you got?	**Que legumes tem?**	ker ler**goo**mersh tayng
I'd like some . . .	**Queria . . .**	ker**reeer**
I'd like some asparagus.	**Queria espargos.**	ker**reeer** ish**pahr**goosh
green beans	**feijão verde**	fay**zhahng**ʷ **veh**rder
mushrooms	**cogumelos**	koo**ġoo**me**hloosh**
carrots	**cenouras**	si**noa**rersh
onions	**cebolas**	ser**boa**lersh
red cabbage	**repolho**	rer**poa**lyoo
spinach	**espinafres**	ishpee**nahf**rersh

rice	**arroz**	erroash
peas	**ervilhas**	errveelyersh
tomatoes	**tomates**	toomahtersh
green salad	**salada de alface**	serlahdher der ahlfahser
potatoes	**batatas**	bertahtersh

Desserts

Nothing more, thanks.	**Mais nada, obrigado.**	mighsh nahdher obree-ğahdhoo
Just a small portion, please.	**Muito pouco, por favor.**	moongʸtoo poakoo poor fervoar
Have you any ice-cream?	**Tem gelados?**	tayng zherlahdoosh
fruit salad	**salada de frutas**	serlahder dher frootersh
fresh fruit	**fruta fresca**	frooter frayshker
cheese	**queijo**	kayzhoo

Drink

What would you like to drink?	**Que deseja tomar?**	ker derzayzher toomahr
I'll have a beer, please.	**Queria uma cerveja, por favor.**	kerreeer oomer serrvayzher poor fervoar
I'll have a whisky, please.	**Queria um whisky, por favor.**	kerreeer oong weeshkee poor fervoar

Wine

I'd like a bottle of wine.	**Queria uma garrafa de vinho.**	kerreeer oomer gerrahfer der veeñoo
red wine	**vinho tinto**	veeñoo teentoo
rosé wine	**vinho rosé**	veeñoo rozay
white wine	**vinho branco**	veeñoo brahngkoo
Cheers!	**Saúde!**	seroodher

The bill (check)

| May I have the bill (check) please? | **Pode dar-me a conta, por favor?** | poadher dahrmer er konter poor fervoar |
| Is service included? | **O serviço está incluído?** | oo serrveesoo ishtah eengklooeedhoo |

216

| Everything's included. | **Tudo incluído.** | **too**dhoo eengkloo**ee**dhoo |
| Thank you, that was a very good meal. | **Obrigado, foi uma boa refeição.** | obree**gah**dhoo foy **oo**mer **boa**er rerfay**sahng**ʷ |

Travelling

Where's the railway station, please?	**Onde é a estação de caminho de ferro, por favor?**	**ond**er eh er ishter**sahng**ʷ der kermee**ñoo** der **feh**roo poor fer**voar**
Where's the ticket office, please?	**Onde é a bilheteira, por favor?**	**ond**er eh er beelyer**tayr**er poor fer**voar**
I'd like a ticket to...	**Queria um bilhete para...**	ker**ree**er oong beelyay**ter** **perr**er
First or second class?	**De primeira ou segunda classe?**	der pree**may**rer oa ser**goon**der **klah**ser
First class, please.	**De primeira, por favor.**	der pree**may**rer poor fer**voar**
Single or return (one way or round-trip)?	**Uma ida ou ida e volta?**	**oo**mer **eed**er oa **eed**er ee **volt**er
Do I have to change trains?	**Devo mudar de comboio?**	**day**voo moo**dahr** der koam**boy**oo
What platform does the train leave from?	**De que cais parte o comboio?**	der ker kighsh **pahr**ter oo koam**boy**oo
Where's the nearest underground (subway) station?	**Onde é a estação de metro mais próxima?**	**ond**er eh er ishter**sahng**ʷ der **meh**troo mighsh **pro**seemer
Where's the bus station, please?	**Onde é a estação dos autocarros?**	**ond**er eh er ishter**sahng**ʷ doosh owtoo**kah**roosh
When's the first bus to...?	**A que horas parte o primeiro autocarro para...?**	er ker **or**ersh **pahr**ter oo pree**may**roo owtoo**kah**roo **perr**er
the last bus	**o último autocarro**	oo **ool**timoo owtoo**kah**roo
the next bus	**o próximo autocarro**	oo **pro**seemoo owtoo**kah**roo
Please let me off at the next stop.	**Por favor, deixe-me sair na próxima paragem.**	poor fer**voar day**shermer sereer ner **pro**seemer per**rah**zhayng

Relaxing

| What's on at the cinema (movies)? | **O que há no cinema?** | oo ker ah noo see**naym**er |

What's on at the theatre?	**O que há no teatro?**	oo ker ah noo ti**ah**troo
What time does the film begin? And the play?	**A que horas começa o filme? E a peça?**	ah ker o**rersh** koo**meh**ser oo **feel**mer. ee er **peh**ser
Are there any tickets for tonight?	**Há bilhetes para esta noite?**	ah beel**yay**tersh **perr**er **ehsh**ter **noy**ter
Where can we go dancing?	**Onde podemos ir dançar?**	**onder** poo**dheh**moosh eer dahn**sahr**
Would you like to dance?	**Quer dançar?**	kehr dahn**sahr**

Introductions

How do you do?	**Bom dia.**	bawng **deeer**
How are you?	**Como está?**	**koa**moo ish**tah**
Very well, thank you. And you?	**Muito bem, obrigado. E você?**	moong^{y}too bayng obree**gah**dhoo. ee vo**say**
May I introduce Miss Philips?	**Apresento-lhe a Menina Philips.**	erprer**zaynt**oolyer er mer**neen**er Philips
My name is ...	**O meu nome é ...**	oo **meh**oo **noa**mer eh
I'm very pleased to meet you.	**Tenho muito prazer em conhecê-lo.**	**tay**ñoo moong^{y}too prer**zehr** ayng koo**ñer**sayloo
How long have you been here?	**Há quanto tempo está cá?**	ah **kwahn**too **tayng**poo ish**tah** kah
It was nice meeting you.	**Tive muito prazer em conhecê-lo.**	**teev**er moong^{y}too prer**zehr** ayng koo**ñer**sayloo

Dating

Would you like a cigarette?	**Quer um cigarro?**	kehr oong see**gah**roo
May I get you a drink?	**Posso oferecer-lhe uma bebida?**	**poss**soo oferrer**sehr**lyer **oo**mer ber**beed**her
Do you have a light, please?	**Tem lume, por favor?**	tayng **loo**mer poor fer**voar**
Are you waiting for someone?	**Espera alguém?**	ish**payr**er ahl**gayng**
Are you free this evening?	**Está livre esta noite?**	ish**tah** **leev**rer **ehsh**ter **noy**ter
Where shall we meet?	**Onde nos podemos encontrar?**	**onder** noosh poo**dheh**moosh ingkoan**trahr**

PORTUGUESE

What time shall I meet you?	**A que horas posso encontra-la?**	er ker orersh **posss**oo ingkoantrahler
May I take you home?	**Posso leva-la a casa?**	**posss**oo lervahler er kahzer
Thank you, it's been a wonderful evening.	**Obrigado por esta noite tão agradável.**	obreegahdhoo poor ehsh-ter noyter tahng^w ergrer-dhahvehl
What's your telephone number?	**Qual é o seu número de telefone?**	kwahl eh oo **seh**oo noomerroo de terlerfoner
Do you live alone?	**Vive só?**	**vee**ver so
What time is your last train?	**A que horas é o seu último comboio?**	er ker orersh eh oo **seh**oo **ool**timoo koamboyoo
Good-night...	**Boa noite...**	boaer noyter

Banks

Where's the nearest bank, please?	**Onde é o Banco mais próximo, por favor?**	onder eh oo **bahng**koo mighsh **proos**eemoo poor fervoar
Where can I cash some traveller's cheques?	**Onde posso trocar alguns cheques de viagem?**	onder **posss**oo troo**kahr** ahl**goong**sh shehks der vyah**zhayng**
What time does the bank open? What time does it close?	**A que horas abre o Banco? A que horas fecha?**	er ker orersh ahbrer oo **bahng**koo? er ker orersh fehsher
I'm expecting some money from home. Has it arrived?	**Aguardo dinheiro da família. Já chegou?**	ergwahrdhoo diñayroo der fermeelyer. zhah shergoa
Can you give me some small change, please?	**Pode dar-me alguns trocos, por favor?**	poadher dahrmer ahl**goong**sh trokoosh poor fervoar

Shops, stores and services

Where is the nearest chemist's (pharmacy)?	**Onde é a farmácia mais próxima?**	onder eh er ferr**mah**seeer mighsh **proos**eemer
the nearest hairdresser's	**o cabeleireiro mais próximo**	o kerberlee**ray**roo mighsh **proos**eemoo
the photo shop	**a loja de artigos fotográficos**	er lozher der errtee**g**oosh footoo**grah**feekoosh
the jeweller's	**a ourivesaria**	er oareevser**reee**er
the department store	**o armazém**	oo ahrmer**zayng**

the police station	o posto de policia	oo **posh**too der **poolee**-seeer
the garage	a garagem	er ger**rahz**hayng
How do I get there?	Como vou lá ter?	**koa**moo voa lah tehr
Is it within walking distance?	Pode-se ir a pé?	**poa**dherser eer ah peh

Service

Can you help me, please?	Pode ajudar-me, por favor?	**poa**dher erzhoo**dahr**mer poor fer**voar**
Can you show me this? And that, too.	Pode mostrar-me isto? e aquilo também.	**poa**dher moosh**trahr**mer **eesh**too ee er**kee**loo tahm**bayng**
It's too expensive/ too big/too small.	É muito caro/muito grande/muito pequeno.	eh **moong**^{y}too **kah**roo/ **moong**^{y}too **grahn**der/ **moong**^{y}too per**keh**noo
Can you show me some more?	Pode mostrar-me mais alguns?	**poa**dher moosh**trahr**mer mighsh ahl**goongsh**
something better	algo melhor	**ahl**ĝoo mil**yoar**
something cheaper	algo mais barato	**ahl**ĝoo mighsh ber**rah**too
How much is this? And that?	Quanto custa isto? E aquilo?	**kwahn**too **koosh**ter **eesh**too? ee er**kee**loo
It's not quite what I want.	Não é exatamente o que quero.	nahng^w eh izahter**mehn**ter oo ker **keh**roo
I like it.	Gosto disto.	**gosh**too **deesh**too

Chemist's (Pharmacy)

| I'd like something for a cold/for a cough/for travel sickness. | Queria qualquer coisa para a constipação/para a tosse/para o enjôo de viagem. | ker**reeer** kwahl**kehr** **koy**zer **perr**er er kawngshtipersahng^w/**perr**er er **to**ser/**perr**er oo ayng**zhoa**oo der vyah**zhayng** |
| Can you recommend something for hay-fever/for sunburn? | Pode indicar-me algo para a alergia do polen/para quei-maduras do sol? | **poa**dher eendee**kahr**mer **ahl**ĝoo **perr**er er erler-**zheeer** doo po**layn**/**perr**er kaymerd**hoo**rersh doo sol |

PORTUGUESE

Toiletry

May I have some razor blades?	Pode dar-me lâminas de barbear?	poadher dahrmer lahmeenersh der berrbyahr
some shaving cream	creme para a barba	kreaymer perrer er bahrber
some toothpaste	uma pasta de dentes	oomer pahshter der dehntish
I'd like some soap.	Queria um sabonete.	kerreeer oom serboonehter
some suntan oil	um óleo para bronzear	oong olyoo perrer bronzeeahr

At the barber's

I'd like a haircut, please.	Quero cortar o cabelo, por favor.	kehroo koortahr oo kerbayloo poor fervoar
Short/Leave it long.	Curto/Deixe-o comprido.	koortoo/daysheroo kompreedoo
A razor cut, please.	A navalha, por favor.	er nervahlyer poor fervoar

At the hairdresser's

I'd like a shampoo and set, please.	Queria um champô e mise, por favor.	kerreeer oong shahmpoa ee meezer poor fervoar
I'd like a bleach.	Queria aloirar o cabelo.	kerreeer erloyrahr oo kerbayloo
a permanent	fazer uma permanente	ferzehr oomer pehrmernehnter
a colour rinse	pintar o cabelo	peentahr oo kerbayloo
a manicure	uma manicura	oomer merneekoorer

Photography

| I'd like a film for this camera. | Queria um rolo para esta máquina fotográfica. | kerreeer oong roaloo perrer ehshter mahkeener footoograhfeeker |
| This camera doesn't work. | Esta máquina não funciona bem. | ehshter mahkeener nahng^w foonsyoaner bayng |

At the post office

Where's the nearest post office, please?	**Qual é o correio mais próximo, por favor?**	kwahl eh oo **koo**rayoo mighsh **proo**seemoo poor fer**voar**
I'd like to send this by express (special delivery)/by air mail.	**Queria enviar isto por expresso/por avião.**	ker**reeer** ayng**vee**ahr **eesh**too poor ish**prehsoo**/ poor erveeahng[w]

Service stations

Where is the nearest service station, please?	**Qual é a estação de serviço mais próxima, por favor?**	kwahl eh er ishter**sahng**[w] der serr**vee**soo mighsh **proo**seemer poor fer**voar**
Fill her up, please.	**Encha o depósito, por favor.**	**ayng**sher oo der**po**zeetoo poor fer**voar**
Check the oil, please.	**Verifique o óleo, por favor.**	verree**fee**ker oo o**lyoo** poor fer**voar**
Would you check the tyres?	**Pode verificar os pneus?**	**poa**dher verreefee**kahr** oosh **pneh**oosh

Street directions

Can you show me on the map where I am?	**Pode mostrar-me no mapa onde me encontro?**	**poa**dher **moosh**trahrmer noo **mah**per **on**der mer ayng**kon**troo
You're on the wrong road.	**Está na estrada errada.**	ish**tah** ner ish**trah**dher er**rah**dher
Go back to . . .	**Volte atrás até . . .**	**volter** er**trahsh** er**teh**
Go straight ahead.	**Sempre em frente.**	**saym**prer ayng **fraynter**
It's on the left/on the right.	**É à esquerda/à direita.**	eh ah ish**kehr**der/ah di**rayter**

Accidents

May I use your telephone?	**Posso telefonar?**	**poss**soo terlerfoo**nahr**
Call a doctor quickly.	**Chame um médico depressa.**	**sher**mer oong **may**deekoo der**preh**ser
Call an ambulance.	**Chame uma ambulância.**	**sher**mer **oo**mer erm-boo**lahng**seeer
Please call the police.	**Chame a polícia, por favor.**	**sher**mer er poo**lee**seeer poor fer**voar**

Numbers

one	**um**	oong
two	**dois**	doysh
three	**três**	traysh
four	**quatro**	kwahtro
five	**cinco**	seengkoo
six	**seis**	saysh
seven	**sete**	sehter
eight	**oito**	oytoo
nine	**nove**	nover
ten	**dez**	dehsh
eleven	**onze**	awngzer
twelve	**doze**	doazer
thirteen	**treze**	trayzer
fourteen	**catorze**	kertoarzer
fifteen	**quinze**	keenzer
sixteen	**dezasseis**	derzersaysh
seventeen	**dezassete**	derzersehter
eighteen	**dezoito**	derzoytoo
nineteen	**dezanove**	derzernover
twenty	**vinte**	veenter
twenty-one	**vinte e um**	veenter ee oong
thirty	**trinta**	treenter
forty	**quarenta**	kwerrehnter
fifty	**cinquenta**	seengkwehnter
sixty	**sessenta**	sersehnter
seventy	**setenta**	sertehnter
eighty	**oitenta**	oytehnter
ninety	**noventa**	noovehnter
one hundred	**cem**	sayng
one thousand	**mil**	meel
ten thousand	**dez mil**	dehsh meel

Days

It's Sunday.	**É domingo.**	eh doomeenggoo
Monday	**segunda-feira**	sergoonder fayrer
Tuesday	**terça-feira**	tehrser fayrer
Wednesday	**quarta-feira**	kwahrter fayrer
Thursday	**quinta-feira**	keenter fayrer
Friday	**sexta-feira**	sayshter fayrer
Saturday	**sábado**	sahberdhoo
yesterday	**ontem**	awngtayng
today	**hoje**	oazher
tomorrow	**amanhã**	ahmerñahng
morning/afternoon	**manhã/tarde**	merñahng/tahrder
evening/night	**noite/noite**	noyter/noyter

PORTUGUESE

Months

January	**Janeiro**	zher**nay**roo
February	**Fevereiro**	fever**ray**roo
March	**Março**	**mahr**soo
April	**Abril**	er**breel**
May	**Maio**	**migh**oo
June	**Junho**	**zhoo**ñoo
July	**Julho**	**zhool**yoo
August	**Agosto**	er**goash**too
September	**Setembro**	ser**tayng**broo
October	**Outubro**	oa**toob**roo
November	**Novembro**	noo**vayng**broo
December	**Dezembro**	der**zayng**broo
Merry Christmas!	**Feliz Natal/Feliz**	fer**leesh** ner**tahl**/fer**leesh**
Happy New Year!	**Ano Novo!**	**ahnoo** **novoo**

RUSSIAN

Guide to Pronunciation

Letter	Approximate pronunciation	Symbol	Example	
Vowels				
а	between the **a** in c**a**t and the **ar** in c**ar**t	ah	как	kahk
е	like **ye** in **ye**t	yeh	где	gdyeh
ё	like **yo** in **yo**nder	yo	мёд	myod
и	like **ee** in s**ee**	ee	синий	**see**nyee
й	like **y** in ga**y** or bo**y**	y	бой	boy
о	like **o** in h**o**t	o	стол	stol
у	like **oo** in b**oo**t	oo	улица	**oo**leetsah
ы	similar to **i** in h**i**t	i	вы	vi
э	like **e** in m**e**t	eh	эта	**eh**tah
ю	like **u** in d**u**ke	yoo	юг	yoog
я	like **ya** in **ya**rd	yah	мясо	**myah**sah

Consonants

б	like **b** in **b**it	b	был	**b**il
в	like **v** in **v**ine	v	ваш	**v**ahsh
г	like **g** in **g**o	g	город	**g**orahd
д	like **d** in **d**o	d	да	**d**ah
ж	like **s** in plea**s**ure	zh	жаркий	**zh**ahrkee
з	like **z** in **z**oo	z	за	**z**ah
к	like **k** in **k**itten	k	карта	**k**ah**r**tah
л	like **l** in **l**ose	l	лампа	**l**ah**m**pah
м	like **m** in **m**y	m	масло	**m**ahsslah
н	like **n** in **n**ot	n	нет	**n**yeht
п	like **p** in **p**ot	p	парк	**p**ahrk
р	like **r** in **r**un	r	русский	**r**oosskee
с	like **s** in **s**ee	s/ss	слово	**s**lovah
т	like **t** in **t**ip	t	там	**t**ahm
ф	like **f** in **f**ace	f	ферма	**f**yeh**r**mah
х	like **ch** in Scottish lo**ch**	kh	хлеб	**kh**lyehb
ц	like **ts** in si**ts**	ts	цена	**ts**eenah
ч	like **ch** in **ch**ip	ch	час	**ch**ahss
ш	like **sh** in **sh**ut	sh	ваша	vah**sh**ah
щ	like **sh** followed by **ch**	shch	щётка	**shch**yotkah

Other letters

ь gives a ''soft'' pronunciation to the preceding consonant. A similar effect can be produced by pronouncing **y** as in **y**et—but very, very short—after the consonant. In our transcription we shall show this with an apostrophe (') after the soft consonant.

ъ is sometimes used between two parts of a compound word, when the second part begins with **я**, **ю**, or **е**, to show that the pronunciation of the word should incorporate a clear separation of the two parts.

Diphthongs

ай	like **igh** in s**igh**	igh	чай	ch**igh**
яй	like the previous sound, but preceded by the **y** in **y**es	yigh	негодяй	nyehgo**dyigh**
ой	like **oy** in b**oy**	oy	вой	v**oy**
ей	like **ya** in **Ya**tes	yay	соловей	solov**yay**
ый	like **i** in b**i**t followed by the **y** in **y**es	iy	красивый	krah**seeviy**
уй	like **oo** in g**oo**d followed by the **y** in **y**es	ooy	луй	d**ooy**
	like the previous sound, but preceded by the **y** in **y**es	yooy	плюй	pl**yooy**

RUSSIAN

The effects of non-stress

If a vowel or diphthong is not stressed, it often changes its pronunciation. This could be called a weakening of the sound.

о	unstressed, is pronounced like Russian **a**	ah	отец	ah**tyehts**
е, я, и, он, ей, ий	unstressed, are pronounced like a short **yee** sound	yee or ee	теперь английский	tyee**pyehr'** ahn**glee**skee

The alphabet

The column at the left shows printed capital and small letters while the centre column shows handwritten capital and small letters. The right-hand column will help you to pronounce the names of these letters in Russian.

А а	*А а*	ah	Р р	*Р р*	ehr
Б б	*Б б*	beh	С с	*С с*	ehs
В в	*В в*	veh	Т т	*Т т*	teh
Г г	*Г г*	geh	У у	*У у*	oo
Д д	*Д д*	deh	Ф ф	*Ф ф*	ehf
Е е	*Е е*	yeh	Х х	*Х х*	khah
Ё ё	*Ё ё*	yoh	Ц ц	*Ц ц*	tseh
Ж ж	*Ж ж*	zheh	Ч ч	*Ч ч*	chah
З з	*З з*	zheh	Ш ш	*Ш ш*	shah
И и	*И и*	ee	Щ щ	*Щ щ*	shchah
Й й	*Й й*	ee **kraht**koyeh	Ъ ъ	*ъ*	**tvyor**diy znahk
К к	*К к*	kah	Ы ы	*ы*	yeh**ree**
Л л	*Л л*	ehl	Ь ь	*ь*	**myah**kee znahk
М м	*М м*	ehm	Э э	*Э э*	eh obo**rot**noyeh
Н н	*Н н*	ehn	Ю ю	*Ю ю*	yoo
О о	*О о*	o	Я я	*Я я*	yah
П п	*П п*	peh			

RUSSIAN

Some basic expressions

Yes.	Да.	dah
No.	Нет.	nyeht
Please.	Пожалуйста.	pah**zhah**loostah
Thank you.	Спасибо.	spah**see**bah
Thank you very much.	Большое спасибо.	bahl'**sho**yee spahseebah
That's all right.	Не за что.	nyee zah **shto**

Greetings

Good morning.	Доброе утро.	dobrahyee **oo**tro
Good afternoon.	Добрый день.	dobri **dyehn'**
Good evening.	Добрый вечер.	dobri **vyeh**chyeer
Good night.	Спокойной ночи.	spah**koy**nigh **no**chee
Good-bye.	До свидания.	dah svee**dah**neeyah
See you later.	До встречи.	dah **vstryeh**chee
This is Mr....	Это господин ...	ehtah gahspah**deen**
This is Mrs....	Это госпожа ...	ehtah gahspah**zhah**
This is Miss ...	Это госпожа ...	ehtah gahspah**zhah**
I'm very pleased to meet you.	Очень приятно.	**o**chyeen' pree**yaht**nah
How are you?	Как дела?	kahk dyeh**lah**
Very well, thank you. And you?	Спасибо, хорошо. Как у Вас?	spah**see**bah khahrah**sho** kahk oo **vahs**
Fine.	Прекрасно.	pryee**krahs**nah
Excuse me.	Простите.	prah**stee**tyee

Questions

Where?	Где?	gdyeh
Where is ... ?	Где ... ?	gdyeh
Where are ... ?	Где ... ?	gdyeh
When?	Когда?	kahg**dah**
What?	Что?	shto
How?	Как?	kahk
How much?	Сколько?	**skol**'kah
How many?	Сколько?	**skol**'kah

Who?	**Кто?**	kto
Why?	**Почему?**	pahchyee**moo**
Which?	**Какой?**	kah**koy**
What do you call this?	**Как это называется?**	kahk **eh**tah nahzi**vah**yeetsah
What do you call that?	**Как это называется?**	kahk **eh**tah nahzi**vah**yeetsah
What does this mean?	**Что это значит?**	shto **eh**tah **znah**cheet
What does that mean?	**Что это значит?**	shto **eh**tah **znah**cheet

Do you speak ... ?

Do you speak English?	**Вы говорите по-английски?**	vi gahvah**reet**yee pah ahn**glee**skee
Do you speak German?	**Вы говорите по-немецки?**	vi gahvah**reet**yee pah nyee**myeht**skee
Do you speak French?	**Вы говорите по-французски?**	vi gahvah**reet**yee pah frahnt**soo**skee
Do you speak Spanish?	**Вы говорите по-испански?**	vi gahvah**reet**yee pah ees**pahn**skee
Do you speak Italian?	**Вы говорите по-итальянски?**	vi gahvah**reet**yee pah eetahl'**yahn**skee
Could you speak more slowly, please?	**Могли-бы вы говорить медленнее?**	mah**glee**bi **vi** gahvah**reet' myeh**dlyeenyehyee
Please point to the phrase in the book.	**Покажите мне, пожалуйста, фразу в книге.**	pahkah**zhee**tyee mnyeh pah**zhah**loostah **frah**zoo v **knee**gyee
Just a minute. I'll see if I can find it in this book.	**Минуточку. Я посмотрю, смогу ли я её найти в книжке.**	meenoo**tahch**koo **yah** pahsmah**tryoo** smah**goo**lee yah yee**yo** nigh**tee** v **knee**zhkyee
I understand.	**Я понимаю.**	**yah** pahnyee**mah**yoo
I don't understand.	**Я не понимаю.**	**yah** nyee pahnyee**mah**yoo

Can ... ?

Can I have ... ?	**Можно ... ?**	**mo**zhnah
Can we have ... ?	**Можно ... ?**	**mo**zhnah
Can you show me ... ?	**Вы мне можете показать ... ?**	vi mnyeh **mo**zhyeetyee pahkah**zaht'**

| Can you tell me . . . ? | Вы мне можете сказать . . . ? | vi mnyeh **mo**zhyeetyee skah**zaht'** |
| Can you help me, please? | Пожалуйста помогите мне. | pahzhah**loostah** pahmah**ghee**tyee mnyeh |

Wanting

I'd like . . .	Я хотел бы . . .	yah khah**tyehl** bi
We'd like . . .	Мы хотели бы . . .	mi khah**tyeh**lee bi
Please give me . . .	Дайте мне, пожа- луйста, . . .	**digh**tyee **mnyeh** pahzhah**loostah**
Give it to me, please.	Дайте мне это, пожалуйста.	**digh**tyee mnyeh **eh**tah pahzhah**loostah**
Please bring me . . .	Принесите мне, пожалуйста . . .	preenyee**see**tyee **mnyeh** pahzhah**loostah**
Bring it to me, please.	Принесите мне это, пожалуйста.	preenyee**see**tyee **mnyeh** **eh**tah pahzhah**loostah**
I'm hungry.	Я голодный.	**yah** gah**lo**dni
I'm thirsty.	Мне хочется пить.	**mnyeh** khochyeetsah **peet'**
I'm tired.	Я устал.	**yah** oostahl
I'm lost.	Я заблудился.	**yah** zahbloo**dee**lsah
It's important.	Это важно.	**eh**tah **vahzh**nah
It's urgent.	Это срочно.	**eh**tah **sroch**nah
Hurry up!	Скорее!	skah**ryeh**yee

It is/There is . . .

The words "it is/there is" are often dropped in Russian. For example, the word холодно (**kho**lahdnah) alone conveys the idea "It is cold".

It is/It's . . .	Это . . .	**eh**tah
Is it . . . ?	Это . . . ?	**eh**tah
It isn't . . .	Это не . . .	**eh**tah nyeh
There is/There are . . .	Есть . . .	yehst'
Is there/Are there . . . ?	Есть-ли . . . ?	**yehst'** lee
There isn't/There aren't . . .	Нет ли . . .	nyeht lee
There isn't any/ There aren't any.	Нет ли.	nyeht lee

RUSSIAN

A few common words

big/small	большой/ маленький	bahl'**shoy**/**mah**lyeen'kee
quick/slow	быстро/медленно	**bi**strah/**myeh**dlyeenah
early/late	рано/поздно	**rah**nah/**poz**nah
cheap/expensive	дёшево/дорого	**dyo**shyeevah/**do**rahgah
near/far	близко/далеко	**blees**kah/dahlyeeko
hot/cold	горячо/холодно	gahr**yah**chyo/**kho**lahdnah
full/empty	полный/пустой	**pol**ni/poo**stoy**
easy/difficult	легко/трудно	lyeekh**ko**/**trood**nah
heavy/light	тяжёлый/лёгкий	tyee**zho**li/**lyokh**kee
open/shut	открыто/закрыто	aht**kri**tah/zah**kri**tah
right/wrong	верно/неверно	**vyehr**nah/nyeevyehrnah
old/new	старый/новый	**stah**riy/**no**vi
old/young	старый/молодой	**stah**ri/mahlah**doy**
beautiful/ugly	красиво/уродливо	krah**see**vah/oorodleevah
good/bad	хорошо/плохо	khahrah**sho**/**plo**khah
better/worse	лучше/хуже	**loo**chyee/**khoo**zhyee

Some prepositions and a few more useful words

at	в	v
on	на	nah
in	в	v
to	к	k
from	от	ot
inside	внутри	vnoo**tree**
outside	снаружи	snah**roo**zhee
up	вверх	**vvyeh**rkh
down	вниз	vnees
before	до	do
after	после	**pos**lyee
with	с	s
without	без	byehss
through	через	**chyeh**ryeess
towards	к	k
until	до	do
during	во время	vah **vryeh**myee
and	и	ee
or	или	**ee**lee
not	не	nyeh
nothing	ничего	neechyee**vo**
none	ни один	nyeh ah**deen**

very	очень	**ochyeen'**
also	тоже	**toz**hyee
soon	скоро	**sko**rah
perhaps	может быть	**mozh**yeet bit'
here	здесь	zdyehs'
there	там	tahm
now	теперь	tyee**pyehr'**
then	тогда	tahg**dah**

Arrival

Your passport, please.	Ваш паспорт, пожалуйста.	vahsh **pahs**pahrt pah**zhah**loostah
Here it is.	Пожалуйста.	pah**zhah**loostah
Have you anything to declare?	У Вас есть что-либо заявить для таможни?	oo vahs yehst' **shto**leebah zahyah**veet'** dlyah **tah**mahzhnyee
No, nothing at all.	Нет, ничего.	nyeht nyee**chee**vo
Porter!	Носильщик!	nah**seel'**shcheek
Can you help me with my luggage, please?	Пожалуйста возьмите мой багаж?	pah**zhah**loostah vahz**mee**tyeh moy bah**gahzh**
That's my suitcase.	Это мой чемодан.	**eh**tah moy cheemah**dahn**
Where's the tourist office?	Где бюро Интуриста?	gdyeh bjooro eentoo**ree**stah
This way, please.	Сюда, пожалуйста.	syoo**dah** pah**zhah**loostah

Changing money

Can you change a traveller's cheque, please?	Можете ли Вы разменять аккредитив?	**mo**zhehtyeh lee vi rahz-mye**hnyaht'** ahkryeh-dyee**tyeev**
Where's the nearest bank, please?	Где ближайший банк?	gdyeh blee**zhigh**sheey bahnk

Car rental

I'd like a car.	Мне нужна машина.	mnyeh noozh**nah** mah-**shee**nah
For how long?	На какое время?	nah kah**ko**yeh **vryeh**myah
A day/Four days/ A week/Two weeks.	На день/на четыре дня/на неделю/на две недели.	nah dyehn'/nah chyeht**ryeh** dnyah/nah nyeh**dyeh**lyoo/nah dvyeh nyeh**dyeh**lee

Taxi

Where can I get a taxi?	Где я могу найти такси?	gdyeh yah mah**goo** night-**yee** tahk**see**
What's the fare to . . . ?	Сколько стоит доехать до . . . ?	**skol**'kah **sto**eet dah**yeh**khaht' dah
Take me to this address, please.	Довезите меня по этому адресу, пожалуйста.	dahvee**zee**tyeh myeh**nya** pah **eh**tahmoo **ah**dryehsoo pahz**hah**loostah
I'm in a hurry.	Я спешу.	yah spee**shoo**
Could you drive more slowly, please?	Могли бы Вы ехать медленнее?	mahg**lee** bi vi **yeh**khaht' **myehd**lyehnnyehyeh

Hotel and other accommodation

My name is . . .	Моя фамилия . . .	mah**yah** fah**mee**leeyah . . .
Have you a reservation?	Вы резервировали номер?	vi ryehz**yeh**hr**veer**ahvahlee **no**myehr
Yes, here's the confirmation.	Да, вот подтверждение.	dah vot pahdtv**yeh**hr**zhdyeh**nyeeyeh
We reserved a single room/ a double room.	Мы забронировали одинарный / двойной номер.	mi zahb**ran**yee**rah**vahlee ahd**yee**nahrniy/dvigh**noy** **no**myehr
a room with a bath/with a shower	номер с ванной/с душем	**no**myehr s **vahn**nigh/ s **doo**shahm
What's my room number, please?	Какой у меня номер комнаты?	kah**koy** oo myeh**nyah** **no**myehr **kom**nahti
Number 123.	Номер 123.	**no**myehr 123

Service, please

Who is it?	Кто там?	**kto** tahm
Just a minute, please.	Одну минуту, пожалуйста.	ahd**noo** mee**noo**too pahz**hah**loostah
Come in! The door's open.	Войдите! Дверь открыта.	vigh**dyee**tyeh! dvyehr' ahtk**ri**tah
May we have breakfast in our room?	Можно получить завтрак в нашей комнате?	**mozh**nah pahloo**cheet' zahv**trahk v **nah**shay **kom**nahtyeh

RUSSIAN

Breakfast

I'll have . . .	Я хотел бы . . .	yah khah**tyehl** bi
I'll have some fruit juice.	Я хотел бы фруктовый сок.	yah khah**tyehl** bi frookto-viy sok
a boiled egg	варёное яйцо	vah**ryo**nahyeh yight**so**
a fried egg	яичницу	yah**yeech**nyeetsoo
some bacon/some ham	бекон/ветчину	**byeh**kon/veecheenoo
some toast	тост	tost
a pot of tea	чай в чайничке	chigh v **chigh**nyeechkyeh
a cup of tea	чашку чая	**chahsh**koo **chah**yah
some coffee	кофе	**ko**fyeh
some chocolate	шоколад	shahkah**lahd**
more butter	больше масла	**bol**'sheh **mahs**lah
some hot water	горячей воды	gah**ryah**chyay vah**di**

Difficulties

The central heating doesn't work.	Центральное отопление не работает.	tsehn**trahl**'nahyeh ah-tah**plyeh** nyeeyeh nyeh rah**bo**tahyeht
the light/the socket the tap/the toilet	свет/штепсель кран/туалет	svyeht/**shtehp**sehl' krahn/tooah**lyeht**
There's no hot water.	Нет горячей воды.	nyeht gah**ryah**chyay vah**di**
May I see the manager, please?	Можно поговорить с администра-тором?	**mozh**nah pahgahvah**reet'** s ahdmeenyee**strah**tahrom

Telephone—Mail

There's a call for you.	Вас к телефону.	vahs k tyehlyeh**fo**noo
Hold the line, please.	Подождите у телефона.	pahdahzh**dyee**tyeh oo tyehlyeh**fo**nah
Operator, I've been cut off.	Девушка, нас прервали.	**dyeh**vooshkah nahs pryehr**vah**lee
Did anyone telephone me?	Мне кто-нибудь звонил?	mnyeh **kto**nyeebood' zvah**nyeel**
Is there any mail for me?	Есть для меня почта?	yehst' dlyah myeh**nyah** **poch**tah
Are there any messages for me?	Мне никто не оставил записки?	mnyeh nyee**kto** nyeh ah**stah**veel zah**pees**kee

Checking out

May I have my bill, please?	Могу ли я получить счёт?	mahgoo lee yah pahloocheet' shchyot
We're in a great hurry.	Мы очень спешим.	mi ochehn' speeshim
It's been a very enjoyable stay.	Пребывание было очень приятным.	preebivahnyeeyeh bilah ochehn' preeyahtnim

Eating out

Good evening, sir/ Good evening, madam.	Добрый вечер, господин/ Добрый вечер госпожа.	dobriy vyehchehr gahspahdyeen/dobriy vyehchehr gahspahzhah
Good evening, I'd like a table for two, please.	Добрый вечер. Я хотел бы столик на двоих.	dobriy vyehchehr. yah khahtyehl bi stoleek nah dvahyeekh
Do you have a fixed-price menu?	У Вас есть меню?	oo vahs yehst' mehnyoo
May I see the à la carte menu?	У Вас есть обеденное меню?	oo vahs yehst' ahbyehdyehnnahyeh mehnyoo
May we have an ashtray, please?	Можно попросить пепельницу?	mozhnah pahprahseet' pyehpyehl'nyee tsoo
some bread	хлеб	khlyehb
a fork	вилку	veelkoo
a knife	нож	nozh
a spoon	ложку	lozhkoo
a plate	тарелку	tahryehlkoo
a glass	стакан	stahkahn
a napkin	салфетку	sahlfyehtkoo
another chair	другой стул	droogoy stool
Where's the gentlemen's toilet (men's room)?	Где мужской туалет?	gdyeh moozhskoy tooahlyeht
Where's the ladies' toilet (ladies' room)?	Где женский туалет?	gdyeh zhehnskeey tooahlyeht

Appetizers

| I'd like some . . . | Я хотел бы . . . | yah khahtyehl bi |
| I'd like some assorted appetizers. | Я хотел бы ассорти. | yah khahtyehl bi ahsortyee |

RUSSIAN

orange juice	апельсиновый сок	ahpyehl'**see**nahviy sok
ham	ветчину	veechee**noo**
melon	дыню	**din**yoo
pâté	паштет	pah**shtyeht**
smoked salmon	сёмгу	**syom**goo
shrimps (shrimp)	креветок	kryeh**vyeh**tahk

Soup

Have you any . . . ?	Есть у Вас . . . ?	yehst' oo vahs
Have you any chicken soup?	Есть у Вас суп с курицей?	yehst' oo vahs soop s **koo**reetsay
vegetable soup	овощной суп	ovahshch**noy** soop
onion soup	луковый суп	**loo**kahviy soop

Fish

I'd like some . . .	Я хотел бы . . .	yah khah**tyehl** bi
I'd like some fish.	Я хотел бы рыбу.	yah khah**tyehl** bi **ri**boo
sole	морской язык	mah**rskoy** yah**zik**
trout	форель	fah**rehl'**
lobster	омаров	o**mah**rahv
crayfish	лангуст	lahn**goost**
prawns	креветок	kryeh**vyeh**tahk
I'd like it . . .	Я бы хотел это . . .	yah bi khah**tyehl** **eh**tah
I'd like it steamed.	Я бы хотел это паровое.	yah bi khah**tyehl** **eh**tah pahrah**voyeh**
grilled	жареное на рашпере.	**zhah**ryehnahyeh nah rah**shpyeh**ryeh
boiled	отварное	ahtvahr**noyeh**
baked	печёное	pyeh**chyo**nahyeh
fried	жареное	**zhah**ryehnahyeh

Meat—Poultry—Game

I'd like some . . .	Я бы хотел . . .	yah bi khah**tyehl**
I'd like some beef.	Я бы хотел говядину.	yahbi khah**tyehl** gah**vyah**dyeenoo
a beef steak	бифштекс	beef**shtehks**
some roast beef	ростбиф	rost**beef**
a veal cutlet	телячью котлету	tyeh**lyah**chyoo kaht**lyeh**too

mutton	баранину	bah**rah**nyeenoo
lamb	мясо барашка	**myah**sah bah**rahsh**kah
a pork chop	свиную котлету	sveenooyoo kaht**lyeh**too
roast pork	жареную свинину	**zhah**ryehnooyoo sveen**yee**noo
hare	зайца	**zigh**tsah
chicken	цыплёнка	tsip**lyon**kah
roast chicken	жареного цыплёнка	**zhah**ryehnahvah tsip**lyon**kah
duck	утку	**oot**koo

Vegetables

What vegetables have you got?	Какие овощи у Вас есть?	kah**kee**eyeh **o**vahshchee oo vahs yehst'
I'd like some . . .	Я бы хотел . . .	yah bi khah**tyehl**
I'd like some asparagus.	Я бы хотел спаржу.	yah bi khah**tyehl** **spahr**zhoo
green beans	бобы	**bo**bi
mushrooms	грибы	**gree**bi
carrots	морковь	mahr**kov'**
onions	лук	look
red cabbage	красную капусту	**krahs**nooyoo kah**poo**stoo
spinach	шпинат	shpee**naht**
rice	рис	rees
peas	горох	gah**rokh**
tomatoes	помидоры	pahmee**do**ri
green salad	зелёный салат	zyeh**lyo**niy sah**laht**
potatoes	картофель	kahr**to**fyehl'

Desserts

Nothing more, thanks.	Больше ничего, спасибо.	**bol'**sheh nyeechyeh**vo** spah**see**bah
Just a small portion, please.	Маленькую порцию, пожалуйста.	**mah**lyehn'kooyoo **por**tsiyoo pah**zhah**loostah
Have you any ice-cream?	У Вас есть мороженое?	oo vahs yehst' mah**ro**zhehnahyeh
fruit salad	салат из фруктов	sah**laht** eez **frook**tahv
fresh fruit	свежие фрукты	**svyehzh**iyeh **frook**ti
cheese	сыр	sir

Do I have to change trains?	Мне надо будет делать пересадку.	mnyeh **nah**dah **boo**dyeht dyeh**l**aht' peereesahdkoo
What platform does the train leave from?	С какой платформы отправляется поезд?	s kah**koy** plaht**form**i ahtprahv**lya**hyehtsah **po**yehzd
Where's the nearest underground station?	Где ближайшая станция метро?	gdyeh blee**zhigh**shahyah **stahn**tsiyah myeh**tro**
Where's the bus station, please?	Где автобусная остановка?	gdyeh ahv**to**boosnahyah ahstah**nov**kah
When's the first bus to . . . ?	Когда идёт первый автобус в . . . ?	kahg**dah** ee**dyot** **pyehr**viy ahv**to**boos v
the last bus	последний автобус	pah**slyehd**nyeey ahv**to**boos
the next bus	следующий автобус	**slyeh**dooshshcheey ahv**to**boos
Please let me off at the next stop.	Дайте мне выйти на следующей остановке, пожалуйста.	**digh**tyeh mnyeh **viy**tee nah **slyeh**dooshchay ahstah**nov**kee pah**zhah**loo-stah

RUSSIAN

Relaxing

What's on at the cinema (movies)?	Что идёт в кино?	shto ee**dyot** v kee**no**
What's on at the theatre?	Что идёт в театре?	shto ee**dyot** v tyeh**ah**tryeh
What time does the film begin?	Когда начинается фильм?	kahg**dah** nahchee**nah**yehtsah feel'm
And the play?	А пьеса?	ah **pyeh**sah
Are there any tickets for tonight?	Есть билеты на вечер?	yehst' beel**yeh**ti nah **vyeh**chehr
Where can we go dancing?	Куда можно пойти танцевать?	koo**dah mozh**nah pigh**tyee** tahntsi**vaht'**
Would you like to dance?	Хотите ли вы потанцевать?	khat**yee**tyeh lee vi pahtahntsi**vaht'**

Introductions

How do you do?	Добрый день?	**dobr**iy dyehn'
How are you?	Как поживаете?	kahk pahzhi**vah**yehtyeh
Very well, thank you. And you?	Спасибо, очень хорошо. А Вы?	spah**see**bah **o**chehn' khahrah**sho**. ah vi
May I introduce Miss Philips?	Разрешите представить мисс филипс?	rahzree**shi**tyeh pryehd**stah**veet' Miss Philips
My name is . . .	Меня зовут . . .	myeh**nyah** zah**voot**
I'm very pleased to meet you.	Очень приятно.	**o**chehn' pree**yaht**nah
How long have you been here?	Вы давно уже здесь?	vi dah**vno** oo**zheh** zdyehs'
It was nice meeting you.	Было очень приятно с Вами встретиться.	**bi**lah **o**chehn' pree**yaht**nah s **vah**mee **vstryeh**teetsah

Dating

Would you like a cigarette?	Хотите сигарету?	khah**tyee**tyeh seegah**ryeh**too
May I get you a drink?	Хотите что-нибудь выпить?	khah**tyee**tyeh **shto**nyeebood' **vi**peet'
Do you have a light, please?	У Вас есть спички?	vahs yehst' **speech**kee
Are you free this evening?	Вы свободны сегодня вечером?	vi svah**bod**ni seevo**d**nyah **vyeh**chehrahm
Where shall we meet?	Где мы встретимся?	gdyeh mi **vstryeh**tyeemsyah
What time shall I meet you?	Когда я Вас встречу?	kahg**dah** yah vahs **vstryeh**choo
Thank you, it's been a wonderful evening.	Спасибо, это был чудесный вечер.	spah**see**bah, **eh**tah bil choo**dyehs**niy **vyeh**chehr
What time is your last train?	Когда уходит Ваш последний поезд?	kahg**dah** oo**kho**dyeet vahsh pah**slyehd**nyeey **po**yehzd
Good-night . . .	Доброй ночи . . .	**do**brigh **no**chee

Banks

Where's the nearest bank, please?	Где ближайший банк?	gdyeh bleezhighshiy bahnk
Where can I cash some traveller's cheques?	Где я могу обменять аккредитивы?	gdyeh yah mahgoo ahbmyehnyaht' ahkryehdyeetyeevi
What time does the bank open/What time does it close?	Когда открывается банк/когда он закрывается?	kahgdah ahtkrivahyehtsah bahnk/kahgdah on zahkrivahyehtsah
I'm expecting some money from home. Has it arrived?	Я жду деньги из дому. Они прибыли?	yah zhdoo dyehn'ghee eezdahmoo. ahnyee preebilee
Can you give me some small change, please?	Дайте мне, пожалуйста, мелочью?	dightyeh mnyeh pahzhahloostah myehlahchyo

Shops, stores and services

Where is the nearest chemist (pharmacy)?	Где ближайшая аптека?	gdyeh bleezhighshahyah ahptyehkah
the nearest hairdresser's	ближайшая парикмахерская	bleezhighshahyah pahreekmahkhehrskahyah
the photo shop	фотомагазин	fotomahgahzeen
the jeweller's	ювелирный магазин	yooveeleerniy mahgahzeen
the department store	универмаг	oonyeevyehrmahg
the police station	отделение милиции	ahtdyehlyehnyeeyeh meeleetsiee
the garage	гараж	gahrahzh
How do I get there?	Как мне туда проехать?	kahk mnyeh toodah prahyehkhaht'
Is it within walking distance?	Можно дойти пешком?	mozhnah dightyee peeshkom

Service

Can you help me, please?	Помогите мне, пожалуйста?	pahmahgheetyeh mnyeh pahzhahloostah
Can you show me this? And that, too.	Покажите мне, пожалуйста, это. И то тоже.	pahkahzhityeh mnyeh pahzhahloostah ehtah. ee to tozheh
It's too expensive/ too big/too small.	Это слишком дорого/слишком велико/слишком мало.	ehtah sleeshkahm dorahgah/sleeshkahm vyehleeko/sleeshkahm mahlo

Can you show me some more?	Вы мне можете показать еще?	vi mnyeh **mo**zhehtyeh pahkah**zaht'** yehsh**chyo**
something better	Что-нибудь получше	**shton**yeebood' pah**looch**sheh
something cheaper	Что-нибудь подешевле	**shton**yeebood' pahdyee**sheh**vlee
How much is this? And that?	Сколько стоит это? И то?	**skol'**kah **sto**eet **eh**tah? ee to?
It's not quite what I want.	Это не совсем то, что я хочу.	**eh**tah nyeh sahv**syehm** to shto yah khah**choo**
I like it.	Это мне нравится.	**eh**tah mnyeh **nrah**veetsah.

Chemist's (Pharmacy)

| I'd like something for a cold/for a cough/for travel sickness. | Я хотел бы что-нибудь от простуды/от кашля/от морской болезни. | yah khah**tyehl** bi **shton**yeebood' aht prah**stoo**di/aht **kahsh**lyah/aht mar**skoy** bal'**yehz**ni |
| Can you recommend something for hay-fever/for sunburn? | Что Вы мне можете рекомендовать от сенной лихорадки/от ожогов? | shto vi mnyeh **mo**zhehtyeh ryehkah-myehndah**vaht'** aht **syehn**nigh leekhah**rahd**kee/aht a**zho**gav |

Toiletry

May I have some razor blades?	У Вас есть лезвия для бритья?	oo vahs yehst' **lyehz**-veeyah dlyah bree**tyah**
some shaving cream	крем для бритья	kryehm dlyah bree**tyah**
some toothpaste	зубная паста	zoob**nah**yah **pah**stah
I'd like some soap.	Мне нужно мыло.	mnyeh **noo**zhnah milah
some suntan oil	крем для загара	kryehm dlyah zah**gah**rah

At the barber's

I'd like a haircut, please.	Я хотел бы постричься.	yah khah**tyehl** bi pah**streech**syah
Short/Leave it long.	Коротко/оставьте длинные.	**ko**rahtkah/ah**stahv'**tyeh **dleen**niyeh
A razor cut, please.	Бритвой, пожалуйста.	**breet**vigh pah**zhahl**oostah

At the hairdresser's

I'd like a shampoo and set, please.	Помойте голову и сделайте укладку, пожалуйста.	pah**moy**tyeh **go**lahvoo ee **sdyeh**lightyeh oo**klahd**koo pah**zhah**loostah
I'd like a bleach.	Мне нужно обесцвечивание.	mnyeh **noozh**nah ahbyeh-**stsvyeh**cheevahnyeeyeh.
a permanent	перманент	pyehrmah**nyehnt**
a colour rinse	оттеночное полоскание	aht**tyeh**nahchnahyeh pahlah**skahn**yeeyeh
a manicure	маникюр	mahnyee**kyoor**

Photography

| I'd like a film for this camera. | Мне нужна плёнка для этого аппарата. | mnyeh **noozh**nah **plyon**kah dlyah **eh**tahvah ahpah**rah**tah. |
| This camera doesn't work. | Этот аппарат не работает. | **eh**taht ahpah**raht** nyeh rah**bo**tahyeht. |

At the post office

| Where's the nearest post office, please? | Где ближайшая почта? | gdyeh blee**zhigh**shahyah **poch**tah |
| I'd like to send this by express (special delivery)/by air mail. | Я хотел бы послать это срочно/авиапочтой. | yah khah**tyehl** bi pah**slaht'** **eh**tah **sroch**nah/ahveeah**poch**tigh |

Service stations

Where is the nearest service station, please?	Где ближайшая станция обслуживания?	gdyeh blee**zhigh**shahyah **stahn**tsiyah ahb**sloozhi**vahnyeeyah
Fill her up, please.	Полный, пожалуйста.	**pol**niy pah**zhah**loostah
Check the oil, please.	Проверьте масло, пожалуйста.	prah**vyehr'**tyeh **mahs**lah pah**zhah**loostah
Would you check the tyres?	Проверьте шины, пожалуйста?	prah**vyehr'**tyeh **shi**ni pah**zhah**loostah

RUSSIAN

244

Street directions

Can you show me on the map where I am?	Вы мне можете показать на карте, где я?	vi mnyeh **mozhehtyeh** pahkah**zaht**' nah **kahr**tyeh gdyeh yah
You're on the wrong road.	Вы едете неверно.	vi **yeh**dyehtyeh nyeh**vyehr**nah
Go back to ...	Вернитесь назад к ...	vyehr**nyeetyehs**' nah**zahd** k
Go straight ahead.	Вам надо прямо.	vahm **nah**dah **pryah**mah
It's on the left/on the right.	Это слева/справа.	**eh**tah **slyeh**vah/**sprah**vah

Accidents

May I use your telephone?	Можно позвонить по Вашему телефону?	**mozh**nah pahzvah**nyeet**' pah **vah**shehmoo tyehlyeh**fo**noo
Call a doctor quickly.	Быстро вызовите доктора.	**bist**rah vi**zah**veetyeh **dok**tahrah
Call an ambulance.	Вызовите санитарную машину.	vi**zah**veetyeh sahnyee-**tahr**nooyoo mah**shi**noo
Please call the police.	Вызовите милицию.	vi**zhah**veetyeh mee**leet**siyoo

Numbers

one	один	ah**dyeen**
two	два	dvah
three	три	tree
four	четыре	chee**ti**ryeh
five	пять	pyaht'
six	шесть	shehst'
seven	семь	syehm'
eight	восемь	**vo**syehm'
nine	девять	**dyeh**vyaht'
ten	десять	**dyeh**syaht'
eleven	одиннадцать	ah**dyee**nahtsaht'
twelve	двенадцать	dvee**nahts**aht'
thirteen	тринадцать	tree**nahtt**saht'
fourteen	четырнадцать	chyeh**tir**nahtsaht'
fifteen	пятнадцать	pyaht**nahts**aht'
sixteen	шестнадцать	shehst'**nahts**aht'
seventeen	семнадцать	syehm**nahts**aht'
eighteen	восемнадцать	vahseem**nahts**aht'

RUSSIAN

nineteen	девятнадцать	dyehvyaht**naht**saht'
twenty	двадцать	**dvah**tsaht'
twenty-one	двадцать один	**dvah**tsaht' ah**dyeen**
thirty	тридцать	**tree**tsaht'
forty	сорок	**so**rahk
fifty	пятвдесят	peedyee**syaht**
sixty	шестьдесят	shehs'dyeh**syaht**
seventy	семьдесят	**syehm**'dyehsyaht
eighty	восемьдесят	**vo**syehm'dyehsyaht
ninety	девяносто	dyehvyah**nos**tah
one hundred	сто	sto
one thousand	тысяча	**ti**syahchah
ten thousand	десять тысяч	**dyeh**syaht' **ti**syahch

Days

It's Sunday.	Воскресенье	vahskryeh**syehn**'yeh
Monday	Понедельник	pahnyee**dyehl**'nyeek
Tuesday	Вторник	**vtor**nyeek
Wednesday	Среда	sryeh**dah**
Thursday	Четверг	chyehtvyehrg
Friday	Пятница	**pyaht**nyeetsah
Saturday	Суббота	soo**bo**tah
yesterday	вчера	vchyeh**rah**
today	сегодня	syeh**vod**nyah
tomorrow	завтра	**zahv**trah
morning/afternoon	утро/после обеда	**oo**trah/**pos**lyeh ah**byeh**dah
evening/night	вечер/ночь	**vyeh**chyehr/noch'

Months

January	январь	yahn**vahr**'
February	февраль	fyeh**vrahl**'
March	март	mahrt
April	апрель	ah**pryehl**'
May	май	migh
June	июнь	eey**oon**'
July	июль	eey**ool**'
August	август	**ahv**goost
September	сентябрь	syehn**tyahbr**'
October	октябрь	ahk**tyahbr**'
November	ноябрь	nah**yahbr**'
December	декабрь	dyeh**kahbr**'
Happy New Year!	Счастливого Нового Года!	schah**stlee**vahvah **no**vahvah **go**dah

RUSSIAN

SERBO-CROATIAN

Guide to Pronunciation

Note that Serbo-Croatian has some diacritical letters—with accent marks—which we do not know in English. On the other hand, **q**, **w**, **x** and **y** do not exist in Serbo-Croatian. A basic rule for handling Serbo-Croatian might be: pronounce it as it's written—every letter is pronounced, and its pronunciation is always the same, regardless of its position in a word.

Letter	Approximate pronunciation	Symbol	Example	
Consonants				
b	like **b** in **b**rother	b	**brat**	braht
c	like **ts** in **ts**e-**ts**e	ts	**cesta**	**tse**hsstah
č	like **ch** in **ch**urch	ch	**čuti**	**choo**tee
ć	like **ch** in **ch**eap (a little further forward in the mouth than **č**; called a "soft" **č**)	ch	**ćerka**	**chehr**kah
d	like **d** in **d**own	d	**dole**	**dol**eh

dž	like j in June	j	džem	jehm
dj	like j in jeep (a "soft" dž); also written đ	j	djak	jahk
f	like f in father	f	figura	feegoorah
g	like g in go	g	gde	gdeh
h	like h in house	h	hleb	hlehb
j	like y in yoke	y	ja	yah
k	like k in key	k	kuća	koochah
l	like l in lip	l	lep	lehp
lj	like l in failure	l^y	ljubav	l^yoobahv
m	like m in mouth	m	most	most
n	like n in not	n	ne	neh
nj	like ni in onion	ñ	njegov	ñehgov
p	like p in put	p	policija	poleetseeyah
r	like r in rope	r	reka	rehkah
s	like s in sister	s/ss	sestra	sehsstrah
š	like sh in ship	sh	šta	shtah
t	like t in top	t	tamo	tahmo
v	like v in very	v	vrlo	verlo
z	like z in zip	z	zvezda	zvehzdah
ž	like s in pleasure	zh	želim	zhehleem

Note: The letter r can also act as a vowel, as for example, in the word **vrlo** or in the name of the island **Krk**; in this case, it should be pronounced rather like a Scottish r, e.g., **Krk** is pronounced kerk.

Vowels

a	like a in car	ah	sat	saht
e	like e in get	eh	svet	sveht
i	like i in it	ee	iz	eez
o	like o in hot	o	ovde	ovdeh
u	like oo in boom	oo	put	poot

The alphabet

Two different alphabets are used in Yugoslavia. Our Roman alphabet is in use in Slovenia and Croatia; elsewhere the Cyrillic alphabet (more or less like the Russian one) is dominant. Given below are the characters which the Cyrillic alphabet, as used in Yugoslavia, comprises. The column at left shows the printed capital and small letters while written letters are shown in the center column. At right the corresponding letters are shown in the Roman alphabet which we're using in this book.

Printed		Written		Roman
А	а	*A*	*a*	a
Б	б	*Б*	*б*	b
Ц	ц	*Ц*	*ц*	c
Ч	ч	*Ч*	*ч*	č
Ћ	ћ	*h*	*h*	ć
Д	д	*Д*	*g*	d
Џ	џ	*Џ*	*џ*	dž (cap. **Dž**)
Ђ	ђ	*ђ*	*ђ*	dj or đ (cap. **Dj** or **Đ**)
Е	е	*Е*	*е*	e
Ф	ф	*ф*	*ф*	f
Г	г	*Г*	*i*	g
Х	х	*X*	*x*	h
И	и	*И*	*u*	i
Ј	ј	*J*	*j*	j
К	к	*K*	*к*	k
Л	л	*Л*	*л*	l
Љ	љ	*љ*	*љ*	lj (cap. **Lj**)
М	м	*M*	*м*	m
Н	н	*Н*	*н*	n
Њ	њ	*њ*	*њ*	nj (cap. **Nj**)
О	о	*O*	*o*	o
П	п	*П*	*ū*	p
Р	р	*Р*	*р*	r
С	с	*С*	*с*	s
Ш	ш	*Ш*	*ш*	š
Т	т	*Т*	*ū*	t
У	у	*У*	*y*	u
В	в	*B*	*в*	v
З	з	*З*	*з*	z
Ж	ж	*Ж*	*ж*	ž

Some basic expressions

Yes.	**Da.**	dah
No.	**Ne.**	neh
Please.	**Molim.**	moleem
Thank you.	**Hvala.**	hvahlah
Thank you very much.	**Hvala Vam mnogo.**	hvahlah vahm mnogo
That's all right.	**Molim.**	moleem

Greetings

Good morning.	**Dobro jutro.**	dobro yootro
Good afternoon.	**Dobar dan.**	dobahr dahn
Good evening.	**Dobro veče.**	dobro vehcheh
Good night.	**Laku noć.**	lahkoo noch
Good-bye.	**Zbogom.**	zbogom
See you later.	**Dovidjenja.**	doveejehnyah
This is Mr....	**Ovo je Gospodin...**	ovo yeh gospodeen
This is Mrs....	**Ovo je Gospodja...**	ovo yeh gospojah
This is Miss...	**Ovo je Gospodjica...**	ovo yeh gospojeetsa
I'm very pleased to meet you.	**Milo mi je da sam Vas upoznao.**	meelo mee yeh dah sahm vahss oopoznaho
How are you?	**Kako ste?**	kahko steh
Very well, thank you.	**Hvala, vrlo dobro.**	hvahlah verlo dobro
And you?	**A Vi?**	ah vee
Fine.	**Dobro.**	dobro
Excuse me.	**Izvinite.**	eezveehneehteh

Questions

Where?	**Gde?**	gdeh
Where is...?	**Gde je...?**	gdeh yeh
Where are...?	**Gde su...?**	gdeh soo
When?	**Kad?**	kahd
What?	**Šta?**	shtah

SERBO-CROATIAN

How?	**Kako?**	kahko
How much?	**Koliko?**	koleeko
How many?	**Koliko?**	koleeko
Who?	**Ko?..**	ko
Why?	**Zašto?**	zahshto
Which?	**Koji/Koja/Koje?**	koyee/koyah/koyeh
What do you call this?	**Kako se ovo zove?**	kahko seh ovo zoveh
What do you call that?	**Kako se zove ono?**	kahko seh zoveh ono
What does this mean?	**Šta ovo znači?**	shtah ovo znahchee
What does that mean?	**Šta ono znači?**	shtah ono znahchee

Do you speak . . . ?

Do you speak English?	**Govorite li engleski?**	govoreeteh lee ehnglehskee
Do you speak German?	**Govorite li nemački?**	govoreeteh lee nehmahchkee
Do you speak French?	**Govorite li francuski?**	govoreeteh lee frahntsooskee
Do you speak Spanish?	**Govorite li španski?**	govoreeteh lee shpahnskee
Do you speak Italian?	**Govorite li italijanski?**	govoreeteh lee eetahleeyahnskee
Could you speak more slowly, please?	**Možete li govoriti sporije molim Vas?**	mozhehteh lee govoreeteh sporeeyeh moleem vahss
Please point to the phrase in the book.	**Pokažite mi molim Vas tu frazu u knjizi.**	pokahzheeteh mee moleem vahss too frahzoo oo kñeezee
Just a minute. I'll see if I can find it in this book.	**Samo trenutak. Videću da li mogu da je nadjem u knjizi.**	sahmo trehnootahk. veedehchoo dah lee mogoo dah yeh nahjehm oo kñeezee
I understand.	**Razumem.**	rahzoomehm
I don't understand.	**Ne razumem.**	neh rahzoomehm

Can ... ?

Can I have ... ?	**Mogu li dobiti ... ?**	mogoo lee dobeetee
Can we have ... ?	**Možemo li dobiti ... ?**	mozhehmo lee dobeetee
Can you show me ... ?	**Možete li mi pokazati ... ?**	mozhehteh lee mee pokahzahtee
Can you tell me ... ?	**Možete li mi reći ... ?**	mozhehteh lee mee rehchee
Can you help me, please?	**Možete li mi pomoći molim Vas?**	mozhehteh lee mee pomochee moleem vahss

Wanting

I'd like ...	**Želeo bih ...**	zhehleho beeh
We'd like ...	**Želeli bismo ...**	zhehlehlee beessmo
Please give me ...	**Molim Vas dajte mi ...**	moleem vahss dahyteh mee
Give it to me, please.	**Dajte mi to molim Vas.**	dahyteh mee to moleem vahss
Please bring me ...	**Molim Vas donesite mi ...**	moleem vahss donehseeteh mee
Bring it to me, please.	**Donesite mi to molim Vas.**	donehseeteh mee to moleem vahss
I'm hungry.	**Gladan sam.**	glahdahn sahm
I'm thirsty.	**Žedan sam.**	zhehdahn sahm
I'm tired.	**Umoran sam.**	oomorahn sahm
I'm lost.	**Zalutao sam.**	zahlootaho sahm
It's important.	**Važno je.**	vahzhno yeh
It's urgent.	**Hitno je.**	heetno yeh
Hurry up!	**Požurite!**	pozhooreeteh

It is/There is ...

It is/It's ...	**To je ...**	to yeh
Is it ... ?	**Da li je to ... ?**	dah lee yeh to
It isn't ...	**To nije ...**	to neeyeh
There is/There are ...	**Ima ...**	eemah
Is there/Are there ... ?	**Ima li ... ?**	eemah lee

There isn't/There aren't...	**Nema ...**	**neh**mah
There isn't any/ There aren't any.	**Nema.**	**neh**mah

A few common words

big/small	**veliko/malo**	**veh**leeko/**mah**lo
quick/slow	**brzo/sporo**	**ber**zo/**spo**ro
early/late	**rano/kasno**	**rah**no/**kahs**no
cheap/expensive	**jeftino/skupo**	**yehf**teeno/**skoo**po
near/far	**blizu/daleko**	**blee**zoo/**dah**lehko
hot/cold	**vruće/hladno**	**vroo**cheh/**hlah**dno
full/empty	**puno/prazno**	**poo**no/**prah**znoh
easy/difficult	**lako/teško**	**lah**ko/**tehsh**ko
heavy/light	**teško/lako**	**tehsh**ko/**lah**ko
open/shut	**otvoreno/zatvoreno**	**ot**vorehno/**zaht**vorehno
right/wrong	**tačno/pogrešno**	**tahch**no/**po**greshno
old/new	**staro/novo**	**stah**ro/**no**vo
old/young	**star/mlad**	**stahr**/**mlahd**
beautiful/ugly	**lepo/ružno**	**leh**po/**rooz**hno
good/bad	**dobro/loše**	**do**bro/**lo**sheh
better/worse	**bolje/lošije**	**bol**^{y}eh/**lo**sheeyeh

Some prepositions and a few more useful words

at	**kod**	kod
on	**na**	nah
in	**u**	oo
to	**ka**	kah
from	**od**	od
inside	**unutra**	oo**noo**trah
outside	**napolju**	nah**pol**^{y}oo
up	**gore**	**go**reh
down	**dole**	**do**leh
before	**pre**	preh
after	**posle**	**pos**leh
with	**sa**	sah
without	**bez**	behz
through	**kroz**	kroz
towards	**prema**	**preh**mah
until	**do**	do
during	**za vreme**	zah **vreh**meh
and	**i**	ee
or	**ili**	**ee**lee
not	**ne**	neh
nothing	**ništa**	**neesh**tah

none	ni jedan	nee **yeh**dahn
very	vrlo	**ver**lo
also	takodje	**tah**kojeh
soon	uskoro	**oos**skoro
perhaps	možda	**mozh**dah
here	ovde	**ov**deh
there	tamo	**tah**mo
now	sada	**sah**dah
then	tada	**tah**dah

Arrival

Your passport, please.	Vaš pasoš, molim Vas.	vahsh **pah**sosh **mol**eem vahss
Here it is.	Izvolite.	eez**vol**eeteh
Have you anything to declare?	Imate li nešto za carinu?	**ee**mahteh lee **neh**shto zah **tsah**reenoo
No, nothing at all.	Ne, nemam ništa.	neh **neh**mahm **nee**shtah
Porter!	Nosač!	**no**sahch
Can you help me with my luggage, please?	Možete li mi poneti prtljag, molim Vas?	**mo**zhehteh lee mee **po**nehtee **pert**l^yahg **mol**eem vahss
That's my suitcase.	To je moj kofer.	to yeh moy **ko**fehr
Where's the bus to the centre of town, please?	Gde je autobus za centar grada, molim Vas?	gdeh yeh ahoo**to**booss zah **tsehn**tar **grah**dah **mol**eem vahss
This way, please.	Ovuda, izvolite.	o**voo**dah eez**vol**eeteh

Changing money

| Can you change a traveller's cheque, please? | Možete li promeniti putni ček, molim Vas? | **mo**zhehteh lee pro**meh**neetee **poot**nee chehk **mol**eem vahss |
| Where's the nearest bank, please? | Gde je najbliža banka, molim Vas? | gdeh yeh **nahy**bleezhah **bahn**kah **mol**eem vahss |

Car rental

I'd like a car.	Želeo bih kola.	**zheh**leho beeh **ko**lah
For how long?	Za koliko dugo?	zah **ko**leeko **doo**go
A day/Four days/ A week/Two weeks.	Jedan dan/Četiri dana/Nedelju dana/Dve nedelje.	**yeh**dahn dahn/**cheh**teeree **dah**nah/**neh**dehl^y oo **dah**nah/dveh **neh**dehl^yeh

Taxi

Where can I get a taxi?	**Gde mogu da dobijem taksi?**	gdeh mogoo dah dobeeyehm tahksee
What's the fare to...?	**Koliko staje do...?**	koleeko stahyeh do
Take me to this address, please.	**Odvezite me na ovu adresu, molim Vas.**	odvehzeeteh meh nah ovoo ahdrehssoo moleem vahss
I'm in a hurry.	**Žurim se.**	zhooreem seh
Could you drive more slowly, please?	**Da li biste mogli da vozite malo sporije, molim Vas?**	dah lee beesteh moglee dah vozeeteh mahlo sporeeyeh moleem vahss

Hotel and other accommodation

My name is...	**Ja se zovem...**	yah seh zovehm
Have you a reservation?	**Imate li rezervaciju?**	eemahteh lee rehzehrvahtseeyoo
Yes, here's the confirmation.	**Da, izvolite potvrdu.**	dah eezvoleeteh potverdoo
I'd like...	**Želeo bih...**	zhehleho beeh
I'd like a single room/a double room.	**Želeo bih sobu sa jednim krevetom/sa dva kreveta.**	zhehleho beeh soboo sah yehdneem krehvehtom/sah dvah krehvehtah
a room with a bath/ with a shower	**sobu sa kupatilom/ sa tušem**	soboo sah koopahteelom/ sah tooshehm

How much?

What's the price per night/per week/per month?	**Koliko staje za jednu noć/jednu nedelju/mesec?**	koleeko stahyeh zah yehdnoo noch/yehdnoo nehdehlʸoo/mehssehts
May I see the room?	**Mogu li da vidim sobu?**	mogoo lee dah veedeem soboo
I'm sorry, I don't like it.	**Nažalost ne dopada mi se.**	nahzhahlost neh dopahdah mee seh
Yes, that's fine. I'll take it.	**Da, dobra je, uzeću je.**	dah dobrah yeh oozehchoo yeh
What's my room number, please?	**Koji je broj moje sobe?**	koyee yeh broy moyeh sobeh
Number 123.	**Broj 123.**	broy 123

Service, please

Who is it?	Ko je?	ko yeh
Just a minute.	Samo jedan trenutak.	sahmo yehdahn trehnootahk
Come in! The door's open.	Udjite! Vrata su otvorena.	oojeeteh. vrahtah soo otvorehnah
May we have breakfast in our room?	Možemo li dobiti doručak u sobi?	mozhehmo lee dobeetee doroochahk oo sobee

Breakfast

I'll have . . .	Želeo bih . . .	zhehleho beeh
I'll have some fruit juice.	Želeo bih voćni sok.	zhehleho beeh vochnee sok
a boiled egg	jedno kuvano jaje	yehdno koovahno yahyeh
a fried egg	jedno prženo jaje	yehdno perzhehno yahyeh
some bacon/some ham	slaninu/šunku	slahneenoo/shoonkoo
some toast	tost	tost
a pot of tea	lonče čaja	loncheh chahyah
a cup of tea	šoljicu čaja	sholʸeetsoo chahyah
some coffee	kafu	kahfoo
some chocolate	čokoladu	chokolahdoo
more butter	još malo putera	yosh mahlo pootehrah
some hot water	vruće vode	vroocheh vodeh

Difficulties

The central heating doesn't work.	Centralno grejanje ne radi.	tsentrahlno grehyahñeh neh rahdee
the light/the socket the tap/the toilet	svetlo/utikač slavina (pipa)/toalet	svehtlo/ooteekahch slahveenah (peepah)/ toahleht
There's no hot water.	Nema tople vode.	nehmah topleh vodeh
May I see the manager, please?	Želeo bih da govorim sa šefom, molim Vas.	zhehleho beeh dah govoreem sah shehfom moleem vahss

Telephone—Mail

There's a call for you.	Imate telefonski poziv.	eemahteh tehlehfonskee pozeey
Hold the line, please.	Ostanite na telefonu, molim Vas.	ostahneeteh nah tehlehfonoo moleem vahss

Operator, I've been cut off.	**Gospodjice, veza se prekinula.**	**goss**pojeetseh **veh**zah seh **preh**keenoolah
Did anyone telephone me?	**Da li me neko tražio telefonom?**	dah lee meh **neh**ko trahzheeo tehlehfonom
Is there any mail for me?	**Ima li pošte za mene?**	**ee**mah lee **posh**teh zah **meh**neh
Are there any messages for me?	**Ima li neka poruka za mene?**	**ee**mah lee **neh**kah **po**rookah zah **meh**neh

Checking out

May I have my bill, please?	**Molim Vas račun.**	**mo**leem vahss **rah**choon
We're in a great hurry.	**Jako se žurimo.**	**yah**ko seh **zhoo**reemo
It's been a very enjoyable stay.	**Boravak je bio vrlo prijatan.**	**bo**rahvahk yeh **bee**o verlo **pree**yahtahn

Eating out

Good evening, sir/ Good evening, madam.	**Dobro veče Gospodine/Dobro veče Gospodjo.**	**do**bro **veh**cheh gospodeeneh/**do**bro **veh**cheh gospojo
Good evening. I'd like a table for two, please.	**Dobro veče. Hteo bih sto za dvoje molim Vas.**	**do**bro **veh**cheh. **hte**ho beeh sto zah **dvo**yeh **mo**leem vahss
Do you have a fixed-price menu?	**Imate li meni?**	**ee**mahteh lee **meh**nee
May I see the à la carte menu?	**Mogu li da dobijem jelovnik?**	**mo**goo lee dah **do**beeyehm **yeh**lovneek
May we have an ashtray, please?	**Molim Vas pepeljaru.**	**mo**leem vahss **peh**pehl^yahroo
some bread	**hleb**	hlehb
a fork	**viljušku**	veel^yooshkoo
a knife	**nož**	nozh
a spoon	**kašiku**	**kah**sheekoo
a plate	**tanjir**	**tah**ñeer
a glass	**čašu**	**chah**shoo
a napkin	**salvetu**	**sahl**vehtoo
another chair	**još jednu stolicu**	yosh **yehd**noo **sto**leetsoo
Where's the gentlemen's toilet (men's room)?	**Gde je toalet za muškarce?**	gdeh yeh **to**ahleht zah **moosh**kahrtseh
Where's the ladies' toilet (ladies' room)?	**Gde je toalet za žene?**	gdeh yeh **to**ahleht zah **zheh**neh

Appetizers

I'd like some...	Hteo bih...	hteho beeh
I'd like some assorted appetizers.	Hteo bih mešano predjelo.	hteho beeh mehshahno prehdyehlo
orange juice	sok od pomorandže	sok od pomorahnjeh
ham	šunku	shoonkoo
melon	dinju	deeñoo
pâté	paštetu	pahshtehtoo
smoked salmon	dimljenog lososa	deeml^yehnog lossossah
shrimps (shrimp)	račiće	rahcheecheh

Soup

Have you any...?	Imate li...?	eemahteh lee
Have you any chicken soup?	Imate li pileću čorbu?	eemahteh lee peelehchoo chorboo
vegetable soup	čorbu od povrća	chorboo od poverchah
onion soup	čorbu od luka	chorboo od lookah

Fish

I'd like some...	Hteo bih...	hteho beeh
I'd like some fish.	Hteo bih ribu.	hteho beeh reeboo
sole	tabinju	tahbeeñoo
trout	pastrmku	pahstermkoo
lobster	jastoga	yahstogah
crayfish	rak	rahk
prawns	kozice	kozeetseh
I'd like it...	Želeo bih...	zhehleho beeh
I'd like it steamed.	Spremljenu na pari.	sprehml^yehnoo nah pahree
grilled	na roštilju	nah roshteel^yoo
boiled	kuvanu	koovahnoo
baked	pečenu	pehchehnoo
fried	prženu	perzhehnoo

Meat—Poultry—Game

I'd like some...	Želeo bih...	zhehleho beeh
I'd like some beef.	Želeo bih govedinu.	zhehleho beeh govehdeenoo
a beef steak	govedju šniclu	govehjoo shneetsloo
some roast beef	govedje pečenje	govehjeh pehchehñeh

a veal cutlet	teleći kotlet	tehlehchee kotleht
mutton	ovčetinu	ovchehteenoo
lamb	jagnjetinu	yahgñehteenoo
a pork chop	svinjski kotlet	sveeñskee kotleht
roast pork	svinjsko pečenje	sveeñsko pehchehñeh
hare	zečetinu	zehchehteenoo
chicken	piletinu	peelehteenoo
roast chicken	pečenu piletinu	pehchehnoo peelehteenoo
duck	patku	pahtkoo

How do you like your meat?	Kako pečeno želite meso?	kahko pehchehno zhehleeteh mehsso
rare	polu-pečeno	poloo pehchehno
medium	srednje pečeno	srehdñeh pehchehno
well done	dobro pečeno	dobro pehchehno

Vegetables

What vegetables have you got?	Kakvo povrće imate?	kahkvo povercheh eemahteh
I'd like some ...	Želeo bih ...	zhehleho beeh
I'd like some asparagus.	Želeo bih špargle.	zhehleho beeh shpahrgleh
green beans	boraniju (mahune)	borahneeyoo (mah-hooneh)
mushrooms	pečurke	pehchoorkeh
carrots	šargarepu	shahrgahrehpoo
onions	luk	look
red cabbage	crveni kupus	tservehnee koopooss
spinach	spanać (špinat)	spahnahch (shpeenaht)
rice	pirinač (rižu)	peereenahch (reezhoo)
peas	grašak	grahshahk
tomatoes	paradajz	pahrahdahyz
green salad	zelenu salatu	zehlehnoo sahlahtoo
potatoes	krompir	krompeer

Desserts

Nothing more, thanks.	Ništa više, hvala lepo.	neeshtah veesheh hvahlah lehpo
Just a small portion, please.	Jednu malu porciju, molim.	vehdnoo mahloo portseeyoo moleem
Have you any ice-cream?	Imate li sladoleda?	eemahteh lee slahdolehdah
fruit salad	voćnu salatu	vochnoo sahlahtoo
fresh fruit	sveže voće	svehzheh vocheh
cheese	sir	seer

Drink

What would you like to drink?	**Šta biste želeli da pijete?**	shtah **bee**steh **zhe**hlehlee dah **pee**yehteh
I'll have a beer, please.	**Ja bih pivo, molim.**	yah beeh **pee**vo **mo**leem
I'll have a whisky, please.	**Ja bih viski, molim.**	yah beeh **vee**skee **mo**leem

Wine

I'd like a bottle of wine.	**Hteo bih jednu flašu vina.**	**hte**ho beeh **yeh**dnoo **fla**hshoo **vee**nah
red wine	**crvenog vina**	**tser**vehnog **vee**nah
rosé wine	**ružice**	**roo**zheetseh
white wine	**belog vina**	**beh**log **vee**nah
Cheers!	**Živeli.**	**zhee**vehlee

The bill (check)

May I have the bill (check) please?	**Molim Vas račun.**	**mo**leem vahss **rah**choon
Is service included?	**Da li je servis uračunat?**	dah lee yeh **seh**rveess **oo**rahchoonaht
Everything's included.	**Sve je uračunato.**	sveh yeh **oo**rahchoonahto
Thank you, that was a very good meal.	**Hvala lepo, jelo je bilo vrlo dobro.**	**hvah**lah **leh**po **yeh**lo yeh **bee**lo **ve**rlo **do**bro

Travelling

Where's the railway station, please?	**Gde je železnička stanica (kolodvor), molim Vas?**	gdeh yeh **zheh**lehzneech-kah **sta**hneetsah (kolod-vor) **mo**leem vahss
Where's the ticket office, please?	**Gde je šalter za karte, molim Vas?**	gdeh yeh **shah**ltehr zah **kah**rteh **mo**leem vahss
I'd like a ticket to . . .	**Želeo bih kartu do . . .**	**zheh**leho beeh **kah**rtoo do . . .
First or second class?	**Prvu ili drugu klasu?**	**per**voo **ee**lee **droo**goo **klah**ssoo
First class, please.	**Prvu klasu molim.**	**per**voo **klah**ssoo **mo**leem
Single or return (one way or round-trip)?	**U jednom pravcu ili povratnu?**	oo **yeh**dnom **prah**vtsoo **ee**lee **po**vrahtnoo

Do I have to change trains?	**Moram li presedati?**	morahm lee **preh**sehdahtee
What platform does the train leave from?	**Sa koga perona polazi voz (vlak)?**	sah **ko**gah pehronah **po**lahzee voz (vlahk)
Where's the nearest underground (subway) station?	**Gde je najbliža stanica podzemne železnice?**	gdeh yeh **nahy**bleezhah **stah**neetsah **pod**zehmneh **zheh**lehzneetseh
Where's the bus station, please?	**Gde je autobuska stanica, molim Vas?**	gdeh yeh ahootobooskah **stah**neetsah **mo**leem vahss
When's the first bus to ...?	**Kad polazi prvi autobus za ...?**	kahd **po**lahzee pervee ahootobooss zah
the last bus	**poslednji autobus**	poslehd**ñee** ahootobooss
the next bus	**sledeći autobus**	**sleh**dehchee ahootobooss
Please let me off at the next stop.	**Sišao bih na sledećoj stanici.**	**see**shaho beeh nah **sleh**dehchoy **stah**neetsee

Relaxing

What's on at the cinema (movies)?	**Šta se daje u bioskopu (kinu)?**	shtah seh **dah**yeh oo **bee**ooskopoo (**kee**noo)
What's on at the theatre?	**Šta se daje u pozorištu (kazalištu)?**	shtah seh **dah**yeh oo **po**zoreeshtoo (**kah**zahleeshtoo)
What time does the film begin?	**U koliko sati počinje film?**	oo ko**lee**ko **sah**tee **po**cheeñeh feelm
And the play?	**A komad?**	ah **ko**mahd
Are there any tickets for tonight?	**Ima li karata za večeras?**	**ee**mah lee **kah**rahtah zah **veh**chehrahss
Where can we go dancing?	**Gde možemo da idemo na ples?**	gdeh **mo**zhehmo dah **ee**dehmo nah plehss
Would you like to dance?	**Želite li da igrate (plešete)?**	**zheh**leeteh lee dah **ee**grahteh (**pleh**shehteh)

Introductions

How do you do?	**Dobar dan.**	**do**bahr dahn
How are you?	**Kako ste?**	**kah**ko steh
Very well, thank you. And you?	**Hvala, vrlo dobro. A Vi?**	**hvah**lah **ver**lo **do**bro. ah vee
May I introduce Miss Philips?	**Mogu li da Vam predstavim Gospodjicu Filips.**	**mo**goo lee dah vahm **prehd**stahveem **go**spojeetsoo Philips

My name is . . .	Ja se zovem . . .	yah seh zovehm
I'm very pleased to meet you.	Drago mi je da sam Vas upoznao.	drahgo mee yeh dah sahm vahss oopoznaho
How long have you been here?	Od kad ste ovde?	od kahdah steh ovdeh
It was nice meeting you.	Bilo mi je zadovoljstvo.	beelo mee yeh zahdovol^ystvo

Dating

Would you like a cigarette?	Želite li cigaretu?	zhehleeteh lee tseegahrehtoo
May I get you a drink?	Da li Vam mogu doneti jedno piće?	dah lee vahm mogoo donehtee yehdno peecheh
Do you have a light, please?	Imate li šibicu, molim Vas?	eemahteh lee sheebeetsoo moleem vahss
Are you waiting for someone?	Da li čekate nekoga?	dah lee chehkahteh nehkogah
Are you free this evening?	Da li ste slobodni večeras?	dah lee steh slobodnee vehchehrahss
Where shall we meet?	Gde ćemo se sastati?	gdeh chehmo seh sahstahtee
What time shall I meet you?	Kad ćemo se videti?	kahd chehmo seh veedehtee
May I take you home?	Smem li Vas otpratiti kući?	smehm lee vahss otprahteetee koochee
Thank you, it's been a wonderful evening.	Hvala Vam, bilo je divno veče.	hvahlah vahm beelo yeh deevno vehcheh
What's your telephone number?	Koji je broj Vašeg telefona?	koyee yeh broy vahshehg tehlehfonah
Do you live alone?	Da li živite sami?	dah lee zheeveeteh sahmee
What time is your last train?	Kad ide Vaš poslednji voz (vlak)?	kahd eedeh vahsh poslehdnee voz (vlahk)
Good-night . . .	Laku noć . . .	lahkoo noch

Banks

| Where's the nearest bank, please? | Gde je najbliža banka, molim Vas? | gdeh yeh nahybleezhah bahnkah moleem vahss |
| Where can I cash some traveller's cheques? | Gde mogu da unov- čim putne čekove? | gdeh mogoo dah oonov- cheem pootneh chehkoveh |

What time does the bank open/What time does it close?	**Kad se banka otvara/Kad se zatvara?**	kahd seh **bahn**kah **ot**vahrah/kahd seh **zah**tvahrah
I'm expecting some money from home. Has it arrived?	**Očekujem novac od kuće. Da li je stigao?**	ochehkooyehm **no**vahtss od **koo**cheh. dah lee yeh **stee**gaho
Can you give me some small change, please?	**Možete li mi dati malo sitnine, molim Vas?**	**mo**zhehteh lee mee **dah**tee **mah**lo **seet**neeneh **mo**leem vahss

Shops, stores and services

Where is the nearest chemist's (pharmacy)?	**Gde je najbliža apoteka?**	gdeh yeh **nahy**bleezhah ahpo**teh**kah
the nearest hair-dresser's	**najbliži frizer**	**nahy**bleezhee **free**zehr
the photo shop	**radnja sa foto materijalom**	**rahd**ñah sah **foto** mahtehree**eyah**lom
the jeweller's	**juvelir**	yoo**veh**leer
the department store	**robna kuća**	**rob**nah **koo**chah
the police station	**policijska stanica**	poleet**see**yskah **stah**neetsah
the garage	**garaža**	gah**rah**zhah
How do I get there?	**Kako mogu da dodjem do tamo?**	**kah**ko **mo**goo dah **do**jehm do **tah**mo
Is it within walking distance?	**Da li se tamo može stići pešice?**	dah lee seh **tah**mo **mo**zheh **stee**chee peh**sheet**seh

Service

Can you help me, please?	**Možete li mi pomoći, molim Vas?**	**mo**zhehteh lee mee po**mo**chee **mo**leem vahss
Can you show me this? And that, too.	**Možete li mi pokazati ovo? I ono takodje.**	**mo**zhehteh lee mee po**kah**zahtee **ovo**? ee **ono** **tah**kojeh
It's too expensive/ too big/too small.	**To je suviše skupo/suviše veliko/suviše malo.**	to yeh **soo**veesheh **skoo**po/**soo**veesheh **veh**leeko/**soo**veesheh **mah**lo
Can you show me some more?	**Možete li mi pokazati još nekoliko?**	**mo**zhehteh lee mee po**kah**zahtee yosh **neh**koleeko
something better	**nešto bolje**	**nehsh**to **bol**ʸeh
something cheaper	**nešto jevtinije**	**nehsh**to **yehv**teeneeyeh

264

How much is this? And that?	Koliko staje ovo? A ono?	koleeko stahyeh ovo? ah ono
It's not quite what I want.	To baš nije ono što ja želim.	to bahsh neeyeh ono shto yah zhehleem
I like it.	Dopada mi se.	dopahdah mee seh

Chemist's (Pharmacy)

| I'd like something for a cold/for a cough/for travel sickness. | Imate li nešto za nazeb/kašalj/putnu bolest? | eemahteh lee nehshto zah nahzehb/kahshahl^y/pootnoo bolehst |
| Can you recommend something for hay-fever/for sunburn? | Možete li pre-poručiti nešto za polensku groznicu/ za opekotine od sunca? | mozhehteh lee prehpo-roocheetee nehshto zah polehnskoo grozneetsoo/ zah opehkoteeneh od soontsah |

Toiletry

May I have some razor blades?	Molim Vas žilete.	moleem vahss zheelehteh
some shaving cream some toothpaste	pastu za brijanje pastu za zube	pahstoo zah breeyahñeh pahstoo zah zoobeh
I'd like some soap.	Molim Vas sapun.	moleem vahss sapoon
some suntan oil	ulje za sunčanje	ool^yeh zah soonchahñeh

At the barber's

I'd like a haircut, please.	Šišanje, molim Vas.	sheeshahñeh moleem vahss
Short/Leave it long.	Kratko/Ostavite malo duže.	krahtko/ostahveeteh mahlo doozheh
A razor cut, please.	Šišanje, molim, bri-jačem.	sheeshahñeh moleem breeyahchehm

At the hairdresser's

| I'd like a shampoo and set, please. | Operite mi kosu i počešljajte me, molim Vas. | opehreeteh mee kosoo ee pochehshl^yahyteh meh moleem vahss |

I'd like a bleach.	**Molim Vas blaj-hanje.**	moleem vahss blahyhahñeh
a permanent	**trajnu ondulaciju**	trahynoo ondoolahtseeyoo
a colour rinse	**preliv**	prehleev
a manicure	**manikir**	mahneekeer

Photography

| I'd like a film for this camera. | **Hteo bih film za ovaj aparat.** | hteho beeh feelm zah ovahy ahpahraht |
| This camera doesn't work. | **Ovaj aparat je pokvaren.** | ovahy ahpahraht yeh pokvahrehn |

At the post office

| Where's the nearest post office, please? | **Gde je najbliža pošta, molim Vas?** | gdeh yeh nahybleezhah poshtah moleem vahss |
| I'd like to send this by express (special delivery)/by air mail. | **Želeo bih da pošaljem ovo ekspres/avionom.** | zhehleho beeh dah poshahl^yehm ovo ehksprehss/ahveeonom |

Service stations

Where is the nearest service station, please?	**Gde je najbliža servisna stanica?**	gdeh yeh nahybleezhah sehrveessnah stahneetsah
Fill her up, please.	**Napunite rezervoar, molim Vas.**	nahpooneeteh rehzehrvoahr moleem vahss
Check the oil, please.	**Proverite ulje, molim Vas.**	provehreeteh ool^yeh moleem vahss
Would you check the tyres?	**Da li biste hteli da proverite gume?**	dah lee beesteh htehlee dah provehreeteh goomeh

Street directions

Can you show me on the map where I am?	**Možete li mi pokazati na karti gde se nalazim?**	mozhehteh lee mee pokahzahtee nah kahrtee gdeh seh nahlahzeem
You're on the wrong road.	**Vi ste na pogrešnom putu.**	vee steh nah pogrehshnom pootoo
Go back to ...	**Vratite se do ...**	vrahteeteh seh do
Go straight ahead.	**Idite pravo napred.**	eedeeteh prahvoo nahprehd
It's on the left/on the right.	**Na levoj je strani/na desnoj.**	nah lehvoy yeh strahnee/nah dehsnoy

Accidents

May I use your telephone?	Mogu li se poslužiti Vašim telefonom?	mogoo lee seh posloozheeteh **vah**sheem tehleh**fo**nom
Call a doctor quickly.	Pozovite brzo doktora.	pozoveeteh **ber**zo **dok**torah
Call an ambulance.	Pozovite kola za hitnu pomoć.	pozoveeteh **ko**lah zah **heet**noo **po**moch
Please call the police.	Pozovite, molim Vas, policiju.	pozoveeteh **mo**leem vahss pol**eet**seeyoo

Numbers

one	jedan	**yeh**dahn
two	dva	dvah
three	tri	tree
four	četiri	**cheh**teeree
five	pet	peht
six	šest	shehst
seven	sedam	**seh**dahm
eight	osam	**o**ssahm
nine	devet	**deh**veht
ten	deset	**deh**seht
eleven	jedanaest	yeh**dah**nahehst
twelve	dvanaest	**dvah**nahehst
thirteen	trinaest	**tree**nahehst
fourteen	četrnaest	**cheh**ternahehst
fifteen	petnaest	**peht**nahehst
sixteen	šesnaest	**shehss**nahehst
seventeen	sedamnaest	seh**dahm**nahehst
eighteen	osamnaest	o**sahm**nahehst
nineteen	devetnaest	deh**veht**nahehst
twenty	dvadeset	**dvah**dehseht
twenty-one	dvadeset jedan	**dvah**dehseht **yeh**dahn
thirty	trideset	**tree**dehseht
forty	četrdeset	chehter**deh**seht
fifty	pedeset	peh**deh**seht
sixty	šezdeset	shehz**deh**seht
seventy	sedamdeset	sehdahm**deh**seht
eighty	osamdeset	osahm**deh**seht
ninety	devedeset	dehveh**deh**seht
one hundred	sto	sto
one thousand	hiljadu	heel^{y}ahdoo
ten thousand	deset hiljada	**deh**seht heel^{y}ahdah

SERBO-CROATIAN

Days

|---|---|---|

Days

It's Sunday.	Nedelja je.	nehdehl[y]ah yeh
Monday	ponedeljak	ponehdehl[y]ahk
Tuesday	utorak	ootorahk
Wednesday	sreda	srehdah
Thursday	četvrtak	chehtvertahk
Friday	petak	pehtahk
Saturday	subota	soobotah
yesterday	juče	yoocheh
today	danas	dahnahss
tomorrow	sutra	sootrah
morning/afternoon	jutro/posle podne	yootro/posleh podneh
evening/night	veče/noć	vehcheh/noch

Months

January	januar	yahnooahr
February	februar	fehbrooahr
March	mart	mahrt
April	april	ahpreel
May	maj	mahy
June	jun	yoon
July	juli	yoolee
August	avgust	ahvgoost
September	septembar	sehptehmbahr
October	oktobar	oktobahr
November	novembar	novehmbahr
December	decembar	dehtsehmbahr
Merry Christmas!	Srećan Božić!	srehchahn bozheech!
Happy New Year!	Srećna Nova godina!	srehchnah novah godeenah

SPANISH

Guide to Pronunciation

Letter	Approximate pronunciation	Symbol	Example	

Consonants

f, k, l, m, n, p, t, y	as in English			
b	1) generally as in English	b	**bueno**	**bway**noa
	2) between vowels, a sound between **b** and **v**	bh	**bebida**	bay**bhee**dhah
c	1) before **e** and **i** like **th** in **th**in	th	**centro**	**thayn**troa
	2) otherwise, like **k** in kit	k	**como**	**koa**moa
ch	as in English	ch	**mucho**	**moo**choa
d	1) generally as in **d**og, although less decisive	d	**donde**	**don**day
	2) between vowels and at the end of a word, like **th** in **th**is	dh	**edad**	ay**dhahdh**

g	1) before **e** and **i**, like **ch** in Scottish lo**ch**	kh	**urgente**	oor**kh**ayntay
	2) between vowels and sometimes inside a word, a weak, voiced version of the **ch** in lo**ch**	ġ	**agua**	ah**ġ**wah
	3) otherwise, like **g** in **g**o	g	**ninguno**	neen**ggoo**noa
h	always silent		**hombre**	ombray
j	like **ch** in Scottish lo**ch**	kh	**bajo**	ba**kh**oa
ñ	like **ni** in on**i**on	ñ	**señor**	say**ñ**or
qu	like **k** in **k**it	k	**quince**	**k**eenthay
r	more strongly trilled (like a Scottish **r**), especially at the beginning of a word	r	**río**	**r**eeoa
rr	strongly trilled	rr	**arriba**	ah**rr**eebhah
s	always like the **s** in **s**it, often with a slight lisp	s/ss	**vista**	bee**s**tah
			cuantos	kwahntoa**ss**
v	1) tends to be like **b** in **b**ad, but less tense	b	**viejo**	**b**yaykhoa
	2) between vowels, more like English **v**	bh	**rival**	ree**bh**ahl
z	like **th** in **th**in	th	**brazo**	bra**th**oa

Vowels

a	like **a** in c**a**r, but fairly short	ah	**gracias**	gr**ah**thyahss
e	1) sometimes like **a** in l**a**te	ay	**de**	d**ay**
	2) less often, like **e** in g**e**t	eh	**llover**	lyoab**eh**br
i	like **ee** in f**ee**t	ee	**si**	s**ee**
o	1) sometimes fairly like **o** in r**o**pe	oa	**sopa**	s**oa**pah
	2) sometimes like **o** in g**o**t	o	**dos**	d**o**ss
u	like **oo** in l**oo**t	oo	**una**	**oo**nah
y	only a vowel when alone or at the end of a word; like **ee** in f**ee**t	ee	**y**	**ee**

N.B. 1) In forming diphthongs, **a**, **e**, and **o** are strong vowels, and **i** and **u** are weak vowels. This means that in diphthongs the strong vowels are pronounced more strongly than the weak ones. If two weak vowels form a diphthong, the second one is pronounced more strongly.
2) The acute accent (´) is used to indicate a syllable that is stressed, e.g., *río* = **ree**oa.
3) In words ending with a consonant, the last syllable is stressed, e.g., *señor* = say**nor**.
4) In words ending with a vowel, the next to the last syllable is stressed, e.g., *mañana* = mah**ñah**nah.

SPANISH

Some basic expressions

Yes.	**Sí.**	see
No.	**No.**	noa
Please.	**Por favor.**	por fah**bhor**
Thank you.	**Gracias.**	**grah**thyahss
Thank you very much.	**Muchas gracias.**	**moo**chahss **grah**thyahss
That's all right.	**No hay de qué.**	noa igh day kay

Greetings

Good morning.	**Buenos días.**	**bway**noass **dee**ahss
Good afternoon.	**Buenas tardes.**	**bway**nahss **tahr**dhayss
Good evening.	**Buenas tardes.**	**bway**nahss **tahr**dhayss
Good night.	**Buenas noches.**	**bway**nahss **noa**chayss
Good-bye.	**Adiós.**	ah**dhyoss**
See you later.	**Hasta luego.**	**ahss**tah **lway**goa
This is Mr....	**Este es el Señor ...**	**ayss**tay ayss ehl say**ñor**
This is Mrs....	**Esta es la Señora ...**	**ayss**tah ayss lah say**ñoa**rah
This is Miss ...	**Esta es la Señorita ...**	**ayss**tah ayss lah sayñoa-**ree**tah
I'm very pleased to meet you.	**Encantado de conocerle.**	ayngkahn**tah**dhoa day koanoa**thayr**lay
How are you?	**Cómo está usted?**	**koa**moa ayss**tah** oos**staydh**
Very well, thank you. And you?	**Muy bien, gracias. ¿Y usted?**	mwee byayn **grah**thyahss. ee oos**staydh**
Fine.	**Bien. Gracias.**	byayn **grah**thyahss
Excuse me.	**Dispénseme.**	deess**payn**saymay

Questions

Where?	**¿Dónde?**	**don**day
Where is ... ?	**¿Dónde está ... ?**	**don**day ayss**tah**
Where are ... ?	**¿Dónde están ... ?**	**don**day ayss**tahn**
When?	**¿Cuándo?**	**kwahn**doa

SPANISH

What?	¿Qué?	kay
How?	¿Cómo?	koamoa
How much?	¿Cuánto?	kwahntoa
How many?	¿Cuántos?	kwahntoass
Who?	¿Quién?	kyayn
Why?	¿Por qué?	por kay
Which?	¿Cuál?	kwahl
What do you call this?	¿Cómo se llama esto?	koamoa say lyahmah aysstoa
What do you call that?	¿Cómo se llama eso?	koamoa say lyahmah aysoa
What does this mean?	¿Qué quiere decir esto?	kay kyayray daytheer aysstoa
What does that mean?	¿Qué quiere decir eso?	kay kyayray daytheer aysoa

Do you speak . . . ?

Do you speak English?	¿Habla usted inglés?	ahbhlah oosstaydh eengglayss
Do you speak German?	¿Habla usted alemán?	ahbhlah oosstaydh ahlaymahn
Do you speak French?	¿Habla usted francés?	ahbhlah oosstaydh frahnthayss
Do you speak Spanish?	¿Habla usted español?	ahbhlah oosstaydh aysspahñol
Do you speak Italian?	¿Habla usted italiano?	ahbhlah oosstaydh eetahlyahnoa
Could you speak more slowly, please?	¿Puede usted hablar más despacio, por favor?	pwaydhay oosstaydh ahbhlahr mahss dayspahthyoa por fahbhor
Please point to the phrase in the book.	Por favor, señale la frase en el libro.	por fahbhor sayñahlay lah frahsay ayn ehl leebhroa
Just a minute. I'll see if I can find it in this book.	Un momento. Veré si lo puedo encontrar en este libro.	oon moamayntoa. bayray see loa pwaydhoa ayngkontrahr ayn aysstay leebhroa
I understand.	Comprendo.	komprayndoa
I don't understand.	No comprendo.	noa komprayndoa

Can...?

Can I have...?	¿Puede darme...?	**pway**dhay **dahr**may
Can we have...?	¿Puede darnos...?	**pway**dhay **dahr**noss
Can you show me...?	¿Puede usted enseñarme...?	**pway**dhay ooss**taydh** ayn-say**ñahr**may
Can you tell me...?	¿Puede usted decirme...?	**pway**dhay ooss**taydh** day-**theer**may
Can you help me, please?	¿Puede usted ayudarme, por favor?	**pway**dhay ooss**taydh** ahyoo**dahr**may por fah**bhor**

Wanting

I'd like...	Quisiera...	kee**syay**rah
We'd like...	Quisiéramos...	kee**syay**rahmoss
Please give me...	Por favor, déme...	por fah**bhor** **day**may
Give it to me, please.	Démelo, por favor.	**day**mayloa por fah**bhor**
Please bring me...	Por favor, tráigame...	por fah**bhor** **trigh**gahmay
Bring it to me, please.	Tráigamelo, por favor.	**trigh**gahmayloa por fah**bhor**
I'm hungry.	Tengo hambre.	**tayng**goa **ahm**bray
I'm thirsty.	Tengo sed.	**tayng**goa saydh
I'm tired.	Estoy cansada.	ayss**stoy** kahn**sah**dhah
I'm lost.	Me he perdido.	may ay pehr**dhee**dhoa
It's important.	Es importante.	ayss eempoar**tahn**tay
It's urgent.	Es urgente.	ayss oor**khayn**tay
Hurry up!	¡Dése prisa!	**day**say **pree**sah

It is/There is...

It is/It's...	Es...	ayss
Is it...?	¿Es...?	ayss
It isn't...	No es...	noa ayss
There is/There are...	Hay...	igh
Is there/Are there...?	¿Hay...?	igh

SPANISH

| There isn't/There aren't... | **No hay ...** | noa igh |
| There isn't any/There aren't any. | **No hay ninguno/No hay ningunos (No hay ninguna/No hay ningunas).** | noa igh neeng**goo**noa/noa igh neeng**goo**noss (noa igh neeng**goo**noah/noa igh neeng**goo**nahss) |

A few common words

big/small	**grande/pequeño**	**grahn**day/pay**kay**ñoa
quick/slow	**rápido/lento**	**rah**peedhoa/**layn**toa
early/late	**temprano/tarde**	taym**prah**noa/**tahr**dhay
cheap/expensive	**barato/caro**	bah**rah**toa/**kah**roa
near/far	**cerca/lejos**	**thehr**kah/**lay**khoass
hot/cold	**caliente/frío**	kah**lyayn**tay/**free**oa
full/empty	**lleno/vacío**	**lyay**noa/bah**thee**oa
easy/difficult	**fácil/difícil**	**fah**theel/dee**fee**theel
heavy/light	**pesado/ligero**	pay**sahd**hoa/lee**khay**roa
open/shut	**abierto/cerrado**	ah**byehr**toa/thay**rrahd**hoa
right/wrong	**correcto/incorrecto**	ko**rrehk**toa/eengko**rrehk**toa
old/new	**viejo/nuevo**	**byay**khoa/**nway**bhoa
old/young	**viejo/joven**	**byay**khoa/**khoa**bhayn
beautiful/ugly	**bonito/feo**	boa**nee**toa/**fay**oa
good/bad	**bueno/malo**	**bway**noa/**mah**loa
better/worse	**mejor/peor**	meh**khor**/pay**or**

Some prepositions and a few more useful words

at	**a**	ah
on	**sobre**	**soa**bhray
in	**en**	ayn
to	**para**	**pah**rah
from	**desde**	**dayz**day
inside	**dentro**	**dayn**troa
outside	**fuera**	**fway**rah
up	**arriba**	ah**rree**bhah
down	**abajo**	ah**bhah**khoa
before	**antes**	**ahn**tayss
after	**después**	dayss**pwayss**
with	**con**	kon
without	**sin**	seen
through	**a través**	ah trah**bhayss**
towards	**hacia**	**ah**thyah
until	**hasta**	**ahss**tah
during	**durante**	doo**rahn**tay
and	**y**	ee
or	**o**	oa

not	**no**	noa
nothing	**nada**	**nah**dhah
none	**ninguno**	neeng**goo**noa
very	**muy**	mwee
also	**también**	tahm**bhyayn**
soon	**pronto**	**pront**oa
perhaps	**tal vez**	tal bayth
here	**aquí**	ah**kee**
there	**allí**	ah**lyee**
now	**ahora**	a**horah**
then	**entonces**	ayn**ton**thayss

Arrival

Your passport, please.	**Su pasaporte, por favor.**	soo pahsah**por**tay por fah**bhor**
Here it is.	**Aquí está.**	ah**kee** ays**stah**
Have you anything to declare?	**¿Tiene usted algo que declarar?**	**tyay**nay oos**staydh ahl**goa kay dayklah**rahr**
No, nothing at all.	**No, nada en absoluto.**	noa **nahd**hah ayn ahb-soa**loo**toa
Porter!	**¡Mozo!**	**moa**thoa
Can you help me with my luggage, please?	**¿Puede usted ayudarme con mi equipaje, por favor?**	**pway**dhay oos**staydh** ahyoo**dhahr**may kon mee aykee**pahk**hay por fah**bhor**
That's my suitcase.	**Esa es mi maleta.**	**ays**sah ayss mee mah**lay**tah
Where's the bus to the centre of town, please?	**¿Dónde está el autobús que va al centro, por favor?**	**don**day ays**stah** ehl ow-toa**booss** kay bah ahl **thayn**troa por fah**bhor**
This way, please.	**Por aquí, por favor.**	por ah**kee** por fah**bhor**

Changing money

| Can you change a traveller's cheque, please? | **¿Puede usted cambiarme un traveller's cheque, por favor?** | **pway**dhay oos**staydh** kahmb**yahr**may oon ''traveller's cheque'' por fah**bhor** |
| Where's the nearest bank, please? | **¿Dónde está el banco más cercano, por favor?** | **don**day ays**stah** ehl **bahng**koa mahss thehr**kah**noa por fah**bhor** |

SPANISH

Car rental

I'd like a car.	**Quisiera un coche.**	kee**syay**rah oon **koa**chay
For how long?	**¿Para cuánto tiempo?**	**pah**rah **kwah**ntoa **tyaym**poa
A day/Four days/ A week/Two weeks.	**Un día/Cuatro días/Una semana/ Dos semanas.**	oon **dee**ah/**kwah**troa **dee**ahss/**oo**nah say**mah**nah/doss say**mah**nahss

Taxi

Where can I get a taxi?	**¿Dónde puedo coger (conseguir) un taxi?**	**don**day **pway**dhoa ko**khehr** (koan**say**geer) oon **tahk**see
What's the fare to . . . ?	**¿Cuánto es la tarifa a . . . ?**	**kwah**ntoa ayss lah tah**ree**fah ah
Take me to this address, please.	**Lléveme a esta dirección, por favor.**	**lyayb**haymay ah **ayss**tah deereh**g**thyon por fah**bhor**
I'm in a hurry.	**Tengo mucha prisa.**	**tayng**goa **moo**chah **pree**sah
Could you drive more slowly, please?	**¿Puede usted ir mas despacio, por favor?**	**pway**dhay oos**staydh** eer mahss dayss**pah**thyoa por fah**bhor**

Hotel and other accommodation

My name is . . .	**Me llamo . . .**	may **lyah**moa
Have you a reservation?	**¿Ha hecho usted una reserva?**	ah **ay**choa oos**staydh** **oo**nah rreh**sehr**bhah
Yes, here's the confirmation.	**Sí, aquí está la confirmación.**	see ah**kee** ayss**tah** lah konfeermah**thyon**
I'd like . . .	**Quisiera . . .**	kee**syay**rah
I'd like a single room/a double room.	**Quisiera una habitación sencilla/una habitación doble.**	kee**syay**rah **oo**nah ahbheetah**thyon** sayn**thee**lyah/**oo**nah ahbheetah**thyon** **doa**blay
a room with a bath/ with a shower	**una habitación con baño/con ducha**	**oo**nah ahbheetah**thyon** kon **bah**ñoa/kon **doo**chah

How much?

What's the price per night/per week/per month?	**¿Cuánto cuesta por noche/por semana/ por mes?**	**kwah**ntoa **kwayss**tah por **noa**chay/por say**mah**nah/por mayss

May I see the room?	¿Puedo ver la habitación?	pwaydhoa bayr lah ahbheetahthyon
I'm sorry, I don't like it.	Lo siento, no me gusta.	loa syayntoa noa may goosstah
Yes, that's fine. I'll take it.	Muy bien, la tomaré.	mwee byayn lah toamahray
What's my room number, please?	¿Cuál es el número de mi habitación, por favor?	kwahl ayss ehl noomayroa day mee ahbheetahthyon por fahbhor
Number 123.	Número 123.	noomayroa 123.

Service, please

Who is it?	¿Quién es?	kyayn ayss
Just a minute.	Un momento, por favor.	oon moamayntoa por fahbhor
Come in! The door's open.	¡Adelante! la puerta está abierta.	ahdhaylahntay! lah pwehrtah aysstah ahbhyehrtah
May we have breakfast in our room?	¿Podemos desayunar en nuestra habitación?	poadhaymoass daysahyoonahr ayn nwaysstrah ahbheetahthyon

Breakfast

I'll have . . .	Quisiera . . .	keesyayrah
I'll have some fruit juice.	Quisiera un zumo de fruta.	keesyayrah oon thoomoa day frootah
a boiled egg	un huevo cocido	oon waybhoa koatheedhoa
a fried egg	un huevo frito	oon waybhoa freetoa
some bacon/some ham	un poco de tocino/un poco de jamón	oon poakoa day toatheenoa/oon poakoa day khahmon
some toast	un poco de pan tostado	oon poakoa day pahn toasstahdhoa
a pot of tea	una tetera de té	oonah taytayrah day tay
a cup of tea	una taza de té	oonah tahthah day tay
some coffee	un poco de café	oon poakoa day kahfay
some chocolate	un poco de chocolate	oon poakoa day choakoalahtay
more butter	más mantequilla	mahss mahntaykeelyah
some hot water	un poco de agua caliente	oon poakoa day ahgwah kahlyayntay

SPANISH

Difficulties

The central heating doesn't work.	La calefacción central no funciona.	lah kahlayfahkthyon thayntrahl noa foonthyoanah
the light/the socket the tap/the toilet	la luz/el enchufe el grifo/el water	lah looth/ehl aynchoofay ehl greefoa/ehl vahtehr
There's no hot water.	No hay agua caliente.	noa igh ahǧwah kahlyayntay
May I see the manager, please?	¿Puedo ver al director, por favor?	pwaydhoa behr ahl deerehktor por fahbhor

Telephone—Mail

There's a call for you.	Hay una llamada para usted.	igh oonah lyahmahdhah pahrah oosstaydh
Hold the line, please.	Espere un momento, por favor.	aysspayray oon moamayntoa por fahbhor
Operator, I've been cut off.	Telefonista, me han cortado.	taylayfoaneesstah may ahn kortahdhoa
Did anyone telephone me?	¿Me ha llamado alguien?	may ah lyahmahdhoa ahlgyayn
Is there any mail for me?	¿Hay correo para mí?	igh korrayoa pahrah mee
Are there any messages for me?	¿Hay algún recado para mí?	igh ahlgoon raykahdhoa pahrah mee

Checking out

May I have my bill, please?	¿Puede darme mi cuenta, por favor?	pwaydhay dahrmay mee kwayntah por fahbhor
We're in a great hurry.	Tenemos mucha prisa.	taynaymoss moochah preesah
It's been a very enjoyable stay.	Ha sido una estancia muy agradable.	ah seedhoa oonah aysstahnthyah mwee ahgrahdhahbhlay

Eating out

Good evening, sir/ Good evening, madam.	Buenas noches, señor/Buenas noches, señora.	bwaynahss noachayss sayñor bwaynahss noachayss sayñoarah
Good evening. I'd like a table for two, please.	Buenas noches. Quisiera una mesa para dos, por favor.	bwaynahss noachayss. keesyayrah oonah maysah pahrah doss por fahbhor

Do you have a fixed-price menu?	¿Tiene usted un menu de precio fijo?	tyaynay oosstaydh oon maynoo day praythyoa feekhoa
May I see the à la carte menu?	¿Puedo ver la carta?	pwaydhoa behr lah kahr-tah
May we have an ashtray, please?	¿Nos puede traer un cenicero, por favor?	noss pwaydhay trahehr oon thayneethayroa por fahbhor
some bread	un poco de pan	oon poakoa day pan
a fork	un tenedor	oon taynaydhor
a knife	un cuchillo	oon koocheelyoa
a spoon	una cuchara	oonah koochahrah
a plate	un plato	oon plahtoa
a glass	un vaso	oon bahsoa
a napkin	una servilleta	oonah sehrbheelyaytah
another chair	otra silla	oatra seelyah
Where's the gentle-men's toilet (men's room)?	¿Dónde está el lavabo de caballeros?	donday aysstah ehl lah-bhahbhoa day kahbhahlyayross
Where's the ladies' toilet (ladies' room)?	¿Dónde está el lavabo de señoras?	donday aysstah ehl lah-bhahbhoa day sayñoarahss

Appetizers

I'd like some...	Quisiera...	keesyayrah
I'd like some assorted appetizers.	Quisiera unos entremeses variados.	keesyayrah oonoss ayntraymaysayss bahreeahdhoss
orange juice	un jugo de naranja	oon khooĝoa day nahrahnkhah
ham	jamón	khahmon
melon	melón	maylon
pâté	pastel de carne	pahsstehl day kahrnay
smoked salmon	salmón ahumado	sahlmon ahoomahdhoa
shrimps (shrimp)	quisquillas	keesskeelyahss

Soup

Have you any...?	¿Tiene usted...?	tyaynay oosstaydh
Have you any chicken soup?	¿Tiene usted sopa de pollo?	tyaynay oosstaydh soapah day poalyoa
vegetable soup	sopa de verduras	soapah day behrdhoo-rahss
onion soup	sopa de cebollas	soapah day thaybhoa-lyahss

SPANISH

Fish

I'd like some . . .	Quisiera . . .	keesyayrah
I'd like some fish.	Quisiera pescado.	keesyayrah paysskahdhoa
sole	lenguado	laynggwahdhoa
trout	trucha	troochah
lobster	langosta	langgosstah
crayfish	cangrejos	kahnggraykhoss
prawns	gambas	gahmbahss
I'd like it . . .	Me gustaría . . .	may goosstahreeah
I'd like it steamed.	Me gustaría al vapor.	may goosstahreeah ahl bahpor
grilled	a la parrilla	ah lah pahreelyah
boiled	cocido	koatheedhoa
baked	asado	ahsahdhoa
fried	frito	freetoa

Meat—Poultry—Game

I'd like some . . .	Quisiera . . .	keesyayrah
I'd like some beef.	Quisiera carne de vaca.	keesyayrah kahrnay day bahkah
a beef steak	un bistec	oon beesstehk
some roast beef	rosbif	rrozbheef
a veal cutlet	una chuleta de ternera	oonah choolaytah day tehrnayrah
mutton	carnero	kahrnayroa
lamb	cordero	kordhayroa
a pork chop	una chuleta de cerdo	oonah choolaytah day thehrdhoa
roast pork	cerdo asado	thehrdhoa ahsahdhoa
hare	liebre	lyaybhray
chicken	pollo	poalyoa
roast chicken	pollo asado	poalyoa ahsahdhoa
duck	pato	pahtoa
How do you like your meat?	¿Cómo le gusta la carne?	koamoa lay goosstah lah kahrnay
rare	poco asada	poakoa ahsahdhah
medium	medio asada	maydhyoa ahsahdhah
well done	bien hecha	byayn aychah

Vegetables

| What vegetables have you got? | ¿Qué verduras tiene usted? | kay behrdhoorahss tyaynah oosstaydh |
| I'd like some . . . | Quisiera . . . | keesyayrah |

SPANISH

I'd like some asparagus.	**Quisiera unos espárragos.**	kee**syay**rah **oo**noss ayss-**pahr**rahĝoss
green beans	**unas judias verdes**	**oo**nahss **khoo**dhyahss **behr**dhayss
mushrooms	**unas setas**	**oo**nahss **say**tahss
carrots	**unas zanahorias**	**oo**nahss thahnah**o**ryahss
onions	**unas cebollas**	**oo**nahss thay**bhoa**lyahss
red cabbage	**lombarda**	loam**bahr**dha
spinach	**unas espinacas**	**oo**nahss ayss**pee**nah**kah**ss
rice	**un poco de arroz**	oon **poa**koa day ahr**roth**
peas	**unos guisantes**	**oo**nos gee**sahn**tayss
tomatoes	**unos tomates**	**oo**nos toa**mah**tayss
green salad	**ensalada de lechuga**	aynsah**lah**dhah day lay-**choo**ĝah
potatoes	**unas patatas**	**oo**nahss pah**tah**tahss

Desserts

Nothing more, thanks.	**Nada más, gracias.**	**nah**dhah mahss **grah**thyahss
Just a small portion, please.	**Una pequeña porción, por favor.**	**oo**nah pay**kay**ñah por-**thyon** por fah**bhor**
Have you any ice-cream?	**¿Tiene usted helado?**	**tyay**nay ooss**taydh** ay**lah**dhoa
fruit salad	**ensalada de fruta**	aynsah**lah**dhah day **froo**tah
fresh fruit	**fruta fresca**	**froo**tah **frayss**kah
cheese	**queso**	**kay**soa

Drink

What would you like to drink?	**¿Qué le gustaría beber?**	kay lay goosstah**ree**ah bay**bhayr**
I'll have a beer, please.	**Tomaré una cerveza, por favor.**	toamah**ray** **oo**nah thehr-**bhay**thah por fah**bhor**
I'll have a whisky, please.	**Tomaré un whisky, por favor.**	toamah**ray** oon **wee**skee por fah**bhor**

Wine

I'd like a bottle of wine.	Quisiera una botella de vino.	keesyayrah oonah boatay-lyah day beenoa
red wine	vino tinto	beenoa teentoa
rosé wine	vino clarete	beenoa klahraytay
white wine	vino blanco	beenoa blahngkoa
Cheers!	¡A su salud!	ah soo sahloodh

The bill (check)

May I have the bill (check) please?	¿Podría darme la cuenta, por favor?	poadhreeah dahrmay lah kwayntah por fahbhor
Is service included?	¿Está incluído el servicio?	aysstah eengklooeedhoa ehl sehrbheethyoa
Everything's included.	Todo está incluído.	toadhoa aysstah eeng-klooeedhoa
Thank you, that was a very good meal.	Gracias. Ha sido una comida muy buena.	grahthyahss. ah seedhoa oonah koameedhah mwee bwaynah

Travelling

Where's the railway station, please?	¿Dónde está la estación de ferrocarril, por favor?	donday aysstah lah aysstahthyon day fehrrokahrreel por fahbhor
Where's the ticket office, please?	¿Dónde está la taquilla, por favor?	donday aysstah lah tahkeelyah por fahbhor
I'd like a ticket to...	Quisiera un billete para...	keesyayrah oon beelyaytay pahrah
First or second class?	¿Primera o segunda clase?	preemayrah o saygoondah klahsay
First class, please.	Primera clase, por favor.	preemayrah klahsay por fahbhor
Single or return (one way or round-trip)?	¿Ida, o ida y vuelta?	eedhah o eedhah ee bwehltah
Do I have to change trains?	¿Tengo que hacer transbordo?	taynggoa kay ahthehr trahnzbhoardhoa
What platform does the train leave from?	¿De qué andén sale el tren?	day kay ahndayn sahlay ehl trayn
Where's the nearest underground (subway) station?	¿Dónde está la próxima estación de metro?	donday aysstah lah prog-seemah aysstahthyon day maytroa

Where's the bus station, please?	¿Dónde está la estación de auto-buses, por favor?	donday aysstah lah ayss-tahthyon day owtoa-boossayss por fahbhor
When's the first bus to...?	¿Cuándo sale el primer autobús para...?	kwahndoa sahlay ehl preemehr owtoabooss pahrah
the last bus	el último autobús	ehl oolteemoa owtoa-booss
the next bus	el próximo autobús	ehl progseemoa owtoa-booss
Please let me off at the next stop.	Por favor, pare en la próxima parada.	por fahbhor pahray ayn lah progseemah pahrah-dhah

Relaxing

What's on at the cinema (movies)?	¿Qué dan en el cine?	kay dahn ayn ehl theenay
What's on at the theatre?	¿Qué dan en el teatro?	kay dahn ayn ehl tayah-troa
What time does the film begin? And the play?	¿A qué hora em-pieza la película? ¿Y la obra?	ah kay oarah aympyay-thah lah payleekoolah? ee lah oabhrah
Are there any tickets for tonight?	¿Quedan entradas para esta noche?	kaydhahn ayntrahdhahss pahrah aysstah noachay
Where can we go dancing?	¿Dónde se peude ir a bailar?	donday say pwaydhay eer ah bighlahr
Would you like to dance?	¿Quiere usted bailar?	kyayray oosstaydh bighlahr

Introductions

How do you do?	Buenos días.	bwaynoss deeahss
How are you?	¿Cómo está usted?	koamoa aysstah ooss-taydh
Very well, thank you. And you?	Muy bien, gracias. ¿Y usted?	mwee byayn grahthyahss. ee oosstaydh
May I introduce Miss Philips?	¿Me permite pre-sentarle la Señorita Philips?	may pehrmeetay pray-sayntahrlay lah sayñoa-reetah Philips
My name is...	Me llamo...	may lyahmoa
I'm very pleased to meet you.	Tanto gusto (en conocerle).	tahntoa goosstoa (ayn koanoathehrlay)

SPANISH

| How long have you been here? | ¿Cuánto tiempo lleva usted aqui? | kwahntoa tyaympoa lyaybhah oosstaydh ahkee |
| It was nice meeting you. | Ha sido un placer conocerle. | ah seedhoa oon plahthehr koanoathehrlay |

Dating

Would you like a cigarette?	¿Quiere usted un cigarrillo?	kyayray oosstaydh oon theegahreelyoa
May I get you a drink?	¿Me permite invitarlo a una bebida?	may pehrmeetay eenbheetahrloa ah oonah baybheedhah
Do you have a light, please?	¿Tiene usted fuego, por favor?	tyaynay oosstaydh fwayǧoa por fahbhor
Are you waiting for someone?	¿Está usted esperando a alguien?	aysstah oosstaydh aysspayrahndoa ah ahlgyayn
Are you free this evening?	¿Está usted libre esta noche?	aysstah oosstaydh leebhray aysstah noachay
Where shall we meet?	¿Dónde quedamos citados?	donday kaydhahmoss theetahdhoss
What time shall I meet you?	¿A qué hora puedo verla?	ah kay oarah pwaydhoa behrlah
May I take you home?	¿Puedo acompañarla a su casa?	pwaydhoa ahkoampahñahrlah ah soo kahsah
Thank you, it's been a wonderful evening.	Gracias, he pasado una velada maravillosa.	grahthyahss ay pahsahdhoa oona bay lahdhah mahrahbheelyoasah
What's your telephone number?	¿Cuál es su número de teléfono?	kwahl ayss soo noomayroa day taylayfoanoa
Do you live alone?	Vive usted sola?	beebhay oosstaydh soalah
What time is your last train?	¿A qué hora sale su último tren?	ah kay oarah sahlay soo oolteemoa trayn
Good-night...	Buenas noches...	bwaynahss noachayss

Banks

| Where's the nearest bank, please? | ¿Dónde está el banco más cercano, por favor? | donday aysstah ehl bahngkoa mahss thehrkahnoa por fahbhor |
| Where can I cash some traveller's cheques? | ¿Dónde puedo cambiar unos traveller's cheques? | donday pwaydhoa kahmbyahr oonoss "traveller's cheques" |

What time does the bank open/What time does it close?	¿A qué hora abren el banco/A qué hora lo cierran?	ah kay **oa**rah **ah**brayn ehl **bahng**koa/ah kay **oa**rah loa thyeh**rrah**n
I'm expecting some money from home. Has it arrived?	¿Estoy esperando dinero de casa. Ha llegado?	ays**stoy** aysspay**rahn**doa dee**nay**roa day **kah**sah. ah yay**gah**doa
Can you give me some small change, please?	¿Puede usted darme algún dinero suelto, por favor?	**pway**dhay ooss**taydh dahr**may ahl**goon** dee**nay**roa **swehl**toa por fah**bhor**

Shops, stores and services

Where is the nearest chemist (pharmacy)?	¿Dónde está la farmacia más cercana?	**don**day ayss**tah** lah fahr**mah**theeah mahss thehr**kah**nah
the nearest hairdresser's	la peluquería más cercana	lah paylookay**ree**ah mahss thehr**kah**nah
the photo shop	la tienda fotográfica	lah **tyayn**dha foatoa**grah**feekah
the jeweller's	la joyería	lah khoayay**ree**ah
the department store	los grandes almacenes	loss **grahn**dayss ahlmah**thay**nayss
the police station	la comisaría	lah koameesah**ree**ah
the garage	el garaje	ehl gah**rah**khay
How do I get there?	¿Cómo podría ir allí?	**koa**moa poa**dhree**ah eer ah**lyee**
Is it within walking distance?	¿Se puede ir andando?	say **pway**dhay eer ahn**dahn**doa

Service

Can you help me, please?	¿Puede usted atenderme, por favor?	**pway**dhay ooss**taydh** ah-tayn**dehr**may por fah**bhor**
Can you show me this? And that, too.	¿Puede usted enseñarme esto? ¿Y aquello también?	**pway**dhay ooss**taydh** ayn-say**ñahr**may **ayss**toa? ee ah**kway**lyoa tahm**byyayn**
It's too expensive/too big/too small.	Es demasiado caro/demasiado grande/demasiado pequeño.	ayss daymah**syah**dhoa **kah**roa/daymah**syah**dhoa **grahn**day/daymah**syah**dhoa pay**kay**ñoa
Can you show me some more?	¿Puede usted enseñarme algo más?	**pway**dhay ooss**taydh** ayn-say**ñahr**may **ahl**goa mahss
something better	algo mejor	**ahl**goa may**khor**
something cheaper	algo más barato	**ahl**goa mahss bah**rah**toa

SPANISH

How much is this? And that?	¿Cuánto es éste? ¿Y ése?	kwahntoa ayss aysstay? ee aysay
It's not quite what I want.	No es exactamente lo que quiero.	noa ayss ehġsahktah-mayntay loa kay kyayroa
I like it.	Me gusta.	may goosstah

Chemist's (Pharmacy)

| I'd like something for a cold/for a cough/for travel sickness. | Desearía algo para el catarro/para la tos/contra el mareo. | daysayahreeah ahlgoa pahrah ehl kahtahrroa/pahrah lah toss/kontrah ehl mahrayoa |
| Can you recommend something for hay-fever/for sunburn? | ¿Podría recomen-darme algo para la fiebre del heno/para las quema-duras del sol? | poadhreeah raykoamayn-dahrmay ahlgoa pahrah lah fyaybhray dehl ay-noa/pahrah lahss kaymah-dhoorahss dehl sol |

Toiletry

May I have some razor blades?	¿Puede darme unas cuchillas para afeitar?	pwaydhay dahrmay oo-nahss koocheelyahss pah-rah ahfaytahr
some shaving cream	una crema para afeitar	oonah kraymah pahrah ahfaytahr
some toothpaste	una pasta de dientes	oonah pahsstah day dyayntayss
I'd like some soap.	Quisiera jabón.	keesyayrah khahbhon
some suntan oil	aceite bronceador	ahthaytay bronthayahdhor

At the barber's

I'd like a haircut, please.	Quisiera cortarme el pelo, por favor.	keesyayrah kortahrmay ehl payloa por fahbhor
Short/Leave it long.	Corto/Déjemelo largo.	kortoa/daykhaymayloa lahrgoa
A razor cut, please.	Un corte a navaja, por favor.	oon kortay ah nahbhah-khah por fahbhor

At the hairdresser's

| I'd like a shampoo and set, please. | Quiero un lavado y marcado por favor. | kyayroa oon lahbhahdhoa ee mahrkahdhoa por fahbhor |

I'd like a bleach.	**Desearía un aclarado.**	daysayahreeah oon ahklahrahdhoa
a permanent	**una permanente**	oonah pehrmahnayntay
a colour rinse	**un reflejo**	oon rayflaykhoa
a manicure	**una manicura**	oonah mahneekoorah

Photography

I'd like a film for this camera.	**Desearía un carrete para esta máquina.**	daysayahreeah oon kahr-raytay pahrah aysstah mahkeenah
This camera doesn't work.	**Esta cámera no funciona.**	aysstah kahmayrah noa foonthyoanah

At the post office

Where's the nearest post office, please?	**¿Dónde está la oficina de correos más cercana, por favor?**	donday aysstah lah oafee-theenah day korrehoss mahss thehrkahnah por fahbhor
I'd like to send this by express (special delivery)/by air mail.	**Quisiera enviar esto por correo urgente/ por avión.**	keesyayrah aybhyahr aysstoa por korrehoa oorkhayntay/ por ahbhyon

Service stations

Where is the nearest service station, please?	**¿Dónde está la estación de servicio más cercana?**	donday aysstah lah ayss-tahthyon day sehrbhee-thyoa mahss thehrkahnah
Fill her up, please.	**Llénemelo por favor.**	lyaynaymayloa por fahbhor
Check the oil, please.	**Compruebe el aceite, por favor.**	komprwaybhay ehl ah-thaytay por fahbhor
Would you check the tyres?	**¿Quiere comprobar los neumáticos?**	kyayray komproabhahr loss nehwmahteekoss

Street directions

Can you show me on the map where I am?	**¿Puede enseñarme en el mapa donde estoy?**	pwaydhay aynsaynahrmay ayn ehl mahpah donday aysstoy
You're on the wrong road.	**Está usted equivocado de camino.**	aysstah oosstaydh aykee-bhoakahdhoa day kah-meenoa

Go back to . . .	**Vuelva a . . .**	bwehlbha a
Go straight ahead.	**Siga todo derecho.**	see**g**ah toadhoa dayray-choa
It's on the left/on the right.	**Está a la izquierda/ a la derecha.**	aysstah ah lah eethkyehr-dhah/ah lah dayraychah

Accidents

May I use your tele-phone?	**¿Puedo utilizar su teléfono?**	pwaydhoa ooteeleethar soo taylayfoanoa
Call a doctor quickly.	**Lláme a un médico rápidamente.**	lyahmay ah oon maydee-koa rahpeedhamayntay
Call an ambulance.	**Lláme a una ambu-lancia.**	lyahmay ah oonah ahm-boolahnthyah
Please call the police.	**Lláme a la policia, por favor.**	lyahmay ah lah polee-theeah por fahbhor

Numbers

one	**uno**	oonoa
two	**dos**	doss
three	**tres**	trayss
four	**cuatro**	kwahtroa
five	**cinco**	theengkoa
six	**seis**	seheess
seven	**siete**	syaytay
eight	**ocho**	oachoa
nine	**nueve**	nwaybhay
ten	**diez**	dyayth
eleven	**once**	onthay
twelve	**doce**	doathay
thirteen	**trece**	traythay
fourteen	**catorce**	kahtorthay
fifteen	**quince**	keenthay
sixteen	**dieciséis**	dyehtheeseheess
seventeen	**diecisiete**	dyehtheesyaytay
eighteen	**dieciocho**	dyehtheeoachoa
nineteen	**diecinueve**	dyehtheenwaybhay
twenty	**veinte**	bayntay
twenty-one	**veintiuno**	bayntioonoa
thirty	**treinta**	trayntah
forty	**cuarenta**	kwahrayntah
fifty	**cincuenta**	theengkwayntah
sixty	**sesenta**	saysayntah
seventy	**setenta**	saytayntah

SPANISH

eighty	**ochenta**	oa**chayn**tah
ninety	**noventa**	noab**hayn**tah
one hundred	**ciento**	**thyayn**toa
one thousand	**mil**	meel
ten thousand	**diez mil**	dyayth meel

Days

It's Sunday.	**Es domingo.**	ayss doa**meeng**goa
Monday	**lunes**	**loo**nayss
Tuesday	**martes**	**mahr**tayss
Wednesday	**miércoles**	**myehr**koalayss
Thursday	**jueves**	**khway**bhayss
Friday	**viernes**	**byehr**nayss
Saturday	**sábado**	**sahb**hahdhoa
yesterday	**ayer**	ah**yehr**
today	**hoy**	oy
tomorrow	**mañana**	mah**ñah**nah
morning/afternoon	**mañana/media tarde**	mah**ñah**nah/**may**dhyah **tahrd**hay
evening/night	**tarde/noche**	**tahrd**hay/**noa**chay

Months

January	**enero**	ay**nay**roa
February	**febrero**	fay**bhray**roa
March	**marzo**	**mahr**thoa
April	**abril**	ah**bhreel**
May	**mayo**	**mah**yoa
June	**junio**	**khoo**nyoa
July	**julio**	**khool**yoa
August	**agosto**	ah**goss**toa
September	**septiembre**	sayp**tyaym**bray
October	**octubre**	ok**toob**hray
November	**noviembre**	noab**hyaym**bray
December	**diciembre**	deeth**yaym**bray
Merry Christmas!	**Felices Pascuas!**	fay**lee**thayss **pahss**kwahss!
Happy New Year!	**Feliz Año Nuevo!**	fay**leeth ah**ñoa **nway**bhoa

SPANISH

SWEDISH

Guide to Pronunciation

Letter	Approximate pronunciation	Symbol	Example	

Consonants

Letter	Approximate pronunciation	Symbol	Example	
b, c, d, f, h, l, m, n, p, v, w, x	as in English			
ch	at the beginning of words borrowed from French, like **sh** in **sh**ut	sh	**chef**	shayf
g	1) before stressed **i**, **e**, **y**, **ä**, **ö** and sometimes after **l** or **r**, like **y** in yet	y	**genast**	**yay**nahst
	2) before **e** and **i** in many words of French origin, like **sh** in **sh**ut	sh	**generös**	shayner**rurss**
	3) elsewhere, generally like **g** in **g**o	g	**gammal**	**gah**mahl
j, dj, gj, lj	like **y** in yet	y	**ja**	yar
k	1) before stressed **i**, **e**, **y**, **ä**, **ö**, generally like **ch** in Scottish lo**ch**, but pronounced in the front of the mouth	kh	**köpa**	**khur**pah
	2) elsewhere, like **k** in **k**it	k	**kål**	koal

kj	like **ch** in Scottish lo**ch**, but pronounced in the front of the mouth	kh	**kjol**	**kh**ool
qu	like **k** in **k**it followed by **v** in **v**at	kv	**Lindquist**	lind**kv**ist
r	slightly rolled near the front of the mouth	r	**råd**	**r**oad
s	1) in the ending **-sion** like **sh** in **sh**ut	sh	**mission**	mi**sh**oon
	2) elsewhere, like **s** in **s**o	s/ss	**smak**	**s**mark
	3) the groups **sch, skj, stj** are pronounced like **sh** in **sh**ut	sh	**schema**	**sh**aymah
sk	1) before stressed **e, i, y, ä, ö,** like **sh** in **sh**ut	sh	**skepp**	**sh**ehp
	2) elsehwere, like **sk** in **sk**ip	sk	**handske**	hahnd**sk**er
t	1) **ti** in the ending **-tion**, is pronounced like **sh** in **sh**ut or like **ch** in **ch**at	sh tsh	**station** **nation**	stah**sh**oon naht**sch**oon
	2) elsehwere, like **t** in **t**op	t	**talk**	**t**ahlk
tj	like **ch** in Scottish lo**ch**, but pronounced in the front of the mouth; sometimes with a t-sound at the beginning	kh	**tjäna**	**kh**ainah
z	like **s** in **s**o	s	**zon**	**s**oon

N.B. In the groups **rd, rl, rn, rs** and **rt,** the letter **r** is generally not pronounced but influences the pronunciation of the **d, l, n, s** or **t,** which is then pronounced with the end of the tongue *not* on the upper front teeth, but behind the gums of the upper teeth.

Vowels

Vowels in stressed syllables are long if followed at most by one consonant, but are short if followed by two or more consonants. Vowels in unstressed syllables are short.

a	1) when long, like **a** in c**a**r	ar	**dag**	d**ar**g
	2) when short, something like the **u** in c**u**t or **o** in American coll**e**ge	ah	**tack**	t**ah**k
e	1) when long, like **ay** in s**ay**, but a *pure* vowel, not a diphthong	ay	**blek**	bl**ay**k
	2) in the stressed prefix **er-**, like **a** in m**a**n, but longer	ææ	**erfara**	**ææ**rfarrah
	3) when short, like **e** in g**e**t	eh	**penna**	p**eh**na
	4) when unstressed, like **a** in **a**bout	er	**betala**	b**er**tarlah
ej	like **a** in m**a**te	ay	**nej**	n**ay**

SWEDISH

i	1) when long, like **ee** in b**ee**	ee	**vit**	v**ee**t
	2) when short, between **ee** in m**ee**t and **i** in h**i**t	i	**bild**	bild
o	1) when long, often like **oo** in s**oo**n, but with the lips more tightly rounded, and with a puff of breath at the end	oo	**sko**	sk**oo**
	2) the same sound can be short	oo	**ost**	**oo**st
	3) when long, it is also sometimes pronounced like **oa** in m**oa**n	oa	**son**	s**oa**n
	4) when short, sometimes like **o** in h**o**t	o	**socker**	s**o**kkerr
u	1) when long, like Swedish **y**, but with the tongue a little lower in the mouth, and with a puff of breath at the end	ew	**hus**	h**ew**ss
	2) when short, a little more like the **u** of p**u**t; a very difficult sound	ew	**ung**	**ew**ng
y	pronounce the **ee** of b**ee** and then round your lips without moving your tongue; the sound can be long or short	ew	**vy** **syster**	v**ew** s**ew**sterr
å	1) when long, like **aw** in r**aw**, but with the tongue a little higher in the mouth	oa	**gå**	g**oa**
	2) when short, like **o** in h**o**t	o	**sång**	s**o**ng
ä	1) when followed by **r**, like **a** in m**a**n, long or short	ææ æ	**ära** **värka**	**ææ**rah v**æ**rkah
	2) elsewhere, like **e** in g**e**t; long or short	ai eh	**läsa** **bäst**	l**ai**sah b**eh**st
ö	like **u** in f**u**r, long or short; when followed by **r**, it is pronounced with the mouth a little more open	ur	**röd** **höst** **öra**	r**ur**d h**ur**st **ur**rah

N.B. The principal stress is generally on the *first* syllable of a word, unless it comes from Latin or French.

SWEDISH

Some basic expressions

Yes.	**Ja.**	yar
No.	**Nej.**	nay
Please.	**Varsågod.**	**vahr**soagood
Thank you.	**Tack.**	tahk
Thank you very much.	**Tack så mycket.**	tahk soa **mew**ker(t)
That's all right.	**Ingen orsak.**	**ingern oor**shark

Greetings

Good morning.	**God morgon.**	goo **mo**ron
Good afternoon.	**God middag.**	goo **mid**dah(g)
Good evening.	**God afton.**	goo **ahf**ton
Good night.	**God natt.**	goo naht
Good-bye.	**Adjö.**	ah**yur**
See you later.	**Vi ses.**	vee sayss
This is Mr....	**Det här är herr...**	day hæær æær hær
This is Mrs....	**Det här är fru...**	day hæær æær frew
This is Miss...	**Det här är fröken...**	day hæær æær **frur**kern
I'm very pleased to meet you.	**Angenämt.**	ahnyer**nehmt**
How are you?	**Hur står det till?**	hewr stoar deht til
Very well, thank you. And you?	**Tack bara bra.** **Och Ni själv?**	tahk **bar**rah brar. o(k) nee shehlv
Fine.	**Fint.**	fint
Excuse me.	**Förlåt.**	furr**loat**

Questions

Where?	**Var?**	varr
Where is...?	**Var är...?**	varr ai
Where are...?	**Var är...?**	varr ai
When?	**När?**	næær
What?	**Vad?**	vard
How?	**Hur?**	hewr
How much?	**Hur mycket?**	hewr **mew**kert
How many?	**Hur många?**	hewr **mong**ah

SWEDISH

Who?	**Vem?**	vaym
Why?	**Varför?**	vahrfurr
Which?	**Vilken?**	vilkern
What do you call this?	**Vad heter det här?**	vard hayterr day hæær
What do you call that?	**Vad heter det där?**	vard hayterr day dæær
What does this mean?	**Vad betyder det här?**	vard bertewderr day hæær
What does that mean?	**Vad betyder det där?**	vard bertewderr day dæær

Do you speak ... ?

Do you speak English?	**Talar Ni engelska?**	tarlahr nee ehngerlskah
Do you speak German?	**Talar Ni tyska?**	tarlahr nee tewskah
Do you speak French?	**Talar Ni franska?**	tarlahr nee frahnskah
Do you speak Spanish?	**Talar Ni spanska?**	tarlahr nee spahnskah
Do you speak Italian?	**Talar Ni italienska?**	tarlahr nee itahliehnskah
Could you speak more slowly, please?	**Kan Ni vara snäll och tala lite långsammare?**	kahn nee varrah snehl o tarlah leeter long-sahmahrer
Please point to the phrase in the book.	**Var snäll och peka på meningen i boken.**	varr snehl o paykah poa mayningern ee bookern
Just a minute. I'll see if I can find it in this book.	**Ett ögonblick, så ska jag se om jag hittar det i den här boken.**	eht urgonblik soa skar jar(g) say om yar(g) hitahr day ee dehn hæær bookern
I understand.	**Jag förstår.**	yar(g) furrshtoar
I don't understand.	**Jag förstår inte.**	yar(g) furrshtoar inter

Can ... ?

Can I have ... ?	**Kan jag få ... ?**	kahn yar(g) foa
Can we have ... ?	**Kan vi få ... ?**	kahn vee foa

SWEDISH

Can you show me...?	**Kan Ni visa mig...?**	kahn nee **vee**sah may
Can you tell me...?	**Kan Ni säga mig...?**	kahn nee **sai**gah may
Can you help me, please?	**Kan Ni vara snäll och hjälpa mig?**	kahn nee **var**rah snehl o **yehl**pah may

Wanting

I'd like...	**Jag skulle vilja ha...**	yar(g) **skew**ller **vil**yah har
We'd like...	**Vi skulle vilja ha...**	vee **skew**ller **vil**yah har
Please give me...	**Var snäll och ge mig...**	varr snehl o yay may
Give it to me, please.	**Var snäll och ge mig den.**	varr snehl o yay may dehn
Please bring me...	**Var snäll och hämta...**	varr snehl o **hehm**tah
Bring it to me, please.	**Var snäll och hämta den.**	varr snehl o **hehm**tah dehn
I'm hungry.	**Jag är hungrig.**	yar(g) æær **hewn**gri(g)
I'm thirsty.	**Jag är törstig.**	yar(g) æær **turr**shti(g)
I'm tired.	**Jag är trött.**	yar(g) æær trurt
I'm lost.	**Jag har gått vilse.**	yar(g) harr got **vil**ser
It's important.	**Det är viktigt.**	day æær **vik**tikt
It's urgent.	**Det är brådskande.**	day æær **bros**kahnder
Hurry up!	**Skynda på!**	**shewn**dah poa

It is/There is...

It is/It's...	**Det är...**	day ai
Is it...?	**Är det...?**	ai day
It isn't...	**Det är inte...**	day ai **in**ter
There is/There are...	**Det finns...**	day finss
Is there/Are there...?	**Finns det...?**	finss day
There isn't/There aren't...	**Det finns inte...**	day finss **in**ter
There isn't any/There aren't any.	**Det finns ingen/Det finns inga.**	day finss **in**gern/day finss **in**gah

A few common words

big/small	**stor/liten**	stoor/**lee**tern
quick/slow	**snabb/långsam**	snahb/**long**sahm
early/late	**tidig/sen**	**tee**di(g)/sayn
cheap/expensive	**billig/dyr**	**bil**li(g)/dewr
near/far	**nära/avlägsen**	**nai**rah/**ahv**lehgsern
hot/cold	**varm/kall**	vahrm/kahl
full/empty	**full/tom**	fewl/toom
easy/difficult	**lätt/svår**	leht/svoar
heavy/light	**lätt/tung**	leht/tewng
open/shut	**öppen/stängd**	**ur**pern/stehngd
right/wrong	**rätt/fel**	reht/fayl
old/new	**gammal/ny**	**gah**mahl/new
old/young	**gammal/ung**	**gah**mahl/ewng
beautiful/ugly	**vacker/ful**	**vah**kerr/fewl
good/bad	**god/dålig**	good/**doa**li(g)
better/worse	**bättre/sämre**	**beh**trer/**sehm**rer

Some prepositions and a few more useful words

at	**vid**	veed
on	**på**	poa
in	**i**	ee
to	**till**	till
from	**från**	froan
inside	**inne**	**in**ner
outside	**ute**	**ewt**er
up	**upp**	ewp
down	**ner**	nayr
before	**före**	**furr**er
after	**efter**	**ehf**terr
with	**med**	mayd
without	**utan**	**ewt**ahn
through	**genom**	**yay**nom
towards	**mot**	moot
until	**till dess**	til dehss
during	**under**	**ewn**derr
and	**och**	ok
or	**eller**	**ehl**lerr
not	**inte**	**in**ter
nothing	**ingenting**	**in**gernting
none	**ingen**	**in**gern
very	**mycket**	**mew**ker(t)
also	**också**	**ok**soa
soon	**snart**	snahrt

perhaps	kanske	kahnsher
here	här	hæær
there	där	dæær
now	nu	new
then	då	doa

Arrival

Your passport, please.	Passet, tack.	pahsert tahk
Here it is.	Varsågod.	vahrsoagood
Have you anything to declare?	Har Ni någonting att förtulla?	harr nee noagonting aht furrtewlah
No, nothing at all.	Nej, ingenting alls.	nay ingernting ahlss
Porter!	Bärare!	bæærahrer
Can you help me with my luggage, please?	Kan Ni vara snäll och hjälpa mig med mitt bagage?	kahn nee varrah snehl o yehlpah may mayd mit bahgarsh
That's my suitcase.	Det där är min väska.	day dæær ai meen vehsskah
Where's the bus to the centre of town, please?	Var är bussen som går till centrum?	varr ai bewssern soam goar til sehntroom
This way, please.	Den här vägen.	dehn hæær vaigern

Changing money

| Can you change a traveller's cheque, please? | Kan Ni växla in en resecheck? | kahn nee vehkslah in ayn rayssershehk |
| Where's the nearest bank, please? | Var ligger närmaste bank? | varr liggerr næærmahsster bahnk |

Car rental

I'd like a car.	Jag skulle vilja hyra en bil.	yar(g) skewller vilyah hewrah ayn beel
For how long?	Hur länge?	hewr lehnger
A day/Four days/ A week/Two weeks.	En dag/Fyra dagar/ En vecka/Två veckor.	ayn darg/fewrah dargahr/ayn vehkah/tvoa vehkor

SWEDISH

Taxi

Where can I get a taxi?	Var kan jag få tag på en taxi?	varr kahn yar(g) foa targ poa ayn **tahk**si
What's the fare to...?	Vad kostar det till...?	vard **koss**tahr day til
Take me to this address, please.	Var snäll och kör mig till den här adressen.	varr snehl o khurr may til dehn hæær ah**drehss**ern
I'm in a hurry.	Jag har bråttom.	yar(g) harr **brott**om
Could you drive more slowly, please?	Skulle Ni kunna köra litet långsammare?	**skew**ller nee **kewn**nah **khurr**ah leetert long-sahmahrer

Hotel and other accommodation

My name is...	Mitt namn är...	mit nahmn ai
Have you a reservation?	Har Ni reserverat?	harr nee raysæær**vay**raht
Yes, here's the confirmation.	Ja, här är bekräftelsen.	yar hæær ai ber**krehf**terlsern
I'd like...	Jag skulle vilja ha...	yar(g) **skew**ller **vil**yah har
I'd like a single room/a double room.	Jag skulle vilja ha ett enkelrum/ett dubbelrum.	yar(g) **skew**ller **vil**yah har eht **ehng**kerlrewm/eht **dewb**berlrewm
a room with a bath/with a shower	ett rum med badrum/med dusch	eht rewm mayd **bard**rewm/med dewsh

How much?

What's the price per night/per week/per month?	Hur mycket kostar det per natt/per vecka/per månad?	hewr **mew**ker(t) **koss**tahr day pær naht/pær **veh**kah/pær **moa**nahd
May I see the room?	Kan jag få se på rummet?	kahn yar(g) foa say poa **rewm**ert
I'm sorry, I don't like it.	Tyvärr, men jag tycker inte om det.	tewvær mayn yar(g) **tewk**kerr **int**er om day
Yes, that's fine. I'll take it.	Ja, det här var bra. Jag tar det.	yar day hæær varr brar. yar(g) tarr day
What's my room number, please?	Vilket rumsnummer har jag?	**vil**kert **rewmss**newmerr har yar
Number 123.	Nummer 123.	**new**merr 123.

Service, please

Who is it?	**Vem är det?**	vaym ai day
Just a minute.	**Ett ögonblick.**	eht urgonblik
Come in! The door's open.	**Kom in. Dörren är öppen.**	kom in durrern ai urppern
May we have breakfast in our room?	**Kan vi få frukost på rummet?**	kahn vee foa frewkost poa rewmert

Breakfast

I'll have ...	**Jag ska be att få ...**	yar(g) skar bay aht foa
I'll have some fruit juice.	**Jag ska be att få litet juice.**	yar(g) skar bay aht foa leeter(t) yooss
a boiled egg	**ett kokt ägg**	eht kookt ehg
a fried egg	**ett stekt ägg**	eht staykt egh
some bacon/some ham	**bacon/skinka**	baykon/shingkah
some toast	**rostat bröd**	rosstaht brurd
a pot of tea	**en kanna te**	ayn kahnah tay
a cup of tea	**en kopp te**	ayn kop tay
some coffee	**kaffe**	kahffer
some chocolate	**choklad**	shooklard
more butter	**mera smör**	mayrah smurr
some hot water	**lite hett vatten**	leeter heht vahtern

Difficulties

The central heating doesn't work.	**Centralvärmen fungerar inte.**	sehntrarlværmern fewnggayrahr inter
the light/the socket the tap/the toilet	**ljuset/kontakten vattenkranen/toaletten**	yewsert/kontahktern vahternkrarnern/twahlehtern
There's no hot water.	**Det finns inget varmvatten.**	day finss ingert vahrmvahtern
May I see the manager, please?	**Kan jag få tala med direktören, tack?**	kan yar(g) foa tarlah mayd direhkturrern tahk

Telephone—Mail

There's a call for you.	**Det är telefon till Er.**	day ai taylayfoan til ayr
Hold the line, please.	**Var god dröj, tack.**	varr good drury tahk

SWEDISH

Operator, I've been cut off.	**Fröken, linjen är bruten.**	frurkern linyern ai brewtern
Did anyone telephone me?	**Har någon ringt mig?**	harr **noa**gon ringt may
Is there any mail for me?	**Finns det post till mig?**	finss day post til may
Are there any messages for me?	**Finns det några meddelanden till mig.**	finss day **noa**gra meh**day**lahndern til may

Checking out

May I have my bill, please?	**Kan jag få räkningen, tack?**	kahn yar(g) foa **rehk**ningern tahk
We're in a great hurry.	**Vi har mycket bråttom.**	vee harr **mew**ker(t) **brott**om
It's been a very enjoyable stay.	**Det har varit mycket trevligt att bo här.**	day har **varr**it **mew**ker(t) **trayv**ligt aht boo hæær

Eating out

Good evening, sir/ Good evening, madam.	**God afton/God afton.**	goo **ahf**ton/goo **ahf**ton
Good evening. I'd like a table for two, please.	**God afton. Jag skulle vilja ha ett bord för två.**	goo **ahf**ton. yar(g) **skew**leh **vil**yah har eht boord furr tvoa
Do you have a fixed-price menu?	**Har Ni en meny?**	harr nee ayn may**new**
May I see the à la carte menu?	**Kan jag få se på à la carte matsedeln?**	kahn yar(g) foa say poa ah lah kahrt **mart**serderln
May we have an ashtray, please?	**Kan vi få en ask-kopp, tack?**	kahn vee foa ayn **ahsk**kop tahk
some bread	**litet bröd**	**lee**ter(t) brurd
a fork	**en gaffel**	ayn **gah**ferl
a knife	**en kniv**	ayn kneev
a spoon	**en sked**	ayn shayd
a plate	**en tallrik**	ayn **tahl**rik
a glass	**ett glas**	eht glarss
a napkin	**en servett**	ayn sær**veht**
another chair	**en stol till**	ayn stool til

SWEDISH

| Where's the gentle-men's toilet (men's room)? | **Var är herr-toaletten?** | varr ai **hær**twahlehtern |
| Where's the ladies' toilet (ladies' room)? | **Var är dam-toaletten?** | varr ai **darm**twahlehtern |

Appetizers

I'd like some ...	**Jag ska be att få ...**	yar(g) skar bay aht foa
I'd like some assorted appetizers.	**Jag ska be att få några smårätter.**	yar(g) skar bay aht foa **noa**grah **smoa**rehterr
orange juice	**apelsinjuice**	ah**per**lseenyooss
ham	**skinka**	**shing**kah
melon	**melon**	may**loon**
pâté	**pastej**	pass**tayy**
smoked salmon	**rökt lax**	rurkt lahks
shrimps (shrimp)	**räkor**	**rai**koor

Soup

Have you any ... ?	**Har Ni ... ?**	harr nee
Have you any chicken soup?	**Har Ni kyckling-soppa?**	harr nee **khewk**lingsopah
vegetable soup	**grönsakssoppa**	**grurn**sahkssopah
onion soup	**löksoppa**	**lurk**sopah

Fish

I'd like some ...	**Jag ska be att få ...**	yar(g) skar bay aht foa
I'd like some fish.	**Jag ska be att få en fiskrätt.**	yar(g) skar bay aht foa ayn **fisk**reht
sole	**sjötunga**	**shur**tewngah
trout	**forell**	fo**rehl**
lobster	**hummer**	**hew**merr
crayfish	**kräftor**	**krehf**toor
prawns	**räkor**	**rai**koor
I'd like it ...	**Jag skulle vilja ha den ...**	yar(g) **skew**ler **vil**yah har dehn
I'd like it steamed.	**Jag skulle vilja ha den ångkokt.**	yar(g) **skew**ler **vil**yah har dehn **ong**kookt
grilled	**grillad**	**gri**lahd
boiled	**kokt**	kookt
baked	**ugnsstekt**	**ewngns**staykt
fried	**stekt**	staykt

SWEDISH

Meat—Poultry—Game

| I'd like some . . . | **Jag ska be att få . . .** | yar(g) skar bay aht foa |
| I'd like some beef. | **Jag ska be att få oxkött.** | yar(g) skar bay aht foa **ooks**khurt |

a beef steak	**en biffstek**	ahn **bif**stayk
some roast beef	**rostbiff**	**rost**bif
a veal cutlet	**en kalvkotlett**	ahn **kahlv**kotleht
mutton	**fårkött**	**foar**khurt
lamb	**lammkött**	**lahm**khurt
a pork chop	**en fläskkotlett**	ahn **flehsk**kotleht
roast pork	**grisstek**	**greess**stayk
hare	**hare**	**har**rer
chicken	**kyckling**	**khewk**ling
roast chicken	**stekt kyckling**	staykt **khewk**ling
duck	**anka**	**ahng**kah

| How do you like your meat? | **Hur vill Ni ha köttet tillagat?** | hewr vil nee har **khur**tert **til**largaht |

rare	**blodig**	**bloo**dig
medium	**lagom**	**lar**gom
well done	**genomstekt**	**yay**nomstaykt

Vegetables

What vegetables have you got?	**Vad för grönsaker finns det?**	vard furr **grurn**sarkerr finss day
I'd like some . . .	**Jag ska be att få . . .**	yar(g) ska bay aht foa
I'd like some asparagus.	**Jag ska be att få sparris.**	yar(g) ska bay aht foa **spah**riss

green beans	**haricots verts**	hahreekoav**æær**
mushrooms	**svamp**	**svahmp**
carrots	**morötter**	moo**rur**terr
onions	**lök**	lurk
red cabbage	**rödkål**	**rurd**koal
lettuce	**sallad**	**sah**lahd
spinach	**spenat**	spay**nart**
rice	**ris**	reess
peas	**ärtor**	**ær**toor
tomatoes	**tomater**	too**mar**terr
green salad	**grönsallad**	**grurn**sahlahd
potatoes	**potatis**	poo**tar**tiss

Desserts

| Nothing more, thanks. | **Ingenting mer, tack.** | **in**gernting mayr tahk |
| Just a small portion, please. | **Bara en liten portion, tack.** | barrah ehn **lee**tern por**choon** tahk |

SWEDISH

Have you any ice-cream?	**Har Ni glass?**	har nee glahss
fruit salad	**fruktsallad**	frewktsahlahd
fresh fruit	**färsk frukt**	færshk frewkt
cheese	**ost**	oost

Drink

What would you like to drink?	**Vad vill Ni ha att dricka?**	vard vil nee har aht drikah
I'll have a beer, please.	**Jag tar en öl, tack.**	yar(g) tarr ehn url tahk
I'll have a whisky, please.	**Jag ska be att få en whisky, tack.**	yar(g) skar bay aht foa ehn wisskew tahk

Wine

I'd like a bottle of wine.	**Jag ska be att få en flaska vin.**	yar(g) skar bay aht foa ehn flahsskah veen
red wine	**rödvin**	rurdveen
rosé wine	**rosévin**	roasayveen
white wine	**vitt vin**	vit veen
Cheers!	**Skål!**	skoal

The bill (check)

May I have the bill (check) please?	**Får jag be om notan, tack?**	foar yar(g) bay om nootahn tahk
Is service included?	**Ingår service?**	ingoar surrviss
Everything's included.	**Allt ingår.**	ahlt ingoar
Thank you, that was a very good meal.	**Tack, det var en mycket god måltid.**	tahk day varr ehn mewker(t) goo moalteed

Travelling

Where's the railway station, please?	**Var är järnvägs-stationen?**	varr ai yærnvehgsstah-shoonern
Where's the ticket office, please?	**Var är biljettluckan?**	varr ai bilyehtlewkahn
I'd like a ticket to ...	**Jag ska be att få en biljett till ...**	yar(g) skar bay aht foa ehn bilyeht til
First or second class?	**Första eller andra klass?**	furrshta ehlerr ahndrah klahss

First class, please.	**Första klass, tack.**	furrshtah klahss tahk
Single or return (one way or round-trip)?	**Enkel eller tur och retur?**	ehngkerl ehlerr tewr o(k) retewr
Do I have to change trains?	**Måste jag byta tåg?**	mosster yar bewtah toag
What platform does the train leave from?	**Från vilken perrong avgår tåget?**	froan vilkern pærong ahv-goar toagert
Where's the nearest underground (subway) station?	**Var ligger närmaste tunnelbanestation?**	varr ligger næærmahster tewnerlbarnerstahshoon
Where's the bus station, please?	**Var är buss-stationen?**	varr ai bewssstah-shoonern
When's the first bus to . . . ?	**När går första bus-sen till . . . ?**	næær goar furrshtah bew-ssern til
the last bus the next bus	**sista bussen/ nästa buss**	sisstah bewssern/ nehsstah bewss
Please let me off at the next stop.	**Var god och låt mig gå av nästa håll-plats.**	varr goo o(k) loat may goa ahv nehsstah hol-plahts

Relaxing

What's on at the cinema (movies)?	**Vad går det på bio?**	vard goar day poa beeoo
What's on at the theatre?	**Vad ger man på teatern?**	vard yayr mahn poa tayarterrn
What time does the film begin?	**När börjar filmen?**	næær burryarr filmern
And the play?	**Och teatern?**	o tayarterrn
Are there any tickets for tonight?	**Finns det några biljetter till i kväll?**	finss day noagrah bilyehterr til ee kvehl
Where can we go dancing?	**Var kan vi gå och dansa?**	varr kahn vee goa o(k) dahnsah
Would you like to dance?	**Får jag lov?**	foar yar(g) loav

Introductions

How do you do?	**Goddag.**	goodarg
How are you?	**Hur står det till?**	hewr stoar day til
Very well, thank you. And you?	**Tack bara bra. Och Ni själv?**	tahk barrar brar. o(k) nee shehlv

SWEDISH

May I introduce Miss Philips?	Får jag presentera fröken Philips?	foar yar(g) prayserntayrah frurkern Philips
My name is...	Mitt namm är...	mit nahmn æær
I'm very pleased to meet you.	Roligt att lära känna Er.	rooligt aht læærah khehnah ayr
How long have you been here?	Hur länge har Ni varit här?	hewr lehnger harr nee varrit hæær
It was nice meeting you.	Det var trevligt att träffas.	day varr trayvligt aht trehfahss

Dating

Would you like a cigarette?	Vill Ni ha en cigarrett?	vil nee har ehn sigahreht
May I get you a drink?	Vill Ni ha något att dricka?	vil nee har noagot aht drikar
Do you have a light, please?	Har Ni möjligen eld?	harr nee muryliggern ayld
Are you waiting for someone?	Väntar Ni på någon?	væntahr nee poa noagon
Are you free this evening?	Är Ni ledig i kväll?	ai nee laydig ee kvehl
Where shall we meet?	Var ska vi träffas?	varr skar vee trehfahss
What time shall I meet you?	När ska vi träffas?	næær skar vee trehfahss
May I take you home?	Får jag följa Er hem?	foar yar(g) furlyah ayr haym
Thank you, it's been a wonderful evening.	Tack, det har varit en underbar kväll.	tahk day har varrit ehn ewnderrbarr kvehl
What's your telephone number?	Vad har Ni för telefonnummer?	vard harr nee furr taylayfoannewmerr
Do you live alone?	Bor Ni ensam?	boor nee aynsahm
What time is your last train?	När går sista tåget?	næær goar sisstah toaget
Good-night...	God natt...	goo naht

Banks

| Where's the nearest bank, please? | Var ligger närmaste bank? | varr ligger næærmahster bahnk |

Where can I cash some traveller's cheques?	**Var kan jag växla in några resecheckar?**	varr kahn yar(g) **vehks**lah in **noa**grah **rays**ser-shehkahr
What time does the bank open/What time does it close?	**När öppnar banken/När stänger den?**	næær **urp**nahr **bahn**kern/næær **stehng**err dehn
I'm expecting some money from home. Has it arrived?	**Jag väntar pengar hemifrån. Har de kommit?**	yar(g) **vehn**tahr **pehng**ahr **hay**mifron. harr day **kom**mit
Can you give me some small change, please?	**Kan jag få litet växel, tack?**	kahn yar(g) foa **lee**ter(t) **vehk**serl tahk

Shops, stores and services

Where is the nearest chemist's (pharmacy)?	**Var finns närmaste apotek?**	varr finss **næær**mahster ahpoo**tayk**
the nearest hairdresser's	**närmaste hårfrisörska**	**næær**mahster **hoar**frisurrshkah
the photo shop	**fotoaffären**	**foo**tooahfairern
the jeweller's	**juveleraren**	yewver**lay**rahrern
the department store	**varuhuset**	**varre**hewssert
the police station	**polisstationen**	poo**leess**stah**shoo**nern
the garage	**garaget**	gahrar**shert**
How do I get there?	**Hur kommer jag dit?**	hewr **kom**merr yar(g) deet
Is it within walking distance?	**Kan man gå dit?**	kahn mahn **goa** deet

Service

English	Swedish	Pronunciation
Can you help me, please?	**Kan Ni vara snäll och hjälpa mig?**	kahn nee **varr**ah snehl o(k) **yehl**pah may
Can you show me this? And that, too.	**Kan Ni visa mig den här? Och den där också.**	kahn nee **vee**sah may dehn hæær? o(k) dehn dæær ok**soa**
It's too expensive/too big/too small.	**Den är för dyr/för stor/för liten.**	dehn ai furr dewr/furr stoor/furr **lee**tern
Can you show me some more?	**Kan Ni visa mig något mer?**	kahn nee **vee**sah may **noa**got mayr
something better	**någonting bättre**	**noa**gonting **beh**trer
something cheaper	**någonting billigare**	**noa**gonting **bil**ligahrer
How much is this? And that?	**Hur mycket kostar den här? Och den där?**	hewr **mew**ker(t) **koss**tar dehn hæær? o(k) dehn dæær

SWEDISH

308

| It's not quite what I want. | **Det är inte precis vad jag tänkt mig.** | day ai **inter praysseess** vard yar(g) tehnkt may |
| I like it. | **Jag tycker om den.** | yar(g) **tew**kerr om dehn |

Chemist's (Pharmacy)

| I'd like something for a cold/for a cough/for travel sickness. | **Jag skulle vilja ha någonting mot förkylning/mot hosta/mot ressjuka.** | yar(g) **skewler vil**yah har **noa**gonting moot turr-**khewl**ning/moot **hoo**stah/moot **rayss**shewkah |
| Can you recommend something for hay-fever/for sunburn? | **Kan Ni rekommendera någonting mot hösnuva/mot solsveda?** | kahn nee raykomehn-**dayr**ah **noa**gonting moot **hurs**newvah/moot **sool**svaydah |

Toiletry

May I have some razor blades?	**Kan jag få några rakblad?**	kahn yar(g) foa **noa**grah **rark**blahd
some shaving cream	**rakkräm**	**rark**krehm
some toothpaste	**tandkräm**	**tahnd**krehm
I'd like some soap.	**Jag ska be att få en tvål.**	yar(g) skar bay aht foa ayn tvoal
some suntan oil	**sololja**	**sool**olyah

At the barber's

I'd like a haircut, please.	**Jag skulle vilja ha håret klippt.**	yar(g) **skewler vil**yah har **hoar**ert klipt
Short/Leave it long.	**Kort/Låt det vara långt.**	kort/loat day **var**rah longt
A razor cut, please.	**Klippning med rakblad, tack.**	**klip**ning mayd **rark**blahd tahk

At the hairdresser's

I'd like a shampoo and set, please.	**Jag ska be att få håret tvättat och lagt.**	yar(g) skar bay aht foa **hoar**ert **tveh**taht o(k) lahgt
I'd like a bleach.	**Jag skulle vilja ha det blekt.**	yar(g) **skewler vil**yah har day blaykt
a permanent	**permanentat**	**pær**mah**nehn**taht
a colour rinse	**tonat**	**too**naht
a manicure	**en manikyr**	ayn mahni**kewr**

Photography

| I'd like a film for this camera. | **Jag ska be att få en film till den här kameran.** | yar(g) skar bay aht foa ayn film til dehn hæær **kar**mayrahn |
| This camera doesn't work. | **Den här kameran fungerar inte.** | dehn hæær **kar**mayrahn fewng**gay**rahr inter |

At the post office

| Where's the nearest post office, please? | **Var ligger närmaste postkontor?** | var **ligg**err **næær**mahster posst**kontoor** |
| I'd like to send this by express (special delivery)/by air mail. | **Jag skulle vilja skicka det här express/med flygpost.** | yar(g) **skew**ler **vil**yah **shi**kar day hæær ehks**prehss**/mayd **flewg**-posst |

Service stations

Where is the nearest service station, please?	**Kan Ni säga mig var närmaste ben-sinstation ligger?**	kahn nee **sai**gah may varr **næær**mahster behn-**seen**stahshoon **ligg**err
Fill her up, please.	**Full tank, tack.**	fewl tahnk tahk
Check the oil, please.	**Kontrollera oljan, tack.**	kontro**layr**ah **ol**yahn tahk
Would you check the tyres?	**Skulle Ni vilja kon-trollera däcken?**	**skew**ler nee **vil**yah kon-tro**layr**ah **deh**kern

Street directions

Can you show me on the map where I am?	**Kan Ni visa mig på kartan var jag är?**	kahn nee **vee**sah may poa **kahr**tahn varr yar(g) ai
You're on the wrong road.	**Ni är på fel väg.**	nee ai poa fayl vaig
Go back to ...	**Kör tillbaka till ...**	khurr til**bar**kah til
Go straight ahead.	**Kör rakt fram.**	khurr rahkt frahm
It's on the left/on the right.	**Det är till vänster/till höger.**	day ai til **vehn**sterr/til **hu**ger

Accidents

| May I use your tele-phone? | **Kan jag få låna Er telefon?** | kahn yar(g) foa **loa**nah ayr taylay**foan** |

SWEDISH

Call a doctor quickly.	**Ring genast efter en läkare.**	ring **yay**nahst **ehf**terr ayn laikahrer
Call an ambulance.	**Ring på ambulansen.**	ring poa ahmbew**lahns**ern
Please call the police.	**Var snäll och ring polisen.**	varr snehl o(k) ring poo**lee**ssern

Numbers

one	**ett**	eht
two	**två**	tvoa
three	**tre**	tray
four	**fyra**	**few**rah
five	**fem**	fehm
six	**sex**	sehks
seven	**sju**	shew
eight	**åtta**	**o**tah
nine	**nio**	**nee**oo
ten	**tio**	**tee**oo
eleven	**elva**	**ehl**vah
twelve	**tolv**	tolv
thirteen	**tretton**	**treh**ton
fourteen	**fjorton**	**fyoor**ton
fifteen	**femton**	**fehm**ton
sixteen	**sexton**	**sehks**ton
seventeen	**sjutton**	**shew**ton
eighteen	**arton**	**arr**ton
nineteen	**nitton**	**nit**ton
twenty	**tjugo**	**khew**goo
twenty-one	**tjugoett**	**khew**gooeht
thirty	**trettio**	**treh**tioo
forty	**fyrtio**	**fewr**tioo
fifty	**femtio**	**fehm**tioo
sixty	**sextio**	**sehks**tioo
seventy	**sjuttio**	**shew**tioo
eighty	**åttio**	**o**tioo
ninety	**nittio**	**nit**tioo
one hundred	**hundra**	**hewn**drah
one thousand	**tusen**	**tew**sern
ten thousand	**tio tusen**	**tee**oo **tews**sern

Days

It's Sunday.	**Det är söndag.**	day ai **surn**dar(g)
Monday	**måndag**	**moan**dar(g)
Tuesday	**tisdag**	**tiss**dar(g)
Wednesday	**onsdag**	**oonss**dar(g)

SWEDISH

Thursday	**torsdag**	**toorsh**dar(g)
Friday	**fredag**	**fray**dar(g)
Saturday	**lördag**	**lurr**dar(g)
yesterday	**i går**	ee goar
today	**i dag**	ee dar(g)
tomorrow	**i morgon**	ee **mo**ron
morning/afternoon	**förmiddag/efter-middag**	**furr**middar(g)/**ehf**ter-middar(g)
evening/night	**kväll/natt**	kvehl/naht

Months

January	**januari**	yahne**wa**rri
February	**februari**	faybre**wa**rri
March	**mars**	mahrsh
April	**april**	ah**preel**
May	**maj**	migh
June	**juni**	**yew**ni
July	**juli**	**yew**li
August	**augusti**	ahew**gew**sti
September	**september**	sehp**tehm**berr
October	**oktober**	ok**too**berr
November	**november**	no**vehm**berr
December	**december**	day**sehm**berr
Merry Christmas!	**God Jul! Gott Nytt År!**	goo(d) yewl! got newt oar
Happy New Year!		

Reference section

Weight conversion

The figure in the middle stands for both kilograms and pounds, e.g., 1 kilogram = 2.205 lb. and 1 pound = 0.45 kilograms.

Kilograms (kg.)		Avoirdupois pounds
0.45	1	2.205
0.90	2	4.405
1.35	3	6.614
1.80	4	8.818
2.25	5	11.023
2.70	6	13.227
3.15	7	15.432
3.60	8	17.636
4.05	9	19.840
4.50	10	22.045
6.75	15	33.068
9.00	20	44.889
11.25	25	55.113
22.50	50	110.225
33.75	75	165.338
45.00	100	220.450

1 kilogram or kilo (kg) = 1000 grams (g)

100 g = 3.5 oz.	½ kg = 1.1 lb.
200 g = 7.0 oz.	1 kg = 2.2 lb.

1 oz. = 28.35 g
1 lb. = 453.60 g

Metres and feet

The figure in the middle stands for both metres and feet, e.g.,
1 metre = 3.281 ft. and 1 foot = 0.30 m.

Metres		Feet
0.30	1	3.281
0.61	2	6.563
0.91	3	9.843
1.22	4	13.124
1.52	5	16.403
1.83	6	19.686
2.13	7	22.967
2.44	8	26.248
2.74	9	29.529
3.05	10	32.810
3.35	11	36.091
3.66	12	39.372
3.96	13	42.635
4.27	14	45.934
4.57	15	49.215
4.88	16	52.496
5.18	17	55.777
5.49	18	59.058
5.79	19	62.339
6.10	20	65.620
7.62	25	82.023
15.24	50	164.046
22.86	75	246.069
30.48	100	328.092

314

Centimetres and inches

To change centimetres into inches, multiply by .39.

To change inches into centimetres, multiply by 2.54.

	in.	feet	yards
1 mm	0,039	0,003	0,001
1 cm	0,39	0,03	0,01
1 dm	3,94	0,32	0,10
1 m	39,40	3,28	1,09

	mm	cm	m
1 in.	25,4	2,54	0,025
1 ft.	304,8	30,48	0,304
1 yd.	914,4	91,44	0,914

(32 metres = 35 yards)

Temperature

To convert Centigrade into degrees Fahrenheit, multiply Centigrade by 1.8 and add 32.

To convert degrees Fahrenheit into Centigrade, subtract 32 from Fahrenheit and divide by 1.8.

The car

Miles into kilometres									
1 mile = 1.609 kilometres (km)									
miles	10	20	30	40	50	60	70	80	90	100
km	16	32	48	64	80	97	113	129	145	161

Kilometres into miles												
1 kilometre (km) = 0.62 miles												
km	10	20	30	40	50	60	70	80	90	100	110	120	130
miles	6	12	19	25	31	37	44	50	56	62	68	75	81

Tire pressure			
lb./sq. in.	kg/cm^2	lb./sq. in.	kg/cm^2
10	0.7	26	1.8
12	0.8	27	1.9
15	1.1	28	2.0
18	1.3	30	2.1
20	1.4	33	2.3
21	1.5	36	2.5
23	1.6	38	2.7
24	1.7	40	2.8

Fluid measures					
litres	imp. gal.	U.S. gal.	litres.	imp. gal.	U.S. gal.
5	1.1	1.3	30	6.6	7.8
10	2.2	2.6	35	7.7	9.1
15	3.3	3.9	40	8.8	10.4
20	4.4	5.2	45	9.9	11.7
25	5.5	6.5	50	11.0	13.0

1 litre (l) = 0.88 imp. quarts = 1.06 U.S. quarts

1 imp. quart = 1.14 l	1 U.S. quart = 0.95 l
1 imp. gallon = 4.55 l	1 U.S. gallon = 3.81 l

This is your size

Ladies

	Dresses/suits					
American	10	12	14	16	18	20
British	32	34	36	38	40	42
Continental	38	40	42	44	46	48

	Stockings						Shoes			
American } British	8	8½	9	9½	10	10½	6	7	8	9
Continental	0	1	2	3	4	5	36	38	38½	40

Gentlemen

	Suits/overcoats						Shirts					
American } British	36	38	40	42	44	46	14	15	15½	16	16½	17
Continental	46	48	50	52	54	56	36	38	39	41	42	43

	Shoes						
American } British	5	6	7	8	9	10	11
Continental	38	39	41	42	43	44	45

In Europe sizes vary somewhat from country to country, so the above must be taken as an approximate guide.

Date Line

1 a.m. 2 a.m. 3 a.m. 4 a.m. 5 a.m. 6 a.m. 7 a.m. 8 a.m. 9 a.m. 10 a.m. 11 a.m. noon p.m. 1 p.m. 2 p.m. 3 p.m. 4 p.m. 5 p.m. 6 p.m. 7 p.m. 8 p.m. 9 p.m. 10 p.m. 11 p.m. mid-night

Eastern European Time

Central European Time

Western European Time (G.M.T.)

Atlantic Time

Eastern Time

Central Time

Mountain Time

Pacific Time

Alaska Time

Countries which have adopted a time differing from that in the corresponding time zone. Note that also in the USSR, official time is one hour ahead of the time in each corresponding time zone. In summer, numerous countries advance time one hour ahead of standard time.

Currency converter

In a world of fluctuating currencies, we can offer no more than this handy do-it-yourself chart. You can get information about exchange rates from banks, travel agents and tourist offices. Why not fill in this chart too, for handy reference?

	£1	$1
Austria (shillings)		
Belgium (francs)		
Denmark (crowns)		
Finland (marks)		
France (francs)		
Germany (marks)		
Greece (drachmas)		
Italy (lire)		
Netherlands (guilders)		
Norway (crowns)		
Poland (zlotys)		
Portugal (escudos)		
Spain (pesetas)		
Sweden (crowns)		
Switzerland (francs)		
USSR (rubles)		
Yugoslavia (dinars)		

Emergency numbers

Ambulance ....

Fire ....

Police ....

Fill in these as well

Embassy ....

Consulate ....

Taxi ....

Airport information ....

Travel agent ....

Hotel ....

Restaurant ....

Babysitter ....

....

....

....

....

....

....

....

Personal data

Passport Nos. ....

....

Checking account No. ....

Credit card Nos. ....

....

Car: Licence plates ....

     Chassis No. ....

     Insurance: Company ....

     Policy No. ....

Travel Insurance: Company ....

     Policy No. ....

Blood type ....

....

....

....

....

....

....

....

....